HOW IS NATURE POSSIBLE?

HOW IS NATURE POSSIBLE?

KANT'S PROJECT IN THE FIRST CRITIQUE

Daniel N. Robinson

continuum

Continuum International Publishing Group

The Tower Building	80 Maiden Lane
11 York Road	Suite 704
London SE1 7NX	New York NY 10038

www.continuumbooks.com

British Library Cataloguing-in-Publication Data
A catalogue record for this book is available from the British Library.

ISBN: PB: 978-1-4411-4851-3
HB: 978-1-4411-7622-6

Library of Congress Cataloging-in-Publication Data
Robinson, Daniel N., 1937-
How is Nature Possible? : Kant's Project in the First Critique / Daniel N.
Robinson.
p. cm.
Includes bibliographical references (p.) and index.
1. Kant, Immanuel, 1724–1804. Kritik der reinen Vernunft. I. Title.
B2779.R55 2011
121–dc23

2011021835

Typeset by Newgen Imaging Systems Pvt Ltd, Chennai, India
Printed and bound in India

As ever,
For Ciny. . .

CONTENTS

That the human mind will ever give up metaphysical researches is as little to be expected as that we should prefer to give up breathing altogether, to avoid inhaling impure air. There will therefore always be metaphysics in the world; nay, every one, especially every man of reflection, will have it, and for want of a recognized standard, will shape it for himself after his own pattern.

(Immanuel Kant, *Prolegomena to Any Future Metaphysics*, 367)

PREFACE

In introducing what came to be his influential exposition and assessment of Kant's *Critique of Pure Reason*, Sir Peter Strawson explained his close study of the work as preparation for the Oxford Core Lectures he was to give on the subject. Those of us who have followed him in this difficult assignment are well aware of the demands the *Critique* imposes and surely share with him what he described as the "commingled sense of great insights and great mystification" it arouses.[1]

Any treatise that would mystify Sir Peter is one that must put on notice the resources of lesser mortals among whom I readily number myself. Perhaps chiefly for this reason, I have not attempted what Sir Peter then referred to as a "unified interpretation" for, both before and after the appearance of *The Bounds of Sense*, there have been many estimable attempts at a unified interpretation. Among the more recent scholars, the names Allison, Ameriks, Beiser, Bennett, Bird, Guyer, and Van Cleve come quickly to mind.

In approaching the work as one who would clarify it for an audience of both generalists and well-prepared students of the text, there are both advantages and liabilities in not being a Kant specialist. The liabilities need little rehearsal. There is no substitute for life-long study if one is to advance original and worthy readings of the works of any major figure in philosophy. Although my interest in Kant covers many years and includes publications on his work, these were not years devoted chiefly to a systematic study of his first *Critique*. However, in addition to a sharply focused and repeated reading of the text, both in translation and in German, I thought I might bring something else to the undertaking: A long immersion in the history of ideas, some decades of research as an experimental scientist specializing in visual perception, and a quite lengthy engagement with the philosophy of Thomas Reid and those philosophically animated exchanges among Reid's and Hume's disciples. Such a preparation does not fall into the margins of Kant's project but actually moves one closer to its very center. A few words here are in order in relation to Reid, to experimental science and to intellectual history as guides to an through the *Critique*. Thomas Reid's misleadingly dubbed "commonsense" school takes the settled and evident arrangements within the overall animal economy as proof enough that nature (expressing as he believed the will of a providential Creator) has provided a ready means by which the conundrums and vexations of philosophers are set aside as life is actually *lived*. One of the keenest and most informed students of science and mathematics, Reid was also confident that any metaphysical theory, doubtful about personal identity and reducing causality to a matter of perceptual coincidences, was simply a philosophical parlor game, but a dangerous one.

As I shall note later in this work, Karl Ameriks finds significant Reidian anticipations in the *Critique*. There is much more to be said on this subject, particularly in the matter of Reid's *Geometry of Visibles* in relation to non-Euclidean space, but this is the subject for another occasion. I note it here to suggest that an exploration of the works of Hume's most formidable contemporary critic in the English-speaking world affords something of a parallel philosophical narrative that augments and clarifies Kant's own understanding of and response to Hume's challenge. In light of this, it is best to regard that well-rehearsed and dismissive sentence in the *Prolegomena* – where Kant lumps Reid, Beattie, and Oswald as feckless in their attacks on Hume – as a bit of academic politics.[2] It should not discourage the sort of comparative analysis suggested here and by Karl Ameriks.

Kant's scientific interests and achievements are a matter of record. When he sets out to distinguish between and among the methods proper to science, mathematics, and philosophy he does so with a perspective shaped by actual and disciplined undertakings in each of these areas. It is an acknowledged bias in the following pages to read the *Critique* as Kant's commitment to secure the special domain of the *scientifically* knowable against various skeptical challenges. This is not to depreciate the commoner mode of understanding as an additional beneficiary, but to make clear that science itself is constructed out of the same epistemic resources employed by scientists even after their instruments have been put away.

As for intellectual history, it is the vast domain that provided Kant with a veritable specimen chest of failed projects, the often aimless *Harumtappen* engaged in by those occupying the pantheon of earlier metaphysicians. He is always searching for the birthdate or pedigree or lineage of an argument or theory, even as he proposes alternatives that are universally and necessarily true.

Scholarship, by which I mean disciplined and systematic study, includes science and is inevitably historically and culturally situated. Nonetheless, one measure of originality is the extent to which a given scholar severs the tribal bonds and moves toward something likely to strike others as either idle or trite, when not downright mystifying. Thus, it matters that Kant's parents were Pietists. that Halle was at once a treasured but suffocatingly orthodox setting, that the partisans of Leibniz and of Newton were at war on more than one front, and that entire domains of scholarly inquiry could be supported or suspended by a stroke of the Prussian royal pen. Of course, it *all* matters, but there must be selection, filtering, distillation, rules of indifference. Much was made of and made with the pages of the *Critique*. Kant would not have approved of all of it and went so far as to correct many attempts that surfaced in his own time. What I hope to present here is what I take to be Kant's own purposes and how he set about to realize them. In various places in the following pages it is instructive to present serious criticisms of ideas and arguments on which the overall project of the *Critique* is said to depend. I strive to not only give them a fair hearing but also to indicate how Kant actually did anticipate and answer them or might plausibly be expected to answer them now. In other words, the treatment is sympathetic but certainly not fawning.

It is said that when Fichte, his fame won, appeared for his lectures, the awe-struck students were silent in their anticipation. "Gentlemen," he is said to have declared from the podium, "withdraw into yourselves." This (somehow) accomplished, they were then instructed to "think the wall." Finally, he urged them ". . . to think that which thinks the wall" if they would understand what the study of human history entails.[3] To read the *Critique* sympathetically is to think him who thinks the wall; it is to share Kant's judgment of what makes a question or issue problematic and then to unravel the analysis he judged to be successful in resolving it or in showing it to fall beyond the ambit of our rational resources.

Needless to say, a sympathetic reading does not guarantee an accurate reading. One recalls Leslie Stevenson's struggling student who would tell us that,

> Descartes held that when he was thinking, his mind could detach itself from his body and think about it completely objectionably.[4]

The thousands of exegetical and critical works addressed to the *Critique of Pure Reason* are no testimonial to its transparency! Thus, to suggest that in the following pages I presume to "think the Kant who thought the *Critique*" should be qualified: It is not to promise an exercise in "depth psychology" but a form of interpretive restraint that calls upon one to eschew all temptations to regard any part of the text as meaningless, incoherent, or patently unsupportable.

It is in the *Prolegomena* that Kant ties the possibility of true and necessary a priori synthetic propositions to the possibility of *nature* itself. Nature thus understood is, he says, "the connection of appearances . . . according to laws" (A216/B263).[5] The central task of the *Critique* is first to establish just how a veritable shower of merely physical impingements is crafted into the lawful realm we comprehend as *nature*, and then—though all this is achieved by way of uniquely human cognitive resources—to establish how the resulting knowledge is nonetheless *objective*. I found the challenge to be irresistible.

Oxford, 2011

CHAPTER 1

PRELIMINARIES

A little more than forty years ago, writing in *The Philosophical Review*, Jonathan Bennett passed what some took to be a final judgment:

> Most of the *Critique of Pure Reason* is prima facie dead, because prima facie dependent on wholly indefensible theories. The commentator's dominant problem is to display the life below the surface.[1]

Clearly, reports of this death were premature. In the years since the autopsy report was filed, it has been obvious to many scholars that the body in question was a case of misidentification. Whole clusters of indefensible theories then proved to be either surprisingly defensible, or not Kant's to begin with. Still other commentators, though agreeing that certain gaps and flaws were, indeed, fatal, nonetheless believed that they possessed a previously unsuspected nostrum with which to restore life and give the patient yet another opportunity to have his merits properly assessed.

A small group—perhaps the smallest—concluded that it was allegiance to the strictures of "analytical philosophy" that had deadened the capacities needed to comprehend Kant's arguments and to engage them on unprejudiced terms. A recent representative of this minority is Kenneth Westphal who states the matter cogently when he discourages attempts to absorb Kant into a contemporary methodology. He recommends that scholars,

> instead of incorporating Kant's transcendental proofs into present-day philosophical attitudes . . . reconsider some of our

current philosophical attitudes in order to understand and benefit from Kant's transcendental proofs.[2]

In whatever camp one finds greatest compatibility, it must be agreed that the *Critique of Pure Reason* is among the most difficult works in the philosophical canon, and ever more so owing to the author's often defensive tone, convoluted arguments, and distracting repetitions. The two editions of the work, separated by a half-dozen years, reveal Kant's pained awareness of the difficulties faced by both hostile and sympathetic readers. There will be further agreement that these difficulties have not been overcome by the immense secondary literature spawned by the *Critique* any more than they were by the extensive correspondence between Kant and his contemporaries. Indeed, those who have bravely (and also those who have somewhat rashly) entered into Kant's thought for the purpose of rendering it accessible to students and nonspecialists have often given the work an even greater mystique and remoteness. As for those who have entered more ambitiously to challenge or enrich the specialist's reading of the *Critique*, the risk here is a greater attachment to how Kant should be read than to what Kant actually wrote. If this is to be avoided, the place to begin may not be with recent decades of Kant scholarship, essential though that is. A more promising approach calls for something of an intellectual biography with close attention to the progress Kant made toward identifying what he took to be the most fundamental questions and how he understood the failure of others to answer them.

Yet even to speak of progress is to overlook the several and diverging paths Kant pursued over a course of years. The evolution of the *Critique* includes a mixed collection of abortive early attempts and more successful but then abandoned productions during his "pre-Critical" years. The earlier efforts were engagements with well-developed perspectives in the academic world of Germany, an academic world marked by strong political and religious attachments, ever alert to departures from orthodoxy. If one is to understand the aims and the very tone of the *Critique*, this part of the overall story becomes important. One should be attentive to the problems and possibilities bequeathed to Kant as well as the special pressures emanating from the political quarters of the German universities. The magnitude of these pressures is conveyed by Kant when he refers peevishly to incompetent judges, who, while they would have an old name for every deviation from their perverse though common opinion, and never judge of the spirit of philosophic nomenclature, but cling to the letter only, are ready to put their own conceits in the place of well-defined notions, and thereby deform and distort them. (*Prolegomena*, 293) [3]

Perhaps the first sign of a more settled position on the task he would undertake is in a letter to a former student. Writing to Marcus Herz a decade before the publication of the first edition, Kant refers to his current efforts on what he has provisionally titled *The Bounds of Sensibility and Reason*. There is an urgency expressed in the letter. He reports that such a project calls for one to be "driven by a mania for systematizing" and that his goal is nothing less than working out "in some detail the foundational principles and laws that determine the sensible world. . . ." [4]

At this time (1771) Kant must make choices between two powerful but radically different modes of inquiry, different modes of understanding; one so productively applied by Newton and another that had established Leibniz as the greatest metaphysician of his age. Just how far can knowledge proceed by way of observation and measurement? Just how far can reason in its theoretical projections enter into and grasp the actual nature of things?

Both sense and reason are limited. Thus, Kant must identify the proper mission and domain of each as well as the manner in which their separate functions come to be integrated in what is finally the intersubjectively settled knowledge of science. The task he faces requires an acknowledgment of the empirical character of science and also a sustained defense of it against skeptical challenges grounded in notions of subjectivity and relativism. Similarly, the grand rational systems so common in traditional metaphysics must be put on notice, but not at the expense of the central place of reason in rendering the world, if incompletely knowable, nonetheless intelligible.

Between the two editions of the *Critique* Kant wrote an exegesis designed to clarify points judged to be obscure in the first edition. This was his *Prolegomena to Any Future Metaphysics* (1783), intended to assist teachers who might wish to adopt the *Critique* but would need a supporting and clarifying summary of the principal arguments. He begins section 14 with the statement, "*Nature* is the *existence* of things, so far as it is determined according to universal laws." A universe of disjointed and random fluctuations cannot qualify as "nature." Rather, nature is possible only insofar as there are in actuality *universal laws of nature* that confer order, predictability, and coherence. Accordingly, there can be "nature" only insofar as there is *a pure science of nature*, and this leads Kant to the question, "How is it possible?" (*Prolegomena*, 295).

If the overall objective of the *Critique* can be collapsed into a single sentence, it is this interrogative: *How is nature possible?* How does the flotsam of mindless physicality become organized into the world as known and knowable?

There is room for confusion on this point, amply illustrated by otherwise authoritative works. On one common construal, Kant's attempt to determine how nature is possible takes a form summarized this way (and criticized) by Graham Bird:

> For Kant nature, empirical reality, is one self-contained realm which requires to be "constituted by" some agency outside that realm, namely a transcendental mind. That non-empirical item is causally affected by things-in-themselves and is causally active in literally constructing nature out of the subjective mental effects of those things-in-themselves. The mind, conceived in this way, will itself belong to that alternative, non-natural, realm of things-in-themselves.[5]

Bird's own position is quite different. His reading leads him to conclude that

> for Kant what is "left out" of a scientific, explanatory, account of reality is now a reference to another causal, or explanatory, account operating in the unknowable realm of things-in-themselves. If a scientific account needs philosophical supplementation it is needed simply as a higher order examination of reality and our knowledge.[6]

As will be shown later, Kant was not oblivious to such attempts to naturalize the mind, citing Locke's attempt to *sensualize* the process by which the resulting lawfulness of nature is achieved (A271/ B327).[7] Kant would surely resist any interpretation that would have nature constructed "out of the subjective mental effects of those things-in-themselves" if, by "constructed out of," one has in mind some determinate relation. On this account, *noumena*—those things as in themselves they really are—are ruled out completely, for the term refers to what is *intelligible* but not sensible. As will be discussed in later chapters, the sensible realm is that of *phenomena*. Just what that ultimate physical constitution of things might be falls beyond the powers of sense. A noumenal realm may be inferred from the very fact of phenomena but cannot be known.

Actually, Kant is utterly uncertain as to whether, once thought has liberated itself from all sensible intuition and thereby engages the concept of *noumena*, "any object whatsoever is left" (A253). He acknowledges and cautions against that tendency by which one is misled into thinking

> the entirely *indeterminate* concept of an intelligible entity . . . as being a *determinate* concept of an entity that allows of being known. (A250/B307)

In all, then, it is doubtful that reality could be constructed out of no more than sensible intuitions and the conceptual elements crafted according to some higher-order examination of empirical knowledge.

But the question persists: *How is nature possible?* The point of the question warrants further consideration of Kant's aims. There is a long history of scholarly controversy on the question of just how Kant's overall project is to be understood, the question of just what it was that he hoped to achieve. An especially clear and economical summary of alternative accounts has been provided by Karl Ameriks.[8] He discusses three major options when attempting to identify Kant's principal objective. One option would have Kant developing a systematic metaphysics serving as a refutation of *skepticism*, as such skepticism emerges from both empiricistic (Locke, Berkeley, Hume) and rationalistic (Descartes) sources. Surely the *Critique* can be viewed in this light, especially granting the importance Kant attaches to the *Refutation of Idealism* he adds to the second edition. On yet another account, a developed metaphysical system such as Kant's might provide philosophical foundations for a species of *scientism* that takes the scientific image of reality as a corrective against the claims of mere common sense, a corrective lest the "manifest image" of reality at the level of ordinary perception be taken as ultimate and authoritative. Finally, there is the enduring problem of *ontology* within metaphysics and the demand or the hope that the right sort of systematic treatment will clarify if not settle questions as to just what there is in reality—and whether human capacities are able to make contact with it.

Ameriks himself argues that Kant was keenly aware of all three of these issues but finally settled on a modest fourth option, the *transcendental option* that would unearth and critically assess the presuppositions and conditions necessary if both the scientific and the manifest images of reality are to be coherent or even possible. There is much to recommend in such a reading of the *Critique*, even if one is repeatedly reminded by Kant that progress in ontology must first overcome skeptical challenges, and that the limits of sense and reason impose constraints that can be identified but not fully overcome.

The orientation adopted throughout these pages is comfortable with Ameriks' interpretation even if less inclined to put any fixed and sharp boundary between "the manifest image" and the scientific image of reality. At the macroscopic level, the boundary is not at all obvious and this, finally, is the level at which "nature" presents itself as something calling for explanation. At what is now understood to be the subatomic level—the level one is tempted to regard as closer to things "as in themselves they really are"—there are not even those *appearances* that stand as the starting point of every epistemic claim.

This will be made clearer in later pages, but at this point it is important to state how Kant's aims are understood in these pages. First, it matters that Kant was a scientist as well as a philosopher, with a lifelong interest in cosmology and physics, and with an abiding concern that the claims of science would never rest securely on what he took to be the available anchoring foundations of philosophy. Haunted by skepticism, the scientific world might seek sanctuary behind the porous screen of appearances, unmindful of the observer's contribution to the pictured world.

Fully aware of the limits and even the distortions imposed by brute empiricism, the scientific world also had a fatal attraction to elaborate rationally constructed models of a reality making little contact with the facts of the world as given. Against this historical background, there was the Age of Newton, the achievements in astronomy, mechanics, physiology—the extraordinary discovery of lawful relationships in every corner of the natural world. How is this to be understood? What makes it even possible?

The question is ever timely. Consider the world as presented to sensitive creatures. The olfactory epithelial cells of canines respond to the dissipation of one molecule of fatty acid. The inner ear is responsive to acoustic energy at the level of Brownian motion. The pigment chemistry of retinal receptors functions at the level of quanta. The ordinary percipient lives in a sea of disconnected physical impingements—incessant, innumerable, and dynamic. Out of all this, and in the manner of discovery rather than invention, a knowable world emerges. Kant's *Critique* sets out to establish how this is so, the implications arising from the very nature of the process and, thus, both the achievements and the limits of sense and reason.

Returning to the ontological question, consider again Kant's division of reality into those *phenomena* that are accessible to perceptual modes of knowing and that other and forever-elusive realm of *noumena* falling utterly beyond the perceptual resources of human cognition. Less clear is just how Kant reaches this conclusion against the small army of once-celebrated metaphysicians who had argued otherwise. Is it really the case, even in this age of superstring theory and journeys to the moon, that Physics cannot reveal what things are *in themselves*? Is Kant's distinction to be understood as an *epistemological* claim regarding limits on one's access to the intricacies of reality, or is it a worrisome *ontological* claim yielding a double reality, a two-worlds theory? The reading encouraged in these pages takes Kant to be proposing the double-aspect character of reality, the (*phenomenal)* aspect accessible by way of sensibility and that other (*noumenal*) aspect that may be reasonably inferred—something thinkable and even considered conjecturally in terms of possibly true or false propositions—but never experienced, never *known*. The *Critique* allows a more daring reading, one considered further in later pages.[9]

By long tradition in science and philosophy the senses are judged to be the paths by which the external world enters into mental life. But how is it that the mental life in question is yours or mine? How does a stream of sensations or perceptions come to be *someone's*, and what presuppositions are necessary for this to be possible? And if, as Kant will argue, time and space are "intuitions" that the percipient brings to the sensible world, rather than finding them outside and independent of oneself, is it the case that time and space are somehow purely subjective, unreal, invented? Then, if this actually is the case, how would nature itself—"so far as it is determined according to universal laws"—be possible? Would not the very temporality of causal relations be reduced to subjectivity? Would not metaphysics become a branch of anthropology? Were the skeptics right all along?

It should be clear that the very purposes of the *Critique* make it arguably the most ambitious treatise in the history of metaphysics, its central arguments still of fundamental importance not only to philosophers but also to scientists. Thus, a recent article in the field of theoretical physics notes that

> In physics it became quite clear in the last 30 years how the cognition of objects can be carried through. Surprisingly, the strategy which is applied in physics for the cognition of objects follows essentially the conceptual program formulated by Kant,—even if the majority of physicists is not aware of this point.[10]

If all knowledge begins with observation, it is clear that the observer makes some sort of contribution. Uncertain as to the nature and degree of this contribution, how finally are epistemic relativism and its skeptical consequences to be avoided? If sense and reason are limited, how can the latter serve as the instrument with which to discover those very limits? Must confidence in the discoveries of science finally be grounded in no more than pragmatic considerations?

How and whether Kant settled these questions frames a lively and enduring dispute among scholars. It will remain so as long as claims to knowledge depend on assumptions and, indeed, on faculties whose nature and limits must put on notice the more certain of our conjectures.

CHAPTER 2

THE LARGER CONTEXT:
GERMANY AND THE ENLIGHTENMENT

Toward the end of his life and reflecting back on years of scholarly writing and teaching, Kant summarized his understanding of the mission of philosophy:

> Philosophy is not some sort of science of representations, concepts, and ideas, or a science of all sciences, or anything else of this sort; rather, it is a science of the human being, of its representing, thinking, and acting—it should present the human being in all of its components, as it is and ought to be, that is, in accordance with its natural determinations as well as its relationship of morality and freedom. . . . The critique of reason has appeared and determined the human being to a thoroughly *active* place in the world. The human being itself is the original creator of all its representations and concepts and ought to be the sole author of all its actions.[1]

Philosophy is a science of the human being. At first blush, this reads as if it were just one of the slogans of the Enlightenment. But within that optimistic message there is an element of resignation. The passage of interest is, ". . . with its natural determinations." Thus are real limits announced. Thus are the limits of "Enlightenment" itself foretold.

The Enlightenment took a different form in different places, but there was this much in common throughout Europe: the received forms of argument, routinely referred to as "Scholastic," were thought to have been put on notice by the scientific achievements of the previous century, the age of Descartes, Newton, and Galileo. To the extent that these achievements seemed to be at the expense of the science of Aristotle, anti-Aristotelianism rose (or sunk) to the level of a cottage industry.

It was Aristotle's physics that was overtaken by the leading scientists of the seventeenth century. Basing his theories on a four-element ontology (earth, air, fire, water), Aristotle's account of natural events was based on what he took to be the tendency of things to move toward their "natural place." Thus, the stone finds its natural place in the earth (thereupon falling down), whereas the flame of a candle continues to point up even when the candle is turned upside down. Moreover, common observation shows that objects, once an impelling force has been removed, come to rest, so motion must require the continued application of force. All this was overturned by the laws associated with Newton and Galileo. Predictably (though without any really relevant argument), the errors in the Physics of Aristotle supported the rejection of what was taken to be at all "Aristotelian." The authority of tradition was now to be replaced by the authority of observation and reason, something Aristotle himself would have applauded had he not been its earliest advocate. As experience and reason were regarded as generously if unevenly distributed, there was growing optimism regarding the ability of the ordinary citizen to engage foundational issues in science and philosophy. This optimism was expressed in several ways: the publication of encyclopedic treatises on technical subjects, the adoption of national languages over and against Latin, and the reformulation of philosophical issues in ways designed to reach a popular audience.

These developments came later to Germany, which had its own culturally and institutionally nurturing conditions and a number of progressive thinkers laboring to overcome the burdens of a long oppressive orthodoxy. Beginning in the seventeenth century with the sermons of Philipp Jakob Spener (1635–1705) the movement known as *Pietism* spread widely through German intellectual and religious circles. Its influence over a course of years was mixed and various. Spener's *Pia Desideria*—pious desires—was published in 1675 as a preface to the teachings of Johann Arndt. His purpose was to establish for the faithful the nature of true piety and the program of required measures for attaining and preserving it. He set down a half-dozen specific measures of which one was the *reform of schools and universities.*[2] That his influence was great was guaranteed in

1729 when King Frederick William I would place the royal stamp of approval on Pietist teaching. It was now mandatory that any theologian aspiring to academic office in any Prussian university first undertake two full years of study at Halle, the geographic and spiritual center of Pietist theology and philosophy. An authority on the subject, F. E. Stoeffler, has noted,

> It would indeed be difficult to find an important Protestant development either in Germany or in Scandinavia which did not react either positively or negatively to Halle's leadership in theology and church politics.[3]

The ascendancy of Prussia within the German-speaking world carried with it the widespread adoption of Pietism within Prussia. At this same time, the University of Königsberg, which would be Kant's institutional home for the entirety of his academic life, had become another influential locus of Pietist teaching. Indeed, Kant's parents were Pietists. Though faithful to Luther's theology, the Pietists were rather indifferent to systematic theology, emphasizing instead strict codes of morality, coupled with severe conceptions of sin and redemption. The Pietist movement in its earlier development included enthusiastic rituals, magic, prophetic visions—just the features that would stand as barriers to serious philosophical reflection. Though this was offset by a spirit of charity and religious devotion, there was simply too much within the movement that stifled scholarly initiative and unprejudiced inquiry.

However, on this very basis there was also the Pietistic aloofness toward academic and systematic theology. Pietism called for the replacement of doctrinal formulas with practical concerns for a morally upright life. These tendencies, maturing even as Enlightenment was expressing itself at the very borders of the German-speaking world, soon left room for a rationalist theology, centered at the University of Halle and now on a collision course with entrenched Pietism. There would be both progressive and regressive movements, but at least for Kant and his contemporaries some portion of the burden of orthodoxy had lifted, if only temporarily.

Beneficiaries of the more progressive developments owed much to Christian Thomasius (1655–1728), a professor of law and philosophy at Halle, who argued against all forms of torture and witch hunting and defended tolerance and intellectual freedom. His father, Jakob

Thomasius (1622–84), had been a highly significant figure in the German intellectual world, numbering Leibniz among his students. He took the lion's share of his son's education, preparing him for the profession of law chiefly through the writings of Grotius and Pufendorf, the leading figures in natural law theory.

The tradition of natural law theory, beginning with Aristotle, developed by Cicero and rendered "official" within Christendom by the works of Thomas Aquinas, reserved to *natural reason* the analytical power sufficient to ground law and morality in the evident nature of human nature itself. Natural reason is distinct from those truths and insights provided by revelation and preserved in scripture. It accounts for the success of the pagans of the classical age in developing moral codes, principles of justice, and enduring political institutions.

Fully educated in this tradition, Christian Thomasius could claim among his accomplishments the installation of philosophy as an academic discipline. His respect for the significant role of revelation was thus moderated by the rich philosophical resources developed within the tradition of natural law. He advocated not only higher education for women but also a clear separation between theological and naturalistic studies. He taught with great distinction at Halle, which he helped to found, lecturing in German rather than Latin, and writing books, as he said, for "all rational persons of whatever social standing and gender."[4] He had reached Halle under the protection of Frederick III, having been threatened with no less than imprisonment at Leipzig for his non-Pietist positions. (Among his political sins was support of marriage between Lutherans and Calvinists.) He was notorious for his sharp criticism of the pedantries exercised by a professoriate that had removed itself from the cares of the real world. His defense of a pragmatic and commonsense philosophy against what was regarded as the overly "academic" tradition marked out one of the boundaries dividing the German academic world of the time. Not a "philosopher" in the sense that would be so perfectly crafted by Kant himself, Thomasius helped restore law and civics to that secular domain once populated by great Roman jurists and senators. As Ian Hunter has observed, Thomasius's writings on the issue of religious orthodoxy and toleration made clear that

> Theologians should concern themselves with eternal salvation, "graciously" leaving this matter to the jurists as the better part of public law.[5]

Thomasius's influence was superseded by that of Christian Wolff (1679–1754), later praised by Kant as the first to show by example "how the secure progress of the science [of metaphysics] is to be attained only through orderly establishment of principles, clear determination of concepts, insistence on strictures of proof, and avoidance of venturesome, nonconsecutive steps in our inferences."[6] It is to Wolff that one looks for establishing what came to be called *Schulphilosophie* with its "insistence upon strictures of proof," as Kant says. It is difficult in a brief space to record the range and degree of Wolff's influence in the German-speaking world of his time. Only Kant and Leibniz stand higher in this regard.

Wolff's background was modest, but he was encouraged to follow an academic calling. After several years teaching at Leipzig, he was awarded a professorship of mathematics at Halle. By this time he was a self-proclaimed disciple of Leibniz's, committed to establish philosophy on rational-mathematical grounds. His lectures and writing were exhortatory, designed to establish the authority of reason, even at the possible expense of scripture and revelation. Once again, the Pietists at Halle were aroused, charging Wolff with a philosophical determinism that ran counter to their conceptions of morality. Wolff had not helped his case by proclaiming the moral superiority of Confucianism, a superiority attained without reliance on Christian theology.

Banned from teaching at Halle by Frederick William—who threatened execution if he did not leave the territory within two days!—Wolff moved on to Marburg, greeted there as a great philosopher and soon earning a small fortune as a lecturer and public figure. Alas, his standing rose still higher, now fortified by the genius of irony: Frederick William's son, the redoubtable Frederick the Great, had become one of Wolff's admirers and, on his accession to the throne, recalled Wolff to Halle where he soon was installed as its Chancellor.

If there is a figure properly identified as a paragon within the German Enlightenment it is surely Wolff. In the patrimony of Leibniz, he fashioned a formal method of inquiry structured in the manner of mathematics. He is the first of leading German philosophers to publish in the German language. Additionally, his scholarly contributions to the field of economics added to his fame beyond the academic world. Within the academic world he shaped the sensibilities of entire generations of scholars by emphasizing the need for specialized professionalism in addressing even the most practical of matters.

As one bridge from Leibniz to Kant, Wolff provided a rigorous philosophical method as well as refined arguments for the development of a scientific metaphysics. His association with Leibniz was direct, including a dozen years of correspondence between the two as well as Leibniz's direct support for Wolff's appointment as professor at Halle. Although the Newton–Leibniz controversy is far more widely known, Wolff made his own contribution to the issues dividing the two giants.[7] Nor should Wolff be judged merely as a "Leibnizian," for his own published works were original in their own right. It should be noted that Leibniz's enduring standing as a philosopher was earned by works published after his death and that Wolff's own contributions were valued less for their "Leibnizian" elements than for their own intrinsic value. His election to London's Royal Society is sufficient evidence of the esteem he enjoyed beyond the German-speaking world.

Wolff's philosophy carefully distinguished between ordinary ways of comprehending reality and genuinely philosophical modes of analysis and explanation.[8] Regarding philosophy's mission as improving and enriching life in practical ways, Wolff was committed to the belief that only systematic and structured modes of philosophical inquiry would render progress possible. Central to the project is a scientific comprehension of the human mind itself—a human science that begins with the recognition that certain cognitive powers are innate and necessary starting points for inquiry itself. Chief among these, following Leibniz, are the law of contradiction and the principle of sufficient reason.

So far, Wolff is seen as a traditional rationalist, faithful to Leibniz and perhaps indifferent to "mere facts." But this would be a caricature, not a proper characterization. It should be remembered that the intellectual world occupied by Wolff had already been largely won over to the science of Newton and to its empiricistic canons as these had been set down by Francis Bacon before Newton and John Locke afterwards. Wolff's philosophy attempted to absorb this perspective into a larger rationalist framework, but not at the expense of systematic observation. As with Leibniz, he insisted that the given fact must find a place within the overall scheme of things by which one records not just the fact but the reason for it. He makes this clear in his *German Metaphysics*:

> Because of that which one knows only by experience, one knows only that it is but does not see how it *is* connected with other truths, in knowledge from experience there is no reason. Hence experience is opposed to reason. . . . We have, then, two ways by which we can reach the knowledge of truth: experience and reason. The former is based on the senses, and the latter on the understanding.[9]

Here and elsewhere, Wolff's philosophical treatises include problems that will be central to Kant's own metaphysical inquiries and arising from debates recently conducted by the disciples of Newton and of Leibniz. The nature of space is just one of these, with the Newtonians taking it to be real and absolute and the Leibnizians taking it as something constructed out of relationships among distinct bodies. Wolff supports the Leibnizian perspective:

> We must take space to be the order of those things that exist at the same time. And thus no space can exist if things are not present to fill it, although it is still distinct from these things.[10]

The combination of the mind's innate powers and the application of rational argument is the means by which metaphysics is developed as a science. This, however, is not the sole engine of discovery and understanding. Though recognizing that the widely adopted empirical philosophy of Locke was inadequate, Wolff fully embraced the proposition that mental life is supplied by experience and that all science must be grounded in systematic observation. In Wolff's work there is a struggle to achieve a balance between the Newtonian and Leibnizian world views, an attempt later and famously carried on by Kant himself.

If Wolff's defense of Leibniz's "pre-established harmony"—cast as a species of determinism—numbered his days at Halle, it did him no harm over the long haul. His influence grew and spread over a course of decades, especially through the support of Frederick the Great. What Wolff sought was an approach that would gain for metaphysics what the natural sciences had won in the previous century. His aim was to ground metaphysics in mathematics, with definitions absorbed into axioms and these then arranged to permit logically permissible inferences.

Kant's encomium continues,

> He was peculiarly well fitted to raise metaphysics to the dignity of a science, if only it had occurred to him to prepare the ground beforehand by a critique of the organ, that is, of pure reason itself.[11]

Wolff, then, was one bridge to Leibniz. Perhaps an even more direct bridge is found in the *Metaphysics* of Alexander Baumgarten (1714–62), the text Kant used as a teacher throughout his academic career. Baumgarten's approach is both Wolffian and Leibnizian with sections devoted to the preestablished harmony and "On the Best World." Perhaps more important is part 3 of the work, "Psychology," which assesses the powers and functions of the senses, the intellect, and reason. Of particular interest is Baumgarten's recognition (at 729–30) of the importance of the percipient being able to distinguish between self and things external to self, a distinction that will figure so centrally in Kant's refutation of idealism. Many things in the external world are represented in consciousness. Were there no means by which to distinguish the representation of "self" from these other representations, solipsism would be the inevitable consequence. There is a hint in these sections of the Kantian argument according to which self-awareness depends on the permanence of objects external to the self. Throughout, Baumgarten approaches core issues in ontology and psychology from the established rationalist perspective, thus providing Kant with just the sort of metaphysical method demanding a critical appraisal.

Kant's exposure to Wolff, to Newtonian science, and to Locke's philosophy cannot be attributed to a single source, but surely one of the most influential of the early sources was Kant's major teacher at Königsberg, Martin Knutzen (1713–51). Something of a prodigy, gaining a professorship at the tender age of 21, it was Knutzen who drew Kant's attention to Newton and the new physics as well as the deficiency of Leibniz's alternative theories. A Wolffian, Knutzen also immersed Kant in the works of Wolff even as Knutzen himself sought to reconcile a thoroughgoing rationalist philosophy to the core principles of Pietism. Perhaps most important, Knutzen's interests in British thought may have been an early source of Kant's own attention to Locke's philosophy.[12]

One of Kant's good friends and persistent critics was the Pietist Johann Georg Hamann (1730–88), a philosopher trained by Knutzen and later a well-known figure in the so-called *Sturm und Drang* movement. This was a literary movement expressly at odds with the rationalistic and scientific character of Enlightenment thought. The movement sought to replace this with an aesthetic of sentiment and primitive expression, eliminating the formalisms of aristocratic taste and installing the earthy authenticity of individual lives. The guide, if it is truth that one is after, is history—even biography—and comparable records of actual persons caught up in the stresses and strains of existence.

Hamman once declared that he looked upon logical proofs ". . . the way a well-bred girl looks upon a love letter." His own philosophical model was, alas, David Hume, though unlike Hume he believed that it is only faith in the divine that saves humanity from the vexations of philosophy.[13] Johann Herder (1744–1803), another leader of the *Sturm und Drang* reaction to Enlightenment rationalism, was a student of Kant's and would become one of the most influential philosophers in the German-speaking world. It would be an exaggeration to credit Pietism with the specific works of Hamman, Herder, and those such as Goethe influenced by them, but the Pietistic emphasis on sensibility, on the inner life with its spiritual resources, did present an alternative to the excessively rationalistic dimensions of Enlightenment orthodoxies.

Here, then, are the larger and smaller pieces of the cultural and philosophical atmosphere surrounding Kant's intellectual development. It leads inevitably to the overarching problem of integrating the rational and the experiential, the subjective and the objective, the personal and the universal, through a systematic metaphysics. At B xiv, he declares metaphysics to be "a speculative science that soars above the teachings of experience, and in which reason is indeed meant to be its own pupil." In the *Prolegomena* he puts it this way:

As concerns the sources of metaphysical knowledge, its very concept implies that they cannot be empirical. Its principles (including not only its maxims, but its basic notions) must never be derived from experience. It must not be physical but metaphysical knowledge, namely, knowledge lying beyond experience. It can therefore have for its basis neither external experience, which is the source of physics proper, nor internal, which is the basis of rational psychology. It is therefore *a priori* knowledge, coming from pure understanding and pure reason.[14] (265)

What this passage makes clear is that the development of metaphysics as a science is not grounded in the empirical facts of the external world or the introspective facts of a Cartesian-Lockean psychology. Rather, metaphysics as an independent science finds its contents in that domain of a priori knowledge that is foundational for both the physical sciences and rational psychology.

But if both the physical and the psychological modes of inquiry are ruled out, what method remains if metaphysics is, as he says, "to enter upon the path of science"? The problem as he sees it is one of method. At Bxv he reduces the prevailing methods of metaphysics to "a merely random groping, and what is worst of all, a groping among mere concepts."

But why should metaphysics be conceived as a "science" in the first place? The significant advances in physics in the seventeenth century stood in vivid contrast to the stagnation of traditional metaphysics. Alternative programs for the development of metaphysics were soon on offer, led in Germany by Wolff, in the patrimony of Leibniz. The controversies arising from these various attempts led to the Prize Competition sponsored by Prussian Royal Academy of Sciences. Kant submitted his *Inquiry Concerning the Distinctness of the Principles of Natural Theology and Morals* late in 1762. The terms of the competition were as follows:

Whether metaphysical truths in general, and especially the first principles of natural theology and morals, are capable of the same degree of proof as geometrical truths, and if they are not capable of such proof, what is the nature of their certainty, and to what degree can they achieve it, and is such certainty sufficient for conviction?[15]

Just what was that "changed fashion," as Kant called it, that heaped such scorn on metaphysics? There was more to the change in fashion than what Newton had brought about in the previous century. There was also the tension between academic and popular approaches to fundamental matters. Within the broader context of German thought, there was a tension between *Schulphilosophie* and *Popularphilosophie*. Kant, during his early Königsberg years, was inclined toward the latter, perhaps owing to the Pietist teachings of his youth. In time, however, he is fully committed to the *Schulphilosophie* of the academic world and increasingly dismissive of anything drawn from the common stock of ideas.

It is thanks in large measure to Wolff that philosophy in Germany had moved away from the commonsense "guide to life" subject that a Christian Thomasius would make accessible to all. *Popularphilosophie*, with its loose, unsystematic structure and open appeal to the ordinary citizen afforded neither the means nor the measure of progress. With Wolff the philosophic agenda was radically transformed, *Popularphilosophie* now replaced by systematic, academic, and even "professional" approaches to issues falling well beyond the ambit of daily life. Consider Kant's all too patronizing dismissal in the *Prolegomena* of Reid, Oswald, and Beattie.[16] It reflects his eagerness to separate his work from any version of a "commonsense" philosophy that might be judged as *Popularphilosophie*. The major works of the Scottish school were surely well known to Kant and had already claimed the allegiance of many of the intellectual leaders of the German world of philosophy. Kant had adopted what still other academic leaders affirmed, namely, that authentic progress reveals itself in the form of grand, encompassing systems, the model here being just what the Age of Newton had produced in science. That this was still very much a matter of concern to him was to be evident when early reviews favored the *Scottish Common Sense* approach of Reid over what seemed to be the argumentative excesses of the *Critique*.[17]

The movement from *Popular* to academic philosophy is understandable. The significant advances in physics in the seventeenth century stood in vivid contrast to the stagnation of traditional metaphysics. The new physics had been won at the expense of the old. Why not a similar development in metaphysics? Alternatives, both conceptual and methodological, were advanced by Newton, Descartes, and Leibniz, and it was to these alternatives that Kant's attention was drawn. Consider what Descartes had achieved in mathematics. He had developed that *Method of Analysis* whereby all of Euclidean geometry could be reduced to algebra. He concluded from this that

> Any problem in geometry can easily be reduced to such terms that a knowledge of the lengths of certain straight lines is sufficient for its construction.[18]

This was part of Descartes's larger commitment to the rational foundations of knowledge, against skeptical challenges based on the uncertainties of sense perception. The startling conclusion was that all of Euclidean geometry can be derived *without looking at figures*! Furthermore, in his *Regulae* he argued that such algebraic representations eliminate appeals to obscure and secret modes of cognition. The analytical method reveals the actual mode of solution.

What of Leibniz? He was, of course, the towering figure of the German Enlightenment, and his work profoundly influenced Kant's understanding of the core problems of metaphysics. To the extent that these problems arise from the competing perspectives of empiricism and rationalism, Leibniz stands in the same relation to Locke that Kant came to stand in relation to Hume. In this connection, consider Leibniz's *New Essays on the Understanding*, completed in 1705 but published only many years later.[19] (We find Kant reading these essays in the 1760s.) It is in this work that Leibniz directly challenges the basic assumptions of Lockean epistemology. Against the traditional empiricist claim that nothing is in the intellect that is not first in the senses (*Nihil in intellectus quod non prius fuerit in sensu*), Leibniz counters, *Nisi intellectus ipse*—nothing but the intellect itself! Here again is the core rationalist assumption: Knowledge necessarily bears the mark and expresses the innate character of intellectual cognition. It was Leibniz, too, whose *Method of Logical Analysis* led to the conclusion that all true propositions are *analytic* of necessity. *Whatever is, is necessarily*! The thesis is summarized in a letter addressed to Arnauld:

> In every affirmative true proposition, necessary or contingent, universal or singular, the notion of the predicate is contained in some way in that of the subject, *praedicatum inest subjecto*. Or else I do not know what truth is.[20]

For Leibniz, all propositions are *analytic*, but their truths may be truths of reason or truths of fact (*Monadology*, 33). Truths of reason are statements of strict identity via the law of universal substitutivity. Such propositions cannot be denied without contradiction. Truths of reason, then, are not influenced by any contingent fact about the world. Truths of fact are also statements of identity, though the grounds for factual truths are not self-evident. Their truth *seems* merely *contingent* since only a complete analysis could show them to be identities. However, it can be shown by way of what Leibniz calls the principle of sufficient reason just how the truths of fact are generated.

Leibniz illustrates the principle by way of Archimedes: Place equal weights on the arms of a fulcrum and the result is total rest. There is no "reason" for one side to behave differently in relation to the other. Nor would it suffice to dismiss all this on the grounds that Leibniz should have simply acknowledged that facts arise from temporally prior causal influences. That would merely beg the question as to why there should be causal dependencies in the first place. For Leibniz, then, the facts of the world are what they are necessarily, for each of them is brought about as a result of there being a sufficient reason for them to be brought about, and a sufficient *reason* is not merely a physical cause by another name.

To understand the difference between conventional notions of causation and Leibniz's principle of sufficient reason it is useful to consider his theory of preestablished harmony. This theory is offered as the correct alternative to conventional causal concepts that are based on the notion of "influxes." According to the *influxus* theory, A causally affects B in virtue of A somehow inserting into B (by way of an "influx") a property otherwise absent from B. Thus, the impinging of A on the surface of B lends some of A's motion to B and thereupon causes B to move.

Leibniz's rejection of this entire line of thinking is tersely advanced in his *Monadology* at #7:

> There is, furthermore, no way to explain how a monad could be altered or changed in its inner make-up by some other created being. For one can transpose nothing in it, nor conceive in it any internal motion that could be excited, directed, increased, or diminished within it, as can happen in composites where

there is change among the parts. Monads have no windows through which something can enter into or depart from them. Accidents cannot be detached, nor wander about outside of substances.[21]

The (in)famous theory of monads is not to be considered here except to say that monads are foundational of Leibniz's ontology. They refer to the ultimate, noncomposite entities out of which other and complex composites are fashioned. As the ultimate constituents of everything—roughly akin to the modern physics of elementary particles—their activity and organization are entirely internal. They are not subject to division, cannot be entered by something else, have no "windows," and, thus, there is no avenue for an external influx. Each monad is thus an image of the cosmos as a whole whose configuration and temporal history are the result of an initially established harmony. As he says in his *New Essays on the Understanding*,

> Each of these souls (monads) expresses in its own manner what occurs outside itself, and it cannot do so through any influence of other particular beings . . . and so necessarily each soul must have received this nature—this inner source of the expression of what lies without—from a universal cause, upon which all of these beings depend and which brings it about that each of them perfectly agrees with and corresponds to the others.[22] (New Essays, 6, 440)

Leibniz is often in the foreground and always in the background of Kant's philosophical labors. Much of the foregoing summary of Leibniz on monads will be revived later when considering Kant's treatment of what he calls the Paralogisms and Antinomies and related "illusions" of reason. But as early as 1749 in his *Thoughts on the True Estimation of Living Forces* (1749) Kant is wrestling with the then hotly contested theories of Descartes and Leibniz on the nature of force. For Descartes, force is the motion of (dead) matter and is thus proportional to mv. Following Galileo, Leibniz took the fundamental relationship to be mv^2—the kinetic energy that Leibniz dubbed *vis viva*. What Kant displays in his *Living Forces* is a *foundationalism* compatible with a Leibnizian physics of intrinsic powers inexplicable in terms of the merely external relations

22

among things. And in that same work, reflecting on metaphysics, he says that it

> has indeed reached only the threshold of a genuinely thorough science. It is not difficult to recognize the weakness in many of the things it attempts.[23]

The point, of course, is that Kant's project arises from an intellectual and scientific context and one in which recourse to the notion of internal principles is an integral part of scientific theory and explanation. Engagement with Descartes and Leibniz takes place also around the concepts of matter, space, and time: Descartes had reduced *matter* to the category of the *res extensa*, according to which every material thing is extended and every extended thing is divisible. Against this, Leibniz insisted that, at the limit, reality must be comprised of the most basic units that are simple, indivisible, and unextended. They are dimensionless mathematical points. So the entire Cartesian world of extended matter is in reality constructed from simple immaterial substances, alas, Leibniz's famous monads. Accordingly Leibniz rejected the Cartesian two-substance dualism of the mental and the material. Specifically, he rejected the notion of genuine, extended material substances, arguing, as did the Scholastic commentators that "being" and "one" are equivalent. Again, in a letter to Antoine Arnauld, he says, "I hold as axiomatic . . . that what is not truly one is not truly one being either"[24] (April 30, 1687).

For something to count as a real being it must be a unity, and for something to be a unity, it must be indivisible and as such indestructible. Hence, though there is matter as such, there is no "real" extended material *substance* of the Cartesian variety. Ultimate reality is monadic. On this understanding, neither space nor time is a fundamental feature of reality. Space and time are unreal, but references to spatial location and temporal duration do provide a convenient shorthand for keeping track of the relations among the consistent set of monads that is the actual world.

Leibniz develops these ideas in opposition to Newtonian science. Against Newton's concept of absolute space and absolute motion, he argues that the motion and position of an object arise solely in relation to other objects, such that all motion is relative. The relation is to other objects, not to space as such, for space as such has no objective representation. Once more, the principle of sufficient reason is invoked. Space as such is entirely homogeneous. No region of empty space is distinguishable from any other region. As with Archimedes' equal weights, this establishes that no sufficient reason enters into the creation of absolute (empty) space, and, therefore, it is not a feature of reality. As Leibniz says in his correspondence with Clarke,

> [Newton] admits, in addition to the matter, an empty space and, according to him, the matter does not occupy more than a very small part of the space . . . to affirm the void in the Nature is to attribute to God a very imperfect production; it is to violate the Principle of necessity of a sufficient Reason.[25]

Put other way, there is never a reason for nothing.

Although seemingly tame now and merely "academic," the tension between the Newtonians and the Leibnizians took on the character of open warfare after Leibniz's death in 1716. The French *philosophes*, in league with their comparably "enlightened" British contemporaries, set out to reduce Leibniz's metaphysical and moral theories to nonsense. His "system of optimism" was turned into effective burlesque in Voltaire's *Candide*, and his monadology was subjected to relentless criticism by such notables as Maupertuis and Euler. The latter's *Letters to a German Princess* (1760–2), written to the daughter of Frederick the Great, dismissed the followers of Wolff as naïve and backward.[26] London's *Royal Society*, along with the lively Salons of Paris, paid little respect to the Berlin Academy, which was still respectful and attentive, but with increasing hesitancy, to the works of the great Leibniz. Surely the most celebrated of the defenders of these works was Moses Mendelssohn (1729–86) who, in a youthful work, said of the master:

> Without your help I would have been lost for ever. I never met you in the flesh, yet your imperishable writings . . . have guided me to the firm path of the true philosophy, to the knowledge of myself and of my origin. They have engraved upon my soul the sacred truths on which my felicity is founded.[27]

The conflict was finally between the emerging empiricism of the school of Bacon and Newton and the seemingly outdated rationalism of the Scholastics, still given life by Leibniz and his followers. Thus was the authority of experience pitted against the authority of reason, a contest providing grist for the Kantian mill. Kant's own quasi-Leibnizian credentials were evident, but so, too, was his allegiance to the new science. He must show that the claims of science are not merely expressions of a peculiar cognitive process, that reality is comprised of what is more than and different from ideas about it, and that the world as a congeries of appearances is nonetheless an objective world capable of being known as such. If it is our fate to have knowledge cobbled out of appearances and a fixed scheme of categories, we are not thereby left to wishful thinking or the mere prejudices of the imagination.

Thanks largely to the persistence of Mendelssohn and the influence of the Leibnizian defenses developed in his *Philosophical Writings*[28] (1761), the Berlin Academy chose for the Prize Competition of 1762 the question, "Whether metaphysical truths . . . are susceptible of the same evidence as mathematical truths?" Mendelssohn won the prize that year, with Kant's essay placed second. The title of Mendelssohn's entry was "On Evidence in Metaphysical Sciences" with Mendelssohn supporting the Leibniz–Wolff mode of philosophical analysis. He defends the proposition that metaphysical and mathematical analysis is conceptually the same:

> Just as there is pure geometry, so there is a pure metaphysics. . . . The procedure of the metaphysician is here the same as that of the geometer. . . . His deductions are quite as unshakeable.[29]

Kant's submission, *Inquiry Concerning the Distinctness of the Principles of Natural Theology and Morals*[30] (1764), tests the feasibility of metaphysical approaches to the fundamental question of the existence of God. More relevant to present purposes, the essay challenges the Wolffian argument that would collapse the differences between mathematical and philosophical modes of analysis. Following Newton's method—which he took to be authoritative— Kant argues for *conceptual analysis* as the first step in putting metaphysics on a scientific footing. Indeed, Kant may be the first post-Newtonian to recognize and integrate fully the mode of conceptual analysis that Newton had brought to bear on the central problems in physics. As Michael Friedman notes,

> More than for any other philosopher of the modern period, the Newtonian concepts of space, time, geometry, and motion were central to Kant's philosophical enterprise.[31]

Commenting on the work of Robert DiSalle, Friedman goes on to say,

> Indeed, it was Kant, for DiSalle, who first grasped the properly "transcendental" character of the Newtonian concepts of space, time, and motion—not as mysterious metaphysical postulations but as necessary presuppositions for a mathematically precise and empirically well-defined physics of forces and interactions."[32]

Kant understood that only with this conceptual analysis successfully completed might metaphysics then aspire to the status of a "synthetic" discipline capable of discoveries on the order of scientific discovery. Moreover, only with that analysis fully completed might metaphysics supply the right sort of objective grounding for science itself.[33] There is no doubt but that between the time he submitted his *Prize Essay* and a decade later in his *Inaugural Dissertation,* he was turning over in his mind, and with great frustration, any number of approaches to the question of epistemology and the limits of human knowledge. Writing to Herder in Spring of 1768 he says with clear disappointment,

> As for my own work, since I am committed to nothing and with total indifference to my own and others' opinions, often turn my whole system upside down . . . I have, since we parted, exchanged many of my views for other insights. My principal aim is to know[34] the actual nature and limits of human capacities and inclinations.

This is not the lamentation of a defeatist who can find no merit in his own work. In the same letter Kant goes on to say that he thinks his efforts in ethics have been successful. Clearly, although he does not specify what has been left undone, it is surely the vast and vexed subject of metaphysics itself.

The *Inaugural Dissertation* (1770) was a required element in his application for the professorship at Königsberg. The submission was titled, *On the Form and Principles of the Sensible and the Intelligible World.*[35] In this work the larger project begins to take shape. He now recognizes that the analysis of concepts is a metaphysical dead-end. The work prefigures the *Critique* as it draws the fundamental distinction between the intelligible world (*mundus intelligibilis*) of metaphysics and the sensible world (*mundus sensibilis*) of the natural sciences. Though lacking the expansive analytical efforts of the mature work, the *Inaugural Dissertation* begins the difficult task of accepting the intuitive and cognitive principles that ground all human knowledge while still preserving that knowledge against skepticism. Many of the central precepts of the *Critique* find earlier expression in the *Inaugural Dissertation*. Illustrative is the section on time:

> *The idea of time does not originate in, but is presupposed by the senses.* Whether things falling under sense-perception be simultaneous or in line of succession cannot be represented but by the idea of time; nor does succession beget the concept of time; it appeals to it. Hence the notion of time, though acquired by experience, is badly defined by a series of actual things existing one *after* another, for what the word *after* means I understand only by the previous concept of time.[36]

Clearly, the project has been engaged. It is not enough to be the subject of perceptions. It is by way of a developed metaphysics that one finally can make sense of experience and thus render knowledge itself intelligible. It is now timely to ask more precisely how Kant would have "metaphysics" understood. In his most economical account, he refers to it as, ". . . nothing but the *inventory* of all our possessions through pure reason, systematically arranged"[37] (Axx). He is guided here, no doubt, by Leibniz's earlier complaint that our ". . . knowledge of nature seems to me like a shop well stocked with goods of all kinds, but lacking any order or inventory."[38] Years after the Prize Competition we find Kant still wrestling with the same question. Thus, in his *Preface* to the first edition he writes that metaphysics, once "the queen of the sciences"—in the now "changed fashion"—brings only scorn.

Again, what of this "changed fashion"? It was Kant's view that the British empiricists, notably Locke, Berkeley, and Hume, had fortified the continuing "scandal" in philosophy, namely, the inability to establish the reality of an external world. But if empiricism leads to skepticism, traditional rationalism leads to empty and misleading conjectures. Kant must, therefore, test the limits of pure reason—what it can establish through its own resources without the benefit of experience. What Kant has come to recognize is the neglect displayed by the rationalists in their reliance on a faculty of reason whose nature and limits had never been subjected to critical appraisal. If, indeed, reason is the instrument of choice, it must be calibrated. The range over which it can be productively employed must be established. If, instead, the senses are the instruments of choice, it is essential to establish the form of knowledge thereby obtained and the manner in which such knowledge is incorporated into the systematic bodies of knowledge claimed by science.

Kant's sheer intellectual integrity would inevitably find him under suspicion in a world led and shaped by kings and princes. Wolff's shifting fortunes had reflected shifting orthodoxies earlier, and now Kant's method of *critique*, when applied to the claims of religion, attracted the attention of those defenders of the faith revived during the reign of Frederick William II. In 1793 Kant published his *Religion within the Limits of Reason Alone* (*Die Religion innerhalb der Grenzen der blossen Vernunft*).[39] In book 4 of the work, he speaks of "the pure religion of reason," whose servants are "all right-thinking men" and who, therefore, cannot be the servants of any "visible church." Here, again, something of an echo is audible of that Pietism that had long challenged the institutional strictures of the prevailing orthodoxy. Religion established by statute is a human affair, marked by the usual ignorance and limitations of humanity at large. He speaks of those whose "allegiance to the historical and statutory element of ecclesiastical faith" as being responsible for a "pseudo-service," a *cultus spurious*, based on blind compliance with "the will of a superior." The essay led summarily to an official Cabinet Order to desist from any further "misuse of Philosophy" and threatened "unpleasant" consequences were Kant to be obstinate. Sensibly, he agreed to write no further in the public domain on religious questions. This will be revisited in the Epilog where Kant's philosophy of religion (if that designation is permissible) is considered.

Kant possessed integrity but not pugnacity. His defense of Enlightenment as *freedom* was typically sober and academic, but it expressed what was clearly the sheer joy of philosophical reflection so evident to those who knew him personally. One such person was Johann Herder, Kant's student and, later as a literary critic, a man whose writings would have profound a influence on Goethe himself. In one of his letters Herder would speak of

> the good fortune to know a philosopher, who was my teacher. In the prime of life he had the happy cheerfulness of a youth, which, so I believe, accompanied him even in grey old age. His forehead, formed for thinking, was the seat of indestructible serenity and peace, the most thought-filled speech flowed from his lips, merriment and wit and humor were at his command, and his lecturing was discourse at its most entertaining. . . . This man, whom I name with the utmost thankfulness, and respect, was Immanuel Kant; his image stands before me to my delight.[40]

Reason, Kant insisted, must become its own student, the one insight that even Wolff had missed. To the extent that metaphysics takes this project as its own, the root question—as acknowledged by those who had framed the Prize Competition—is whether metaphysics can present itself as a science. In light of powerful arguments to the contrary, Kant must test whether metaphysics in the traditional sense is even possible. The *Critique* is the extraordinary result of that attempt.

CHAPTER 3

THE POSSIBILITY OF METAPHYSICS

Those encountering translations of the *Critique* for the first time confront the word *intuition* as early as the Introduction to the first edition. Here Kant is promising the fuller inventory of what reason as such can supply "entirely out of itself." Taking his lead from Leibniz, it is an *inventory* whose contents, he says, are not determined "by any experience or by *special* intuition."[1] It is this early in the reader's labor that an unusual term, one that will be deployed scores of times throughout the work, seems to refer to something profoundly significant but not entirely clear.

How are Kantian *intuitions* to be understood? Dictionary definitions are not especially helpful. In the Merriam-Webster the word refers to "1: quick and ready insight; 2 a: immediate apprehension or cognition b: knowledge or conviction gained by intuition c: the power or faculty of attaining to direct knowledge or cognition without evident rational thought and inference. Turning from this to the German, the match is less than close. The German word in the *Critique* translated as "intuition" is *Anschauung*. Its verb form, *anschauen,* is simply "to look at." Were one to ask another, in a philosophical discussion, "What is your world-view?," the interrogative in German would be, "*Was ist deine Weltanschauung*?" How do you look at things? The question seeks to unearth just how the person is predisposed to see or comprehend the state of the world in general. It surely does not refer to an undeliberated or nonrational disposition but pertains instead to a settled mode of apprehending things and events.

The English word that comes closer is "outlook," but Kant would have *Anschauung* convey more than this. Thus, as the more commonly used words suffer various limitations, translators settled early on "intuition" whose Latin verb root is *intueor*: to look at attentively, to gaze at, to consider, to contemplate. Faithful to the Latin origin, asking about one's *Weltanschauung* is, indeed, to ask how one considers the world in general or is disposed to see it. The problem, then, is not with "intuition" in its earlier acceptation but rather with the word as it tends to be used today.

What, then, of *pure* intuitions? "Pure" is easier to deal with, for here Kant is explicit and consistent. Whether the subject is pure reason (*reinen Vernunft*) or pure intuition (*reinen Anschauung*), the "purity" refers to the absence of any and all empirical grounding or influence. Pure reason is the power of reason as such, neither guided nor deflected nor determined by sensory commerce with the external world. Pure intuition is that mode of apprehension that determines how the external world must be beheld by creatures of a certain kind. Rather than being the result of sensations, it is a necessary condition for sensibility itself. As such, *pure intuitions* comprise the framework within which any experience can occur. They are the necessary conditions of receptivity itself. In their absence a creature would be subject to stimulation and even complex physiological responses to it but surely not to *experience*.

At first blush, this all seems to be an argument for the inescapable subjectivity of knowledge and the relativism and contextualism that stalk any claim to epistemic adequacy. If, for creatures of a certain kind, what is sensible is necessarily represented spatiotemporally, then the spatiotemporal domain both of common experience and the laws of science is, as it were, *put* there rather than *found* there by the observer. On such an account, there is no direct access to the actual world, only a mediated access that imposes on reality features reflective of the peculiarities of the percipient and not the features of the real world. In light of such implications, it becomes a major aim of the *Critique* to save science from just this fate and to do so by mounting a complex and sustained appraisal of subjectivist theories in general and of *idealism* specifically. That he is aware of the power of subjectivist theories is clear when he refers to the "continuing scandal" in metaphysics: the inability of philosophy to establish the reality of the external world!

The problem of idealism is reserved for Chapter 5, but the contours of the problem can be drawn here. In the most general respects, the *ism* is based on the proposition that knowledge claims refer directly and immediately to the contents of one's mind (to one's "ideas") and only indirectly and mediately to the (presumed) objects and events in the external world. At first blush, the Kantian *pure intuitions* would seem to reduce the spatial and temporal features of (presumed) objects and events to something ineliminably subjective. As such, the spatiotemporal aspects of (presumed) reality would be unfit as supports for science. The *Critique* is Kant's attempt to establish both the possibility and the limits of knowledge and the means by which it rises above mere subjectivity. At the same time, Kant must identify and acknowledge the necessary elements of cognition on which all knowledge depends. But this gets ahead of the story. Commentators often refer to Kant's aims and achievements as his so-called Copernican Revolution. This is yet another place calling for caution in attempts to understand the *Critique*. Copernicus is not even mentioned in the first edition of the work and then only briefly in the Introduction to the second edition. In the latter, however, he refers not to a "revolution" inaugurated by Copernicus but to Copernicus's "first thought": *den ersten Gedanken des Kopernicus.*

It is important to be clear on just what Kant found in the mode of analysis adopted by Copernicus. Kant was not only fully versed in the science of astronomy but was also a contributor to it. There is no doubt that his reference to this "first thought" was based on something deeper than an insight into Copernicus's cognitive processes. On more than one occasion Copernicus had been asked by the Church to develop a correct calendar. He respectfully declined on the grounds that there was insufficient agreement among mathematicians as to the length of a year. Older calendars, extending back to Julius Caesar and to Egypt much earlier, were by now hopelessly unsynchronized with the seasons. Caesar's addition of one day every four years worked well enough over a short period of time, but by the sixteenth century the vernal equinox had slipped by ten days. In a Christian world demanding the accurate dating of such feasts as Easter Sunday such variations were unacceptable. It was Pope Leo X who undertook to reform the calendar. By this time Copernicus was confident that the problem called for a rethinking of just how the heavens behave. His "first thought," as Kant put it, was to develop a model based on the motion of the planets as it would appear to one located on the sun as a stationary platform. What Copernicus understood was that reality *as known* reflects the modes of receptivity by which events in the external world become translated into experience. The observer is not the *tabula rasa* of radical empiricism. Rather, the observer arrives on the scene with an assortment of suppositions, orientations, and expectations. How one "beholds" the heavens is different when standing on the sun from what it is when standing on the earth. Such alterations in perspective are not to be abandoned but, as it were, "factored in" if the observations are to be correctly incorporated into a comprehensive system.

Copernicus knew further that it was only by testing various conjectures against the data of experience that a mere casting about gives way to systematic knowledge valid beyond the narrow world of the individual observer. To ask how the solar system appears to one standing on the sun compared with what is seen by one standing on the earth is to acknowledge that the appearance itself is grounded in nonempirical factors. This recognition does not lead to skepticism regarding the "reality" of the sun, moon, and planets. Rather, it establishes how that very reality is cognized by the situated observer. Kant himself does not speak of a "Copernican revolution." At Bxvi Copernicus is cited for the first and only time:

> We must therefore make trial, whether we may not have more success in the tasks of metaphysics, if we suppose that objects must conform to our knowledge. This would agree better with what is desired, namely, that it should be possible to have knowledge of objects *a priori*, determining something in regard to them prior to their being given. We should then be proceeding precisely on the lines of Copernicus's primary hypothesis. Failing of satisfactory progress in explaining the movements of the heavenly bodies on the supposition that they all revolved around a spectator, he tried whether he might not have better success if he made the spectator to revolve and the stars to remain at rest.

Even here the authoritative translations (e.g., Kemp-Smith) are misleading. Kant does not refer to any "primary hypothesis" framed by Copernicus but, as noted, only his first (or perhaps principal) *idea* or *thought* regarding the sources of confusion in the matter of the length of the solar year. Kant's statement that his own attempt to rescue metaphysics from the incessant groping (*Harumtappen*) of metaphysicians suggests a parallel with Copernicus's efforts. As with Copernicus, Kant will "make another trial" (*auf anliche weise Versuchen*). He would have the Copernicus passage and the method to which it refers understood rather as a loose analogy. With few exceptions—notably Aristarchus in ancient times—astronomers assumed that their observer is passive and provides objective records of the actual motions of heavenly bodies. It was not assumed that anything in the observer decisively affected what was observed. To put this in the idiom of philosophy, their assumption was that the events observed were mind independent. Copernicus made a different assumption, namely, that the motion of the observer accounted for quantitative features of the observed events.

Kant identified his own method with just this sort of shift in perspective. The Kantian observer is not the passive recording instrument of the empiricists, but one who brings to reality (a priori) an assortment of cognitive-perceptual powers that will establish the very possibility of sensibility, knowledge, and understanding. Consider these two passages from the second edition:

(1) Understanding has rules which I must presuppose as being in me prior to objects being given to me, and therefore as being given a priori. (Bxvii–xviii)
(2) Nothing in a priori knowledge can be ascribed to objects save what the thinking subject derives from itself. (Bxxiii)

Asserted here is not a skeptical reduction of reality to mere mental contents but the recognition that any explanation of the phenomena of the external world must include the sensual and cognitive framework provided by the observer. What must be uncovered are the *enabling* conditions, absent which there can be no experience of objects at all. None of this should be confused with a theory of innate knowledge. As will be noted often, knowledge for Kant requires experience of the external world. So it is not knowledge that is innate but only certain rules by which experiences are formed and combined.

Kant goes on to say that an experiment akin to Copernicus's

can be tried in metaphysics, as regards the intuition of objects. If intuition must conform to the constitution of the objects, I do not see how we could know anything of the latter *a priori*; but if the object (as object of the senses) must conform to the constitution of our faculty of intuition, I have no difficulty in conceiving such a possibility.

None of this should be confused with a theory of innate knowledge. Knowledge for Kant requires experience of the external world. So it is not knowledge that is innate but only certain rules by which concepts are combined.

This point is repeated frequently in the *Critique* and must be clarified if only briefly at the outset. When Kant undertakes the essential task of refuting traditional arguments for idealism he returns to the distinction between modes of apprehension that are determined by the properties of objects and, contrasted with these, the properties of objects as these are determined by the pure intuitions.

Kant insists that if the physical properties of objects actually did determine experience directly, there could be no means by which to establish even the reality of such objects. Imagine a device that records with undeviating accuracy the physical properties of entities delivered to its sensory processes. Assuming thought on the part of such a device, it could not distinguish between the arrival of actual (external) objects and the mere internal generation of events. In a word, it could not establish the reality of an external world and would thus perpetuate philosophy's "continuing scandal." If this is to be avoided, what must be added are powers or processes not determined by the stimuli but determining instead how such stimuli will and can be received.

Thus, as early as the Introduction to the *Critique* Kant is found preparing readers for the necessity of a nonempirical framework if knowledge is to be shielded from skepticism regarding objects in the external world. Absent such a framework nothing about objects could be known a priori, not even their externality. There would be no basis on which to separate successive events in time nor could such objects be located in space, for neither time nor space is a "given" property of stimuli. If, however, the observer's very mode of apprehension is spatiotemporal, then it becomes possible to know at least some features of objective reality a priori.

The possibility of knowledge a priori is tantamount to the possibility of metaphysics itself. This is made clear as early as (Bxiv) where Kant declares metaphysics to be a speculative science that soars above the teachings of experience and in which reason is meant to be "its own pupil." The point is also developed in the *Prolegomena* where he says,

> As concerns the sources of metaphysical knowledge, its very concept implies that they cannot be empirical. Its principles (including not only its maxims, but its basic notions) must never be derived from experience. It must not be physical but metaphysical

knowledge, namely, knowledge lying beyond experience. It can therefore have for its basis, neither external experience, which is the source of physics proper, nor internal, which is the basis of rational psychology. It is therefore *a priori* knowledge, coming from pure understanding and pure reason. (265)

Metaphysics is not grounded in the empirical facts of the external world or the introspective facts of a Cartesian-Lockean psychology. The science that is grounded in our experience of the external world is physics proper. The science that would derive its subject matter from internal (introspectively reached) experiences is rational psychology. Metaphysics is different from both. It is an independent discipline finding its contents in that domain of a priori knowledge that is foundational for both the physical sciences and the rational psychology. There must be a conceptually prior system or science that establishes the limits of empirical knowledge and rationality alike. To the extent that such a system is possible, metaphysics itself is possible. Failing in this, our empirical claims must otherwise and always fail to be immunized against skepticism, even as reason, with blind circularity, presumes to judge itself.

But if both the physical and the psychological modes of inquiry are ruled out, what method remains if metaphysics is, as he says, "to enter upon the path of science"? As Kant sees it, the problem is finally one of method. At Bxv he reduces the prevailing methods of metaphysics to "a merely random groping (*Harumtappen*) and, what is worst of all, a groping among mere concepts." Kant intends the *Critique* as a whole to be his own discourse on method rather than a settled and complete metaphysical system in its own right. Thus, at Bxxi he says,

> This attempt to alter the procedure which has hitherto prevailed in metaphysics, by completely revolutionizing it in accordance with the example set by the geometers and physicists, forms indeed, the main purpose of this critique of pure speculative reason. It is a treatise on the method, not a system of science itself.

This passage lends itself to misunderstanding. Some of Kant's contemporaries (e.g., Fichte) criticized the work as failing to generate a complete and scientific philosophy, and the lines from (Bxxi) would seem to admit of incompleteness. Kant was plainly peeved by such accusations and made this known in a "public declaration" appearing in 1799:

> The assumption that I have intended to publish only a *propaedeutic* to transcendental philosophy and not the actual system of this philosophy is incomprehensible to me. . . . I took the completeness of pure philosophy within the *Critique of Pure Reason* to be the best indication of the truth of that work.[2]

So, is it a method rather than a complete system, or is it the "completeness of pure philosophy"? This may be finally a distinction without a clear *Kantian* difference. A system is "complete" when it has been developed as far as the nature of things will permit. Sense and reason have limits; the *Critique* exhaustively examines and identifies these. The mode of examination is that of *transcendental philosophy*, taken to be the right method of analysis. Once that method has been applied to the widest range of epistemic claims, the account is *complete*. To ask for more is to be literally *unreasonable*. It is to go beyond the bounds of sensibility and reason.

As noted, the *Critique* is not simply what in contemporary philosophy is referred to as "conceptual analysis." Kant began with such a project in mind but he abandoned it. His early attempt in the *Prize Essay* competition bore the title, *Inquiry Concerning the Distinctness of the Principles of Natural Theology and Morals* (1764), where he tested the feasibility of metaphysical approaches to the fundamental question of the existence of God. Kant here followed Newton's method of *conceptual analysis* as the first step in putting metaphysics on a scientific footing. Only with this phase successfully completed might metaphysics then aspire to the status of a "synthetic" discipline capable of discovery—capable of overcoming that "scandal" that renders an external world merely hypothetical.

This abiding "scandal" calls for renewed if brief attention. The attempt to prove beyond doubt the existence of a world external to and independent of mental representations has ancient roots, but these would ultimately give rise to even more formidable skeptical arguments such as those Descartes sets down in his *Meditations*. In the third *Meditation* he acknowledges that he knows

> by experience that these ideas do not depend on my will, and hence that they do not depend simply on me. Frequently I notice

them even when I do not want to: now, for example, I feel the heat whether I want to or not, and this is why I think that this sensation or idea of heat comes to me from something other than myself, namely the heat of the fire by which I am sitting. (*Mediations*, 3, at 7:38)

But then he moves directly to the skeptical challenge:

Then again, although these [apparently adventitious] ideas do not depend on my will, it does not follow that they must come from things located outside me. Just as the impulses which I was speaking of a moment ago seem opposed to my will even though they are within me, so there may be some other faculty not yet fully known to me, which produces these ideas without any assistance from external things; this is, after all, just how I have always thought ideas are produced in me when I am dreaming. (*Meditations,* 3, at 7:39)

Here is the classic expression of the rationalist's reluctant skepticism. It generates what, in the Introduction to the second edition of the *Critique*, Kant identifies as *the general problem of pure reason*. There, at Bxix, he says, "The proper problem of pure reason is contained in the question: How are *a priori* synthetic judgments possible?" The story behind this general problem has ancient roots but can be picked up with the appearance of Locke's *An Essay Concerning the Human Understanding*, specifically in book 4, chapter 2, "Of the Degrees of Our Knowledge." There Locke distinguishes between and among three modes of knowing. To wit: Some things are known immediately, and known to be true necessarily, without the need for or benefit of experience. Locke referred to this form of knowledge as *intuitive*. It is on this basis, for example, that we know the law of contradiction. Locke puts it this way:

sometimes the mind perceives the agreement or disagreement of two ideas immediately by themselves, without the intervention of any other: and this I think we may call intuitive knowledge. . . . Thus the mind perceives that white is not black, that a circle is not a triangle, that three are more than two and equal to one and two. Such kinds of truths the mind perceives at the first sight of the ideas together, by bare intuition. . . . It is on this intuition that depends all the certainty and evidence of all our knowledge.

There are still other propositions known to be true with certainty but not known to be true immediately. Rather, their truth arises from a successful demonstration. Here we find the truths of geometry, and hence, *demonstrative* knowledge. But *factual* knowledge depends entirely on experience. It is solely through experience that the mind is furnished with facts. Nothing of a factual nature could be known absent experience. This is the mode of knowing that Locke refers to as *sensitive*. He is now in a position to address the question as to how one gains, "sensitive knowledge of the particular existence of finite beings without us." Intuition and demonstration constitute the ultimate degree of knowledge— certainty itself.

> Whatever falls short of this, with what assurance so ever embraced, is but faith or opinion, but not knowledge, at least in all general truths.

Granting such limitations, Locke then considers "another perception of the mind" by which one becomes aware of external objects. This perceptual act provides knowledge that never goes "beyond bare probability." It never attains certainty, but it nonetheless qualifies as knowledge. The evidence that bona fide knowledge is the outcome of such perceptions is that they are accompanied by "the actual entrance of ideas from them." This, of course, is not a serious contender among attempts to defeat skepticism. It is instead the conventional empiricist position that leaves unaddressed what Kant takes to be the general problem of pure reason, namely, "How are *a priori* synthetic judgments possible?" How can the truth of any factual proposition be established independently of experience? Another way of framing the question might be, "How can what Locke takes to be the result of perception come to have the character of an intuition?" Asked yet another way, and more generally, how are Locke's three modes of knowing related to each other?

The whole tendency of such empiricistic conceptions of knowledge and experience as advanced by Locke would culminate in David Hume's influential writings that so famously awakened Kant from his dogmatic slumber.[3] If it is the case that one does not experience objects directly but only by way of some sort of mediated mental representation, then the resulting experience might well be the product of a dream. In any case, the knowledge claims arising from such a process are never self-justifying. To the extent that all knowledge arises from just such experiences there must be a vicious circularity in every attempt to tether knowledge to anything firmer than particular habits and tendencies of mental life.

Hume's arguments continue to inspire productive debate in philosophy. As the most insightful and formidable defender of empiricism he remains to this day the author whose success determines the fate of the *ism* itself. He was well aware of the possession of veritable volumes of knowledge that owe nothing to experience. After all, it is not only a certainty that every number is equal to itself but something known without the need or benefit of experience. Examined closely, however, knowledge of this sort proves to be entirely verbal. Put another way, such knowledge is nothing but the awareness of relations obtaining between ideas. Nothing new or factual is acquired this way; nothing is known beyond the meaning of the terms themselves. Once one is instructed that all bachelors are unmarried, one possesses no more than knowledge of an identity-relation between two terms.

Knowledge that may claim for itself possession of actual facts regarding the world beyond the dictionary is quite another matter: It is but a record of experience, fashioned into complex ideas by way of the laws of association. Even so foundational a concept as causation is finally cobbled together from a history of constant conjunctions in experience. The sequence of A-then-B, repeated often enough, creates a habit in the mind such that the presentation of A immediately suggests B as a reliable effect. Such a process arises within a system constituted in a certain way; other and radically different systems would surely acquire quite different concepts. Hence, anything might be the "cause" of anything.

Reduced to a schematic, Hume's thesis is that knowledge comes in two forms. There is the purely logical and lexical form that supplies true propositions a priori, their truth being both necessary and certain. Such propositions are "analytic," the term here as used by Kant meaning a proposition whose predicate term is contained in the meaning of the subject term. "Bachelor" and "unmarried man" provide the textbook illustration of analytic propositions. Here we have a clear example of what Hume means by "relations of ideas." But claims regarding any and every fact of the real world are set down in the form of *synthetic* propositions whose truth is neither necessary nor certain. Whereas the truth of analytic propositions can be known prior to any experiential encounter, the truth of synthetic propositions requires observation. The proposition, if true, is true owing to a record of verifying observations. The facts of the external world are just what they are but surely could have been different. Thus, what may be said truthfully of them can rise no higher than a *contingent* truth, for it is surely not by necessity that the world happens to be constituted in one way rather than another. Objects that fall to earth might float endlessly on the moon. In a word, all the knowledge on which science depends arises after the fact of experience (a posteriori) and is set down in the form of synthetic propositions the truth of which is neither necessary nor unconditional but always contingent and probable.

What leads to a vexing skepticism in such an account is the mediated nature of experience itself. If the content of synthetic propositions is experiential and the sole means by which to establish the truth of such propositions is also experiential, then the entire enterprise is but psychology by another name! The grounds on which one might avoid the dream-state option will be pragmatic and utilitarian: Getting on with what one takes to be important simply leaves no room for a skepticism otherwise validated by philosophy.

It is useful to consider again the analytic-synthetic distinction and the larger implications Hume would draw from it. The importance of the distinction is announced very early in the *Critique* (A7–10/B11–18) where Kant draws attention to its significance in relation to the overall project:

> In all judgments in which the relation of the subject to the predicate is thought . . . this relation is possible in two different ways. Either the predicate B belongs to the subject A, as something which is (covertly) contained in this concept A; or B lies outside

the concept A, although it does indeed stand in connection with it. In the one case, I entitle the judgment analytic, in the other synthetic.

At Bx Kant notes that the distinction has not been adequately considered. On Kant's account, the two major philosophers who failed to distinguish between the two properly are Leibniz and Hume. Leibniz, the textbook rationalist, takes the law of contradiction to be foundational for all knowledge, which he divides into what he calls *truths of reason* and *truths of fact*. The former are derived directly from the law of contradiction. Truths of fact lack this same certainty, but only because of our failure to form sufficiently clear ideas and then perform the necessary logical analysis. For Leibniz, truths of fact must ultimately be subsumed under truths of reason, leading to the recognition that whatever is the case is so necessarily. All true statements in the end are tautologies. (It is a short step from here to his famous conclusion that this is the best of all possible worlds!)

Hume also recognizes truths of reason, referring to these as *relations of ideas*. He distinguishes these from *matters of fact*, these being entirely artifacts of experience. Where Leibniz and Hume agree is in classifying truths of reason as knowable a priori and as necessary. For Hume, however, all matters of fact are a posteriori, and never more than probable. There is, then, a seemingly unbridgeable divide between *analytic* propositions whose truth is known a priori, merely through an analysis of the terms, and *synthetic* propositions, knowable only a posteriori and entirely dependent on experience. Hume goes so far as to reduce causation itself to an artifact of experience, thus stripping it of its necessity and of rational proofs of its mind-independent reality.

If Hume is correct in regarding causality as an entirely a posteriori concept,—its a priori proof being impossible—then, says Kant,

> metaphysics is a mere delusion whereby we fancy ourselves to have rational insight into what, in actual fact, is borrowed solely from experience.

The casualty claimed by such a view would of course be science itself. What is central to the entire project of the *Critique* is establishing the legitimacy of scientific knowledge and this, in turn, requires establishing the possibility of *synthetic* propositions known to be true a priori, at once universal and necessary. The task, then, is to prove that at least some synthetic judgments are true a priori, lest metaphysics sink to the level of mere delusion.

The specific part of Hume's thesis that awakened Kant is in the account of causation as a concept exhausted by constant conjunctions and the formation of mental associations. In the Introduction to the *Prolegomena* Kant reports that, having been suddenly challenged by such a thesis,

> I tried whether Hume's observation could not be made general, and soon found that the conception of the connection of cause and effect was not by a long way the only one by which the understanding cogitates *à priori* the connections of things, but that metaphysics consists entirely of such. I endeavoured to ascertain their number, and as I succeeded in doing this to my satisfaction, namely, out of a single principle, I proceeded to the deduction of these conceptions, which I was now assured could not, as Hume had pretended, be derived from experience but must have originated in the pure understanding.[4]

What Kant was awakened from was the "dogma" that conferred on rationality the power to oppose skepticism either on the basis of commonsense or of mere conjectures or by way of practical consequences. "Reason," however, understood as a tool (so to speak) had remained too coarse for the task at hand. Some projects can be completed, Kant says, with a hammer and chisel, but others call for an etching needle.[5] Until reason stands as its own student there is no way to determine its ability to rescue knowledge from the skeptical conclusions arising from Hume's thesis.

The objective Kant set for himself was not to reassure ordinary percipients that their knowledge is trustworthy but to defend the structured claims of science against skeptical and contextualizing challenges. He begins, then, with that key question: Whether it is possible to establish the truth of synthetic propositions a priori. Are there universal and necessary cognitive powers by which sensibility and understanding become possible, such that the factual reach of sensibility and understanding can be known a priori by way of these enabling powers? Addressing such a question is a task not for science but for metaphysics. The following passage is then the right starting point for tracing out the required method and conclusions on this central point:

> Whatever the origin of our representations, whether they are due to the influence of outer things, or are produced through inner causes, whether they arise a priori or, being appearances, have an empirical origin, they must all, as modifications of the mind, belong to inner sense. All our knowledge is thus finally subject to time, the formal condition of inner sense. In it [time] they must all be ordered, connected and brought into relation. This is . . . quite fundamental. (A99)

This fundamental insight begins to address the question of how nature is possible. Though current debates among Kant scholars are instructive, it is finally to Kant himself that one must turn first if only to discover just what is debatable. "How is nature possible?" is a question bearing directly on the very fact of the developed sciences. Kant's model, of course, is physics. What it presents is not a thick collection of empirical facts, more or less organized into categories. Instead, there is a strict and rationally coherent set of laws by which empirical findings come to be understood as necessary. How this comes about is not something that physics itself can establish. Rather, what is needed is a *metaphysical* foundation for physics itself. Recall in this connection Kant's distinction between metaphysics and physics, the latter pertaining to knowledge of the external world; further, there is the distinction between metaphysics and psychology, with the latter based on knowledge of inner experience. What, then, of metaphysics? Unless there is the possibility of a systematic discipline based on what is synthetic but also known a priori metaphysics is chimerical. As he stated (in his characteristically labored way) in his *Metaphysical Foundations of Natural Science* (1786),

> What may be called natural science proper presupposes a metaphysics of nature; for laws, i.e., principles of the necessity of that which belongs to the *existence* of a thing are occupied with a conception which does not admit of construction, because its existence cannot be represented in any *a priori* intuition; natural science, therefore, presupposes metaphysics.[6]

Note in this passage that "laws" are understood as necessitating the defining aspects of what belongs to the very existence of any "this" or "that." To say that such a thing "does not admit of construction" is to contrast the empirical fact of the thing with those abstract mathematical constructions of the geometer. Geometric axioms can, indeed, be represented by way of a priori intuitions, but the orbital velocity of a given planet cannot. Just *how* the proper objects and events of the natural sciences are represented and how such representations match up objectively with the empirical facts constitute the task of a metaphysics of the natural sciences.

Clearly, the distinction between analytic and synthetic judgments is pivotal to the entire argument of the *Critique.* The very possibility of synthetic a priori judgments raises three interrelated points. First, in the absence of such judgments it would not be possible for thought, as such, to reach any new knowledge whatever. All thought would be either a mere rehearsal of experiences or of dictionary definitions. As Kant insisted, "If intuition must conform to the constitution of the objects, I do not see how we could know anything of the latter *a priori.*" If judgments are hostage to the external empirical properties of objects—these known solely through *appearances*—the empirical version of (skeptical) idealism is unavoidable, for only appearances could be known, all the rest being mere conjecture. Third, if a priori synthetic judgments regarding the outer world are possible, then metaphysics actually can stand as an independent but complementary resource for the understanding and including especially a scientific understanding of the real world.

Much ink has been spilled on the essential nature of analytic and synthetic propositions and the differences between them. The truth of analytic propositions has been dismissed as merely definitional, as an "empty" tautology, as a necessary truth, and so on. Clearly, if it is the law of contradiction that grounds all analytic propositions, then the denial of any of them would constitute a formal contradiction. It has often been claimed that analytic propositions are thus *necessarily* true—true in all possible worlds—whereas the truth of synthetic propositions never rises higher than a mere and contingent probability. There are surely imaginable possible worlds in which the most durable of earth-bound scientific laws do not obtain.

Kant's contemporary critics expressed confusion and frustration on his discussion of synthetic propositions. In a long letter to Karl Leonhard Reinhold (May 12, 1789) he refers to Herr Eberhard's complaint that "One seeks in vain for Kant's *principle for synthetic judgments.*" Kant says that the principle is advanced ". . . unequivocally . . . in the whole *Critique.*" He adds that if one requires some sort of formula, it is this:

> All synthetic judgments of theoretical cognition are possible only by the relating of a given concept to an intuition.

And then he goes on to say,

> If the synthetic judgment is an experiential judgment, the underlying intuition must be empirical; if the judgment is a priori synthetic, the intuition must be pure. Since it is impossible (for us human beings) to have pure intuitions other than merely of the form of the subject (since no object is given) and of his receptivity to representations, that is, his capacity to be affected by objects, the reality of synthetic a priori propositions is sufficient itself to prove that these propositions concern only sensible objects and cannot transcend appearances.[7]

In this same letter Kant further qualifies what is made possible by way of synthetic a priori judgments. In relating a given concept to an intuition (or, more clearly, in subsuming sensations under the pure categories) we remain tied to the realm of the sensible. There is no path to the suprasensible. However, the same cognitive apparatus can be employed on "things in general," thereby generating not knowledge but what Kant refers to as "practical Ideas of reason." Much more is to be said on this in the next chapter, but it is important to be mindful here of how Kant would have the "*a priori* synthetic" understood as both a limitation on knowledge proper and as a fruitful process in the generation of ideas as distinct from knowledge.

Tied to the distinction between analytic and synthetic propositions is what Kant took to be the quite different distinction between that which is established a priori and that which depends on one or another empirical mode of confirmation. Closer examination, however, has raised doubts about the neatness of such classifications. Saul Kripke, for example, has defended the notion of truths that, though a priori, are contingent and others, though a posteriori, are necessary. Thus, a given stick (S), at a given time

(t_0), is 1 meter in length. One might argue that in any and every possible world, 1 meter is 1 meter, an instance of what Kripke takes to be a "rigid designator." But any given object might well be sensitive to various conditions such that its properties in one world are different in another. Heat might make the given stick longer than 1 meter. Thus, the particular stick—which is designated as *the standard meter* is not *necessarily* but only *contingently* a meter long, a fact established only a posteriori. Or, consider H_2O. Just in case water is H_2O then water and H_2O are identical wherever found, in any and every world. However, truths of identity are necessary truths, but in this case a posteriori. Only by way of scientific investigation was it established that "water" is, in fact, chemically H_2O. The main point Kripke makes is that the distinction between a priori and a posteriori is an epistemological distinction, whereas the distinction between necessity and contingency is metaphysical. Whether something is or can be known a priori is different from the question of whether what is known could be otherwise.[8]

Was Kant fundamentally confused on this main point? Perhaps not, but the issue goes beyond present purposes. "Water," unlike H_2O, bears properties beyond the elemental combination of hydrogen and oxygen atoms. It is viscous, transparent, potable, necessary for life, and so on. One might challenge the claim that "water" and H_2O are identical in the sense required by Kripke. Presumably, the latter is mind independent whereas the former bears properties that are not exhaustively supplied by chemistry; for example, water "Causes pain at 120 degrees, and cools the body at 50 degrees" makes no sense unless a given kind of living body is presupposed.

It is sufficient here to acknowledge that there are difficulties in the Kantian position once exacting work is performed on his classification of propositions. Additionally, Kant is far from clear on the sense in which a predicate "belongs" to a subject or is "contained" in its meaning. It is obvious that what he has in mind is a high degree of conceptual kinship, but there is no precise guidance in the text. Thus, "All bodies are extended" is traditionally regarded as an analytic proposition, the concept "extended" being contained in the concept "body." As such, the proposition is classically regarded as a tautology and, therefore, uninforming. Consider instead, "All bodies are heavy." This is a different matter, for the concept of "body" is not synonymous with "heavy." Rather, in all experiences of bodies, there is the property of weight, and thus, the two are conceptually connected (A8/B12). This, however, is an instance of an a posteriori synthesis, accomplished only after some amount of relevant experiences. Analytic propositions require no such empirical confirmation. Their truth is settled a priori; they are "true by definition," or are "conceptual truths." Following Leibniz, it can be seen that analytic propositions are governed by the law of contradiction: As Kant says,

> For, *if the judgment is analytic* . . . its truth can always be adequately known in accordance with the principle of contradiction. (A151)

On the traditional empiricistic view, the truth of a synthetic proposition cannot be thus established. So, when Kant says that,

> If intuition must conform to the constitution of the objects, I do not see how we could know anything of the latter *a priori*

he should be understood as contrasting two possibilities: either a mode of apprehension determined by the objects apprehended or that "Copernican" perspectival shift that yields an apprehension of objects determined a priori by the mode of apprehension itself. If the latter is the case, then the truth of some synthetic propositions is established a priori.

Suppose instead that all that is apprehended is what inheres in the objects themselves, ontologically independent of any and every observation. In that case there is simply no basis on which to establish the reality of an external world. The "scandal" persists. As the observer's relationship to objects is first by way of appearances, there would be no way for the observer to validate claims about an external world. All talk would be about appearances, these taken to be (but not shown to be) accurate representations of the real attributes of (allegedly) external objects.

Perhaps the difficulty can be set aside by simply rejecting the distinction between synthetic and analytic propositions. Willard Quine dismissed this whole line of analysis as simply mistaken. In his *Two Dogmas of Empiricism* he challenges the distinction on the grounds that it is confined to subject–predicate propositions and rests on an undeveloped conception of "meaning." What does it mean to say that a predicate is included in the "meaning" of the subject? As Quine sees things, how such propositions are classified is a matter of preferred usage and not a discovery about the real world. The distinction thus collapsed, Quine then concludes that there is no a priori knowledge of the sort that matters.[9]

Though long influential, Quine's rejection of the distinction—based chiefly on the rather protean nature of "synonymy" and "meaning"—leaves the distinction itself largely untouched at the *metaphysical* level at which Kant installed it. The sense in which one knows a priori that bachelors are unmarried men is distinguishable from the sense in which one knows that the Euclidean character of the external world as appearance is guaranteed a priori. Quine's criticism is put in useful perspective by C. D. Broad in an essay that actually appeared decades before Quine's own words on the subject:

> But there is always a tendency for empiricists to base their denial of synthetic a priori propositions on some tacitly assumed epistemological premise which is certainly synthetic and which they take to be self-evident. A notorious example is Hume's principle that every simple idea resembles and is due to a previous simple impression; a proposition which Hume, on his own principles, could not possibly know and could not have any empirical ground for believing. And I strongly suspect that some people accept the theory that there are no synthetic a priori propositions because the epistemological principle that a synthetic proposition *could not possibly* be self-evident (which is certainly a synthetic proposition) *does in fact* seem to them self-evident.[10]

Nonetheless, Quine would have the distinction regarded as merely terminological, denying that even such intuitive truths as *lawyers are attorneys* are analytic. He defends this by noting the ambiguities surrounding the concept of synonymy itself. This is a matter calling for a more detailed analysis than is warranted in the present context, but at least a hint is needed if Kant's immunity is to be established. Consider first Quine's conclusion that there is no such thing as an analytic truth. He bases this on the assumption that the very definitions that would yield the required synonymy are subject to challenge and modification arising from additional empirical findings. However, the process of defining is not anarchic. One must

defend and justify a given definition. Of course, the process of definition will itself be parasitic on the analytic-synthetic distinction.
Moreover, just in case Quine is right, such that there are, properly
speaking, no propositions that are unambiguously analytic, then all
propositions laying claim to truth must presumably be synthetic. If
that is so, then an argument establishing the a priori truth of any
of them would do precisely the work required by Kant's project for
metaphysics.

As for Hume's insistence that there can be no synthetic proposition whose truth can be known a priori, C. D. Broad would seem
to provide a sufficient challenge. To this point at least Kant's grand
voyage navigates its way through the turbulence, still on course,
shifting winds duly noted. What is clear is that both Quine (who
rejects the distinction) and Hume (who takes it to be "self-evident"
that all synthetic propositions are a posteriori) leave Kant's analysis largely untouched.

CHAPTER 4

THE PURE INTUITIONS AND
THE ANALOGIES OF EXPERIENCE

From its first appearance Kant's *Critique* gripped the imagination of an entire intellectual world and generated a secondary literature that has grown exponentially. Erich Adikes's bibliography of 1894 of works citing it includes some 2,800 entries by 1887.[1] That number would now be a substantial multiple of that. As already noted, it is a dense and difficult work. Sebastian Gardner's entry in the Routledge *Guidebook* alerts the unsuspecting:

> Virtually every sentence of the critique presents difficulties. Attempts have been made to provide commentaries comprehensively illuminating each individual section of the work, and some of these run to several volumes without getting near its end.[2]

One frustrated reader described the assignment this way:

> A disagreeable task, because the work is dry, obscure, opposed to all ordinary notions, and long-winded as well.

And that reader? Kant![3]

In working through the details of his own analysis, Kant repeatedly laments the abiding stagnation of metaphysics, which he attributed to irresolvable disputes between empiricists and rationalists. In pitting the metaphysics of the Locke–Hume school against that of the Descartes–Leibniz school, he begins by examining the core assumptions of each. Both rationalism and empiricism labor to avoid paralyzing forms of skepticism, which would take reality to be utterly unknowable. The major disagreement between them pertains to the epistemic resources with which to establish the nature of that reality and the means by which to acquire valid knowledge of it.

The textbook empiricist proceeds on the understanding that all substantive knowledge of the real world is gained by sensory commerce with that world, absent which nothing would be known. In this, Hume's distinction between "relations of ideas" and "matters of fact" sets the general boundary conditions for empiricism. The certainties claimed by way of reason alone, on this account, are just those tautologous certainties obtaining among ideas related in a certain way.

With or without regrets, empiricism at the end of its conceptual tether tends toward one or another form of idealism that soon concludes in skepticism. The path is uneven, but the destination is inevitable: To assume, as traditional empiricism does assume, that access to reality is unavoidably *mediated* by perceptual or sensory processes implies that what is directly known is only the contents of consciousness. There is then no means of testing the agreement between these contents and reality, for all the evidence that might be collected for the purpose becomes just further conscious content. Skepticism waits at the end of the process, for every knowledge claim is ultimately challenged by the recognition that what is known is only what is found in conscious experience. "Reality" as such falls beyond this.

Rationalism suffers its own limitations, not least of which is something of a distain for "mere facts." Recognizing the limitations of perceptual modes of knowing, the rationalists often go beyond caution and simply rule out the senses as at all relevant to the search for "truth," which is assumed to be in the form of ever more general and grand systems. Kant, by the time of the *Critique,* has concluded that the legitimate aims of metaphysics must go beyond an analysis and clarification of concepts and must fall short of all encompassing theories. It's method is that of *critique* and its very possibility is tied to the domain of a priori knowledge (B18). Accordingly, at least *in intention*, metaphysics, should be comprised entirely of a priori synthetic propositions. Were it comprised entirely of a priori analytic propositions, it would amount to little more than a collection of definitions—Hume's relations of ideas. Were it comprised entirely of a posteriori synthetic propositions, it would be a branch of empirical science. But knowledge requires content and that is supplied by experience. This much of the empiricist account is unexceptionable, though it leaves unsettled the very grounding of experience. It barely distinguishes between experience and mere sensations.

The passive relationship between physical impingements and sensory responses does not establish "experience," for the latter is an ordered, unified, and coherent conscious event. For there to be experience as such there must be governing principles that ordain the manner in which external impingements will be registered. The resulting order and organization are not "given" by the stimuli themselves but are determined by the very mode of sensibility. Thus, empiricists are correct in regarding knowledge as *arising* from experience and rationalists in recognizing that such knowledge is nonetheless not *grounded* in experience.

In the Preface to his *New Essays on Human Understanding*, Leibniz had summarized the more or less standard rationalist account of the limits of sensory modes of knowing. He says that the senses report the mere instances of phenomena but that

> all the instances which confirm a general truth, however numerous they may be, are not sufficient to establish the universal necessity of this same truth. . . . From which it appears that necessary truths, such as we find in pure mathematics, and particularly in arithmetic and geometry, must have principles whose proof does not depend on instances, nor consequently on the testimony of the senses. (150–1)

It is not much of leap from passages such as this to Kant's attempt to show how mathematical propositions are at once synthetic but known a priori and understood to be at once necessarily and universally true. If, indeed, the actual world as knowable by human beings is structured by their very modes of representation and judgment, then true synthetic propositions can be framed a priori, for they will recover from the known world what the cognizer has put there. The heavy burden that is added to this requires proof that the resulting judgments are nonetheless not "subjective" for all of that.

When Kant repeatedly reminds readers that the very possibility of metaphysics depends on establishing the truth of synthetic propositions *a priori* he is calling attention to the often overlooked foundations on which both the scientific and the manifest images of reality depend. All too often an impoverished metaphysical account defends what in fact is a true proposition but in a manner that is blind to the necessary and universal conditions of its truth. In this connection, consider how Kant frames of the problem of causation as set by Hume:

> Upon what . . . am I to rely when I seek to go beyond the concept A, and to know that another concept B is connected with it? Through what is the synthesis made possible? (A9–10/B13–14)

Henry Allison formulates the question this way:

> How is it possible to extend one's knowledge (in the material sense) beyond a given concept, independently of any experience of the object thought through that concept. (78)

Again, are there synthetic (factual) propositions the truth of which can be known *a priori* and, if so, how is this possible? Of course, the problem does not arise with analytic propositions. One knows *a priori* that every number is equal to itself and that not one bachelor is married. The salient question has to do with *synthetic* propositions, those that stand as contributions to factual knowledge. Kant begins his analysis by noting that in both mathematics and the natural sciences such true synthetic *a priori* judgments are abundant. (B15–18) In arithmetic, for example, the concept "12" is surely not "contained" in the meaning of "5 + 7," meaning the proposition, "5+7 = 12," is not analytic. This is even clearer when very large numbers are considered, for the concept "4,873" is obviously not "contained" in the concept "1,234 + 1,300 + 1,439." That a straight line is the shortest distance between two points is also synthetic, for the *quality* of straightness does not stand in synonymous relation to the *quantity* of length.

In physics, too, there are such *a priori* synthetic propositions as, "in all changes of the material world quantity of matter remains unchanged" (B17), that is, the conservation of matter. The concept of "matter" does not contain within its meaning that of object-permanence, so the proposition is clearly synthetic. Moreover, the truth of the proposition is a *necessary* truth to the extent that it is true in all possible worlds. But just how is such true *a priori* knowledge possible? The fact of it is a challenge to the empiricistic thesis that takes all such knowledge as the gift of experience, but the rationalists are on no firmer ground for it not by way of the law of contradiction or Aristotelian logic that such knowledge is attained.

If progress is to move beyond the phase of point and counter-point, a different philosophical approach would appear to be required. What Kant proposes is a revolutionary shift, one deriving inspiration from mathematics and the natural sciences. Thus, at Bxxi he says,

> This attempt to alter the procedure which has hitherto prevailed in metaphysics, by completely revolutionizing it in accordance with the example set by the geometers and physicists, forms indeed, the main purpose of this critique of pure speculative reason. It is a treatise on the method, not a system of science itself.

As a "treatise on method," the *Critique* takes on the organizational features of a handbook. But although Kant's style is often labored and wooden, his repetitions frequent and often oddly placed, there is a reasonably efficient overall structure that repays close attention. First, there are two main divisions of unequal length and significance. Kant refers to these as the *transcendental doctrine of elements* and the much shorter *transcendental doctrine of method*.

As noted in previous chapters, the term "transcendental" is used by Kant in an uncustomary way. It has been yet another item of controversy in philosophy, not solely as to how the term is to be understood but whether the problems it purports to solve are problems at all. Both of these issues surrounding the term were addressed with commendable clarity some years ago by Barry Stroud.[4] Begun with the declarative claim that there is a tomato on the table, this is voiced in the presence of a skeptic who insists that the speaker is hallucinating. To defeat that challenge, the speaker reports that another person also agrees that there is, indeed, a tomato on the table. It should be clear that, to one insisting that the speaker is subject to hallucinations, it is useless to produce yet another version of the story that would have a tomato on the table, for the hallucinating speaker is just as prone to hallucinating in the account of a verifying witness.

Stroud then invites assistance from the school of logical positivism, in this case from Rudolph Carnap and the distinction between claims arising from positions "inside" and "outside" an accepted framework.[5] There is a tried and true conventional framework within which standard empirical claims of the sort, "There is a tomato on the table," are understood and tested. Of course, the committed skeptic is prepared to reject the framework itself and, therefore, will raise questions that are simply meaningless from the perspective of those inside the framework. However, a position such as Carnap's would probably seem ironic to Kant, for what does it mean to be "inside" a given framework except to have one's perceptual and cognitive powers sufficiently fixed by *a priori* principles for contestants to know that there are multiple frameworks?

What Kant intends by a *transcendental* form of argument is a positive contribution to antiskepticism. It is intended to provide answers to two distinct but related questions: questions of *fact* (*quid facti*) and questions of *right* (*quid juris*). The former reach the means by which knowledge has content, the latter offering a justification for asserting the *necessity* of the framework and the processes on which such knowledge rises to the level of understanding. Briefly put, an argument is transcendental in Kant's sense when it establishes the very presuppositions on which a set of claims *necessarily* depends. The usual deployment in the *Critique* starts with a factual and indubitable statement about perception or thought and then presents what are assumed to be the necessary enabling conditions on which such a fact depends. Thus, the *transcendental doctrine of elements* refers to the necessary conditions for there to be the elements in question. Several common criticisms of this overall approach are reserved to the conclusion of this chapter.

The elements referred to in the major division of the *Critique* are the elements or constituents of cognition itself. Subsumed under them are the three major cognitive powers to be subjected in turn to a further transcendental analysis, an analysis that is not empirical but framed in terms of what is taken to be the necessary and universal character of each. Thus, the *Transcendental Aesthetic* is intended to establish the necessary conditions for sensibility, the *Transcendental Analytic* is to establish the necessary conditions for understanding, and the *Transcendental Dialectic* serves this same function in relation to reason proper and its "discipline." The three powers cited here—sensibility, understanding, and reason—are limited, limited by the nature of their enabling conditions as these are (metaphysically) justified by transcendental arguments.

The *Doctrine of Method* has as its objective, in Kant's words, "the determination of the formal conditions of a complete system of pure reason" (A708/B736). If there is to be such a complete system of pure reason, there must be a necessary grounding or framework within which rationality functions and, alas, by which it is limited. There must be rules that govern the manner in which reason is employed. The doctrine of method is then analyzed in four chapters, the contents of which Kant identifies as "a *discipline*, a *canon*, an *architectonic*, and finally a *history* of pure reason" (A708/B736). The *discipline* of pure reason is Kant's exploration of the manner in which reason's reach is kept within the legitimate bounds of its powers. The method here is that of *critique*—, and hence, the *critique* of pure reason. The *canon* of pure reason is defined by Kant as "the sum of *a priori* principles governing the correct use of certain cognitive powers as such" (A796/B824). These *a priori* principles are the standard fare of traditional Aristotelian logic. To this is added the logic referred to by Kant as *analytic,* which contains the *a priori* synthetic principles of the understanding. Pure reason, in its theoretical deployment, lacks such *a priori* synthetic principles. (How this is to be understood will become clearer in later pages.) The *architectonic* of reason is a term Kant inserts at various places in the *Critique.* What he has in mind is the structure of a given rational representation or comprehension of something. As for the *history* of pure reason, Kant critically assesses approaches to metaphysics before his own.

In his development of the doctrine of method Kant rejects what he calls the "School Concept"—what he takes to be the Aristotelian and scholastic reliance on a set of categories arbitrarily chosen to match up with various properties of objects and then incorporated within tight logical arguments. His alternative architectonic begins with those *pure categories of the understanding,* which determine the very possibility and character of the understanding, the conditions necessary for it. Putting all this together schematically yields a table of organization:

Critique of Pure Reason						
Transcendental Doctrine of Elements			*Transcendental Doctrine of Method*			
Aesthetic	Analytic	Dialectic	Discipline	Canon	Architectonic	History
Sensibility	*Understanding*	*Reason*	*Critique*	*Necess. Principles*	*Pure Categ.*	*Errors*

With this framework the overall project can be considered more fully: First, the aim of the *Critique* is to establish the basis on which to distinguish what is knowable from what is merely conjectural and hypothetical; to establish the limits of sense and of reason, and thus, the limits of scientific understanding itself. It is always useful to employ "scientific" as the modifier when referring to the knowledge and understanding Kant would defend against skepticism. It should be recalled that Kant's very productive "precritical" years were devoted in large measure to issues at the border of theoretical physics (chiefly cosmology and dynamics) and the metaphysical foundations of the physical sciences. During this period he published works on fire, on the axial rotation of the earth, and on the formation of the solar system. The last of these efforts survives as the *Kant–Laplace nebular hypothesis* based on suppositions not unlike those now associated with the "Big Bang" theory. The point, of course, is that the Kant of the *Critique* is also the Kant of the nebular hypothesis and the nature of earthquakes. Thus, a philosophy incapable of establishing the reality of an external world is either hopelessly defective or that body of scientific knowledge that connects lawfully nearly all that is found in the external world is somehow imperiled.

It is the mission of metaphysics to render the world intelligible, in order to explain how a structured and rule-governed *nature* arises from the sensible contents of the world. The bridge between the intelligible world (*mundus intelligibilis*) of metaphysics and the sensible world (*mundus sensibilis*) of the natural sciences is nowhere to be found within the texts of traditional empiricism. They offer access only to the sensible world. If it were the case that the very form of sensibility must conform to the objects of sense experience, all a priori knowledge would be ruled out, for in that case what would be known would be no more than what might be gleaned from reflections on the content of one's perceptions. The armchair would be shared with Descartes's demon, now free to stage any performance within the walled theater of consciousness.

Knowledge pertains to the external world. All that is knowable in that realm is what is finally accessible to experience, but this calls for more than bare sensations. Kant would have knowledge understood in a quite restricted sense, referring to the joint operation of experience and understanding. The question, "Does a dog see a tree?," helps to illustrate the difference between and among perception, experience, and *knowledge*. Only when the contents of perception are subjected to the categories of the understanding is there the *experience* of a "this" or "that." To "see" is merely to record a portion of what is visible in the external world. To see *this*, however, is to comprehend just what it is that is seen. Any given "this," however, arises from a combination of properties not directly given in the mere physics of stimulation. Kant identifies two fundamental powers of the mind from which knowledge arises:

> The first is the capacity of receiving representations . . . the second is the power of knowing an object through these representations. (A50/B74)

Knowledge proper requires experience, and experience is more than sensation. Rather, for there to be experience the sensations must first be "packaged" by way of the spatiotemporal intuitions, now generating appearances that must in turn be subsumed under a conceptual scheme. It is for this reason that Kant stands in close agreement with Hume, to the effect that all knowledge *arises* from experience, but, as he will argue, this is different from the claim that knowledge is *grounded* in experience. A clear statement of this is found at B147 where he states that the pure categories of the understanding

> do not afford us any knowledge of things; they do so only through their possible application to empirical intuition.

Kant's concept of experience is not only at the very center of the overall argument of the *Critique* but stands as one of the most difficult aspects of that argument—and Kant knew it. In a letter to Jacob Beck (January 20, 1792), he acknowledges Beck's "thorough investigation of what is just the hardest thing in the whole *Critique*, namely, the analysis of an experience in general and the principles that make experience in general possible."[6]

He goes so far as to suggest that yet another treatise might be composed to meet the difficulties. Such a work, he says, would begin with the pure categories. These are supplied with content solely by way of the pure intuitions of space and time. The analysis would then show that

> no experience of objects of the senses is possible except insofar as I presuppose a priori that every such object must be *thought* of as a magnitude, and similarly with all the other categories. . . . Out of this there emerges a whole science of Ontology as *immanent* thinking; i.e., a science of things the objective reality of whose concepts can be securely established.[7]

The "whole science of Ontology" is thus grounded in the intrinsic and necessary structure of thought, for everything that might be said of real being must finally be constructed from what is provided by the categories. It is by way of the categories that anything is *thinkable* at all, and it is because of this that the whole science of ontology is understood to be *immanent* thinking. For "objects of the senses" to rise to the level of an experience—for them to be thinkable—the a priori categories are necessary. Much more is needed to complete the process, and these additional requirements are treated in Chapters 7 and 8. Here, however, it is sufficient to see how Kant's analysis of experience demands foundations seemingly unsuspected by the school of Locke and Hume.

Kant goes on to say of the categories,

> they serve only for the possibility of *empirical knowledge*; and such knowledge is what we entitle experience.

Experience, then, is grounded in fixed modes of apprehension—in "pure intuitions"—such that all appearances are spatiotemporally framed. Only by way of empirical intuition are the categories applied in a manner generative of knowledge as such. If the categories are to serve as the grounding of knowledge, they must be applied to the contents of empirical intuition in just the right way. But just how are they properly deployed? As will be clear in later pages, Kant has several converging approaches to this question. One that appears sparingly but importantly in the *Critique* invokes the concept of *spontaneity*. Kant identifies two fundamental powers of the mind from which knowledge arises:

The first is the capacity of receiving representations . . . the second is the power of knowing an object through these representations. (A50/B74)

This second power—the power of knowing an object through representations—is *spontaneity*. It is the freedom with which this power operates that permits conceiving of that which is impossible or extending concepts beyond the range of possible experience, for example, the concept of God (A96). The overall process is summarized as follows:

> If each representation were completely foreign to every other, standing apart and in isolation, no such thing as knowledge would ever arise. For knowledge is essentially a whole in which representations stand compared and connected. . . . Receptivity can make knowledge possible only when combined with spontaneity. (A97)

Spontaneity is integral to the process of synthesis, pulling together into organized wholes what would otherwise leave each representation foreign to every other. The synthesis by which knowledge is achieved is threefold: It is found in the *apprehension* of representations as modifications of the mind caused by stimulation; it is found in the *reproduction* of representations in imagination; it is found in the *recognition* of representations in a concept.

Recall from Chapter 3 that *Anschauung* relates to the very mode of apprehension, the necessary conditions for sensibility itself, and further, that intuitions are "pure" insofar as they are not empirical. They are the enabling conditions *for* sensibility, but they are not given *in* experience. Kant develops the argument for this in steps: First, stimulation of the visual sense leads to an indeterminate *appearance*. This is an empirical item and is thus subject to empirical intuition. Stimulation as such can give rise to nothing *determinate* in an appearance. Think of it as an array of photons striking the retina. Nothing in that burst of activity would be determinate. Thus,

> That in the appearance which corresponds to sensation I term its *matter*. (A20/B34)

For a determinate outcome—which is to say an *appearance*—a condition must be imposed that is not in the stimulus. Appearances are relationally ordered. Thus,

> That which so determines the manifold of appearance that it allows of being ordered in certain relations, I term the *form* of appearance.

This cannot itself be a sensation. An appearance arises from the material condition of sensation and as formed by the relational ordering of the manifold. Accordingly,

> While the matter of all appearance is given to us *a posteriori* only, its form must be ready for the sensations *a priori* in the mind, and so must allow of being considered apart from all sensations.[8]

The "forms of sensibility" are thus *pure* in the transcendental sense (nonempirical) and stand as *pure intuitions*. Note, then, that there are both *empirical* and *pure* intuitions. The pure intuitions are time and space. Kant's task in the matter of space and time is to show that neither is a mind-independent property of objects as in themselves they really are. He must show that they are "pure intuitions"—that is, nonempirical—but nonetheless able to yield true synthetic propositions and not mere tautologies.

To be sure, one may concede that time and space are "intuitions," but might contend that nevertheless they are all empirical, based wholly on experience. Kant rejects this, for if either time or space were empirical it would lack the very *necessity* and *universality* contained in such propositions as follows: *Two straight lines cannot enclose a space.* Nothing of an empirical nature is what it is necessarily. Moreover, the empiricistic account gains credibility only by way of the very Kantian requirements that it opposes. "Space," on an empirical understanding, must refer to something sensed or experienced as "out there." But clearly,

> Space is not an empirical concept which has been derived from outer experiences. For in order that certain sensations be referred to something outside me, that is, to something in another region

of space from that in which I find myself, and similarly in order that I may be able to represent them as outside and alongside one another, and accordingly as not only different, but as in different places, the representation of space must be presupposed. Space is a necessary *a priori* representation, which underlies all outer intuitions. . . . We can never represent to ourselves the absence of space, though, we can quite well think it as empty of objects. It must therefore be regarded as the condition of the possibility of appearances, and not as a demonstration dependent upon them. (A23–4/B38–9)

Kant is not claiming that in order to have awareness of the external world there must be space. Rather, the point is that in order to distinguish objects *as distinct from oneself* there must be the pure, which is to say *nonempirical* intuition of space. He argues further that, as space is the pure intuition of *outer sense* (*ausser uns*), time is the pure intuition of *inner sense* (*in uns*). His major contemporary critics on this point were J. H. Lambert and Moses Mendelsohn, both concerned to affirm the reality of time against what they took to be Kant's subjectivist thesis. They argued along these lines:

a. Mental representations undergo change.
b. Even if such representations are illusory, change requires time.
c. If there is such change, then time is *real*.

Kant begins his defense by agreeing:

I grant the whole argument. Certainly time is something real, namely the real form of inner intuition. It has therefore subjective reality in respect of inner experience; that is, I really have the representation of time and of my determinations in it. (A37/B54)

He then offers the following three arguments against the claim that time has a *mind-independent* reality and in defense of the alternative that asserts the "transcendental ideality of time."
First argument:

Time is not an empirical concept that is somehow drawn from experience. For simultaneity or succession would not themselves come into perception if the representation of time did not ground them *a priori.* Only under its presuppositions can one represent that several things exist at one and the same time (simultaneously) or in different times (successively). (A30/B46)

The contents of perception could not be simultaneous or successive were they not grounded in time. This same argument works well against Hume's notion of constant conjunction. One event following another presupposes succession in time.

Second argument:

Time is a necessary representation that grounds all intuitions. In regard to appearances in general one cannot remove time, though one can very well take the appearances away from time. Time is therefore given *a priori.* In it alone is all actuality of appearances possible. The latter could all disappear, but time itself, as the universal condition of their possibility, cannot be removed. (A31/B46)

Third argument:

The a priori necessity [of time] also grounds the possibility of apodictic principles of the relations of time, or axioms of time in general. It has only one dimension: different times are not simultaneous, but successive. . . . These principles could not be drawn from experience, for this would yield neither strict universality nor apodictic certainty. We would only be able to say: This is what common perception teaches, but not: This is how matters must stand. These principles are valid as rules under which experiences are possible at all, and instruct us prior to them, not through them. (A31/B47)

Apodictic certainty: That which is demonstrably and unconditionally certain. And *how matters must stand*! The argument as developed to this point supports the conclusion that all knowledge is necessarily grounded in formal principles, which could not be given by experience and on which experience itself depends.

The question arises again as to how it is that the objects of experience are placed within the relevant or "right" categorical framework. As noted, *spontaneity* is the power or process by which various aspects of the manifold can be categorically assigned, but, if this is not to be haphazard, the process must be governed by rules. As he says at A132/B171,

> If understanding in general is to be viewed as the faculty of rules, judgment will be the faculty of subsuming under rules; that is, distinguishing whether something does or does not stand under a given rule.

He takes this to be a talent, not something that can be taught, but only practiced. He refers to it as the gift of so-called *mother-wit*, something of a catch-all device to be further discussed in Chapter 7. Whatever is involved, it is clearly not a form of deliberation or practice, for the right match between experiences and concepts would already have to be in place in order to be practiced. Kant settles for mother-wit just as Thomas Reid took recourse to principles of commonsense. Indeed, the more open one is to the possibility of two radically different modes of philosophical analysis being grounded in a very similar perspective, it is appealing to find clear Reidian resonances in this part of the *Critique*.[9]

It is clear that concepts as such have nothing in common with that which is empirically intuited. The pure concepts of the understanding, as he says, can never be met with in any specific entity. He accepts that "no one will say that a category, such as that of causality, can be intuited through sense and is itself contained in appearance" (A177/B). As with Hume, Kant too would accept that no "cause" can be seen between the movement of one billiard ball and the one it strikes. So how is it possible that perceived objects and events are in fact subsumed under the pure concepts? Kant's answer to this question is in the form of what he calls the *schematism* of pure understanding. It is an intrinsic feature of cognition as such to impose on the objects of sensibility a schematic organization. The core principle is this: Whenever an object is subsumed under a concept, the representation of the object must be homogeneous with the concept. He illustrates this with a dinner plate. The empirical concept of the plate is homogeneous with the pure (nonempirical) geometrical concept of a circle. More generally,

No image could ever be adequate to the concept of the triangle in general. It would never attain that universality of the concept which renders it valid of all triangles, with the right angled, obtuse angle, or acute angle; it would always be limited to a part only. . . . The schema of the triangle can exist nowhere but in thought. It is a rule of synthesis of the imagination, in respect to pure figures in space.

At he makes this even clearer when he says,

Everything that can be presented to us as an object must conform to rules. For without such rules appearances would never yield knowledge of an object corresponding to them. What experience gives is the instance which stands under the rule. (B198)

James Van Cleve provides an economical and clear account of how Kant's *schemata* are to be applied. There is a general form of the rules that apply to the schematizing of the pure categories. It is, "Apply C to X if and only if X has T" where "T" is a *schema* having temporal properties. On this account, Van Cleve says,

The rule for substance is "apply the concept of substance to x if x is permanent, that is, exists throughout the whole of time." (A143/B183, A241/B300)[10]

It is the task and the achievement of transcendental philosophy that it not only specifies the rules governing the understanding but also specifies a priori the instances to which the rules are applied. Note, then, a transcendental philosophy presupposes the reality and even the necessity of a priori synthetic propositions. So once again, if the pure categories of the understanding constitute the a priori and necessary scheme for understanding, there must be rules that determine the correct employment of these categories. Kant presents these rules in the form of a table of principles beginning with the *axioms of intuition* The core principle of the axioms of intuition is that *all intuitions are extensive magnitudes*. A magnitude is extensive when the representation of the parts of something necessarily precede the representation of the whole.

Next in the table of principles is what Kant refers to as the *anticipations of perception*, which he defines thus:

> All knowledge by means of which I am enabled to know and determine a priori what belongs to empirical knowledge may be entitled an anticipation. (A167/B209)

An "anticipation" is the set, the cognitive anticipatory starting point from which, prior to any sensations whatever, there is a required condition that must be satisfied. This, too, exemplifies Kant's "transcendental" form of argumentation. There is no question but that we know in advance what can possibly qualify as "empirical" knowledge. For us to know this a priori there must be a principle applicable to the overall domain of possible knowledge that would qualify any candidate entry as "empirical" as such. This principle "anticipates" perception in the sense that it is the precondition for perception to have content. The core principle is that, in all appearances, in all that is a possible object of sensation, there is intensive magnitude, that is, a degree. Kant draws this interesting inference, ruling out the possibility that there could be an empirical proof of empty space:

> If all . . . perception has a degree, between which and negation there exists an infinite gradation of ever smaller degrees, and if every sense must likewise possess some particular degree of receptivity of sensations, no perception, and consequently no experience, is possible that could prove, either immediately or mediately, no matter how far ranging the reasoning may be, a complete absence of all reality in the field appearance. In other words the proof of an empty space or of empty time can never be derived from experience. (B214)

Third in the table of principles are the famous three *analogies of experience*. These are of central importance to the entire work, for they serve as additional proofs against Hume-type skepticism. The foundational principle of the analogies is that "Experience is possible only through the representation of a necessary connection of perceptions" (B218). Absent this connection, coherent experience is simply impossible. Thus, to the extent that Hume's empiricism restricts knowledge to experience, empiricism succeeds only by accepting the very grounding of experience itself.

There is an additional general principle on which all three analogies rest:

the necessary unity of apperception, in respect of all possible pure consciousness, that is, of all perception, at every instant of time . . . this unity lies *a priori* at the foundation of empirical consciousness.

Reading through the tangled wording, one sees that knowledge must inhere in a consciousness and that the various elements or pieces of that knowledge must be unified in that consciousness. Thus, the very experiences on which empiricism depends presuppose as a necessary condition the unity of apperception. As for the analogies, Kant says,

An analogy of experience will therefore be only a rule in accordance with which unity of experience is to arise from perceptions (not as a perception itself. (A180/B223)

Kant's choice of this term has been a matter of discussion and debate. He may well have been influenced by Locke's *Essay* (book 4, chapter 16, section 12):

Concerning the manner of operation in most parts of the works of nature, wherein though we see the sensible effects, yet their causes are unknown, and we perceive not the ways and manner how they are produced. *Analogy* in these matters is the only help we have, and it is from that alone that we draw all our grounds of probability.

One might favor this as the source of Kant's usage, for especially in the second analogy the "rule" that will operate to achieve unity of experience is the rule of causality itself, as will be noted below. Turning to the analogies themselves, the first analogy states: *In all change of appearances, substance is permanent; its quantum in nature is neither increased nor diminished.* Kant's proof of this is based on the proposition that all appearances are in time and that there must be something permanent, in relation to which all time relations are themselves determined. This "something permanent" is *substance.* There is a mundane way of making this point. For there to be an alteration in the appearance of something, there must be a *something.* Were there not a substantial "it," it would not be possible for the appearance of "it" to undergo alteration. In this Kant is rehearsing the old distinction between essential and accidental properties, the distinction Aristotle draws attention to in stating that Coriscus is a man and is musical. "Coriscus is a man" identifies the essential ("substantial") entity that undergoes alterations but not *change.* Gold can be melted and shaped, but it remains gold throughout. Relations in time presuppose a permanent standard against which variations in time might occur. That permanent is *substance.*

According to the second analogy: *Everything that happens, that is, begins to be, presupposes something upon which it follows according to a rule.* Or, as Kant expressed it in the second edition, *all alterations take place in accordance with the law of connection of cause and effect.* The proof is as follows: First, time as such cannot be perceived. Thus, relations in time are not empirically given. Accordingly, the very possibility of experience—empirical knowledge—comes about only in so far as we subject the succession of appearances to the law of causality. Again, to put the matter more simply, for there to be Hume's "constant conjunction," there must already be in place a principle by which otherwise distinct appearances are organized as antecedent and consequent. This is the only basis on which—to use Hume's phrase—one object succeeds another.

This is such a crucial part of the overall argument as to warrant a more detailed discussion.[11] Hume's laws of association might be thought of as accomplishing the work Kant accomplishes by way of the second analogy. On Hume's account, any pair of events reliably associated in experience result in a mental habit of sorts such that the antecedent occurrence is taken to be the cause of what reliably follows. Kant is satisfied that such an account fails utterly to explain what is virtually universal in human experience, a universality that could not be traced to a uniformity of associational histories. The aim of the second analogy is to explain how, by way of a priori grounds, representations are coherently joined. Begin with the fact that what is present to the mind are *representations.* The task now is to explain the basis on which we posit an actual *object* as being external to ourselves and known only by way of the same sort of representations (A197/B242). The task, then, is to avert that "continuing scandal" that prevents metaphysicians from establishing even the reality of the external world. But anything might be willy-nilly connected with anything else as a result of no more than

Hume's "constant conjunctions." If this is so, then it is unclear as to how any of the common objects of experience could ever become part of the predictable, intersubjectively known world. In other words, the Humean account cannot handle the evidence that a fair-minded jury would expect in regarding accounts of causality to be compatible with the facts.

Or, consider a house:

> The house is not a thing in itself, but only an appearance, that is, a representation. . . . What, then, am I to understand by the question: how the manifold may be connected in the appearance itself, which yet is nothing in itself? (A190/B236)

Kant's answer is that the transition from appearance to object must occur according to a rule,

> necessitating us to connect them in some one specific manner: and conversely, that only in so far as our representations are necessitated in a certain order, as regards their time-relations do they acquire objective meaning. (A197/B242)

Of course, the parts of the house can be arranged only in specific ways if the result is to be constitutive of a house. With a static object such as a house, the different parts may be apprehended in a manner independent of temporal order or sequence. With dynamic events, however, the principle of causation is illustrated directly. Kant attempts to show this with the example of a boat on a river. First, consider the static object, the house. The parts of a house are apprehended successively, for the obvious reason that it takes time to examine first one part then another and so on. However, the overall object remains a house, whatever the particular order of perceptions. Dynamic events are different:

> For instance, I see a ship move down stream. My perception of its lower position follows upon the perception of its position higher up in the stream, and it is impossible that in the apprehension of this appearance the ship should first be perceived lower down in the stream and afterwards higher up. . . . There is always a rule that makes the order in which the perceptions

follow upon one another a necessary order. . . . Thus only can I be justified in asserting, not merely of my apprehension, but of appearance itself, that a succession is to be met with in it. (A193/B238)

The second analogy thus answers the empiricist who would have a mere succession of perceptions give rise to ordered and intersubjectively shared experiences. The process requires more than a "constant conjunction," for there are a priori rules that legislate certain "conjunctions" out of bounds.

The third analogy asserts that "all substances, in so far as they can be perceived to coexist in space, are in thoroughgoing reciprocity." Kant's proof for this is as follows: One can look first at the moon and then at the Earth, or, conversely, first at the Earth and then to the moon. Perceptions can thus follow each other reciprocally. It is on this basis that they are said to be coexistent. Such coexistence is the existence of the manifold at one and the same time. But time itself cannot be perceived. Therefore, there is no basis on which to assume, simply from things being set in the same time, that perceptions of them can follow each other reciprocally. However, in the absence of this form of reciprocity, directing attention first to one thing and then another would result in the conclusion that the second follows the other in time. Accordingly, there could be no simultaneity.

As one focuses on one object and then another, and then back to the first, and then back to the second, one is able to comprehend a coexistence of the two objects rather than a causal relationship between them. This again requires an a priori temporal framework within which simultaneity is possible. Taken together, the analogies of experience challenge the central precepts of Hume's epistemology.

It is in the *Prolegomena* that Kant ties his project to what he takes to be Hume's problem: For Hume,

the question was not whether the concept of cause was right, useful, and even indispensable for a knowledge of nature, for this Hume had never doubted; but whether that concept could be thought by reason, a priori, and consequently, whether it possessed an inner truth, independent of all experience. (*Prolegomena*, 259)

The second analogy is an answer to the question. Experience is possible only through the representation and necessary connection of perceptions (B218).

The *analogies* thus noted, there is then the fourth and final entry in the table of principles—*the postulates of the empirical thought in general*, of which there are three: First, whatever agrees with the formal conditions of experience is *possible.* Whatever is bound up with sensation is *actual.* Finally, whatever is connected to the actual in conformity with the universal conditions of experience is *necessary.* To substance, causality, and reciprocity Kant now adds the modal categories of possibility, actuality, and necessity, thereby establishing the conditions on which are based all cognitive representations of objective reality. To the extent the analysis holds, Kant has shown that the claims of science are not merely expressions of a peculiar cognitive process, that reality is comprised of what is more than and different from ideas about it, and that the world as a congeries of appearances is nonetheless an objective world capable of being known as such. If human beings are fated to have a knowledge cobbled out of appearances and a fixed scheme of categories, they are not thereby left to wishful thinking or the prejudices of the imagination.

To the extent that the analysis holds, with all the "elements" now in place, as well as the rules of their deployment, what remains to be shown is that the resulting cognitive representations of reality are valid. It must be established that the proper deployment of cognitive powers is generative of objective knowledge. The linchpin as always is to establish the possibility of true a priori synthetic propositions. On this vital point, surely one of the more daring aspects of Kant's analysis would have him argue that the propositions of mathematics are synthetic.

A useful starting point here is Leibniz. In the famous battle of the geniuses, Leibniz rejected the Newtonian concept of absolute space. He based his conclusions on his rational method of analysis grounded in *the principle of sufficient reason.* Recall Leibnitz's reference to Archimedes. If two perfectly equal weights are balanced on a fulcrum, they remain motionless. Only by introducing a difference, a discontinuity, a disruption, is a change of state brought about. For anything ever to happen, there must be a sufficient reason for it. Empty space is nothingness—and nothing will come of nothing.

In light of the extraordinary achievements arising from Newtonian science, it surely would require more than a neat rational argument to reduce the Newtonian concept of space to some sort of logical error. It is not one of the gifts of unaided reason to settle factual questions regarding the nature of physical reality. Kant sets about to discipline "reason" first by making clear that, absent experiential content, concepts are empty. Recall again the two classes of propositions, those that are analytic and those that are synthetic. Leibniz taught that the logical principle governing propositions is the law of contradiction. However, synthetic propositions, intended to enlarge and expand knowledge, are different. Whereas the negation of an analytic proposition leads to a logical contradiction (e.g., not all bachelors are unmarried), negating synthetic propositions does not (e.g., mass is unaffected by velocity). So the metaphysical question of moment is whether and how synthetic propositions can be known to be true a priori and of necessity.

The transcendental aesthetic answers that question in the matter of sensibility. That time and space are the universal form of all sensibility is taken to be necessarily true and makes possible true propositions regarding the facts of perception. Far less plausible is Kant's thesis that mathematical propositions are also synthetic and that their truth is known a priori.

It is at this point that Kant is able to enter the debate between rationalists such as Leibniz and empiricists such as Locke and Hume. Leibniz contended that the issues dividing his and Newton's physics could be settled by the right sort of rational analysis. Kant must make clear that reason has no means by which to engage reality unless it is supplied with the empirical content of that reality. His position on this matter long predated the publication of the *Critique*. Paul Guyer's study of the early works presents a Kant who

> criticized from the outset the rationalist assumption that the *a priori* knowledge characteristic of general and special metaphysics could be derived from . . . the laws of logic alone. . . . Sufficient reasons for the determinations of real objects could not be established just by the analyses of what are in fact merely concepts.[12]

However, were the required empirical content received directly as it is in itself (i.e., *noumenally*) without the participation of the observer, nothing could be known a priori of the objective external world. The observer would be a passive recipient of incident energy unable even to order events in time, let alone distinguish between conscious states and a world beyond them. However, Kant must also make clear that the observer's contribution by way of the pure intuitions and the categories does not thereby render the resulting knowledge a mere subjective creation. He must account for the manner in which appearances are brought under concepts such that judgments match up with the facts, the result being the possession of a priori truths such as those abundant in mathematics.

The starting point here is geometry. It is quite clear that the concept of space is necessary for geometry itself. Traditionally rationalists have regarded geometry as one of the crowning achievements of reason, not at all dependent on sensation or perception. Exemplifying the perspective, Leibniz argued that by reason alone the Newtonian concept of absolute space could be shown to be mistaken. Kant proceeds to illustrate the defects of this perspective by having the reader hold a hand up to a mirror. Any attempt to rotate the left hand in three dimensional space in order to make it the right hand as seen in the mirror will fail. No such rotation will succeed. As he says in section 13 of the *Prolegomena,*

What can be more similar in every respect, and in every part more alike to my hands . . . than their images in a mirror? And yet I cannot put such a hand as is seen in the glass in the place of its original; for, if this is a right hand, that in the glass is a left one . . . which never can take the place of the other. There are in this case no internal differences which our understanding could determine by thinking alone. Yet the differences are internal as the senses teach, for, notwithstanding their complete equality and similarity, the left-hand cannot be enclosed in the same bounds as the right one (they are not congruent); the glove of one hand cannot be used for the other. What is the solution? These objects are not representations of things as they are in themselves and as some mere understanding would know them, but sensuous intuitions, that is, appearances.

Kant then generalizes from this to geometry at large, arguing that,

> Pure mathematics, and especially Euclidean geometry, can
> have objective reality only on condition that they refer merely
> to objects of sense. But in regard to the latter, the principle
> holds good that our sense representation is not a representation
> of things in themselves, but of the way in which they appear to
> us. Hence it follows that the propositions of geometry are not
> the results of a mere creation of our . . . imagination, and that
> therefore they cannot be referred with the assurance to actual
> objects; but rather that they are necessarily valid of space, and
> consequently, of all that may be found in space, because space
> is nothing else than the form of all external appearances, and it
> is this form alone in which objects of sense can be given to us.
> (*Prolegomena*, 286–7)

On the "left-right" issue, Martin Gardner noted years ago that in
this Kant was among the first to see the philosophical implications
of the fact that there is no formal or logical definition of "left" and
"right." The hands are illustrative of what are called *chiral* entities,
which are those whose mirror images cannot be superimposed.

Gardner illustrates the point with a thought experiment involving those of us living on Earth and residents of a distant planet. We
establish radio contact. Let us assume that they are like us in all
physical and physiological respects. What we want to find out is
whether their world is a mirror image of ours. We know they have
hearts, for example, and we would like to know whether their hearts
are slightly displaced to the left in their chests as are ours. Is our
left shoe their left shoe? But as there is no logical or formal criterion
by which to establish left and right, we would be entirely unable by
purely rational means to have our questions answered.[13]

Recall the steps in the argument:

Even if in some sense modeled after mathematics and the developed sciences, metaphysics is nonetheless distinct from both. It is
incumbent on Kant, therefore, to make clear what the method of
metaphysics must be and how it is different from (while compatible
with) the methods of mathematics and science. What in metaphysics might correspond to the synthetic a priori judgments in science
and mathematics?

The answer to this question is developed in *The Transcendental Doctrine of Method* (A709/B737). Here Kant notes that mathematics offers a splendid example of a successful extension of pure reason without the aid of the experience and then asks whether philosophy can achieve the same end. To answer the question he must distinguish between philosophical and mathematical knowledge. Whereas philosophical knowledge is gained by reason from concepts, mathematical knowledge is gained by reason from what Kant calls the *construction* of concepts. It is important to follow the argument that distinguishes between the methods proper to each.

To construct a concept is to exhibit a priori the intuition that corresponds to it. Kant presents a long and somewhat tortured attempt to clarify this (A713/B741), but the distinction is made clearer in the *Prolegomena* (part 1, 281–6) where he says straight away,

> For the construction of the concept we need a non-empirical intuition.

The point is that, for there to be any geometric construction whatever, there must be nonempirical and necessary conditions of sensibility or else there is simply no starting point. Without such conditions of sensibility mathematics would come to an end. It is the *pure intuition of space* that makes the very objects of geometry possible, as it is the *pure intuition* of time that makes arithmetic possible. Nothing in a physical object carries with it a location "in space," nor does such an object include among its own properties duration or identity over time. Absent the pure intuition of time arithmetic itself is inconceivable, for the very process of addition is sequential and sequences are temporal.

Regarding geometry, consider the single figure drawn by the geometer. The figure is empirical, yet it serves to express the universal concept "triangle." For in this empirical intuition we consider only the act whereby we construct a concept. Differences in the many manifestations of "triangle" (for instance, in the magnitude of the sides and angles) are quite indifferent and do not alter the concept of "triangle" itself. Whereas philosophical knowledge considers the particular only in the universal, mathematical knowledge considers the universal in the particular, or even in the single instance, though still always a priori and by means of reason.

Kant gives the philosopher the concept of a triangle to see what might be done with it (A716/B744). The concept, of course, includes only a figure enclosed by three straight lines. Now ask the philosopher what the relationship is between the sum of the angles in this figure and a right angle. Kant says that no degree of meditation will lead to an answer. The philosopher can analyze the concept of triangle till blue in the face, and nothing will come of it. Enter the mathematician. The mathematician begins by constructing a triangle. Knowing that the sum of two right angles is exactly equal to the sum of all the adjacent angles that can be constructed from a single point on a straight line, the mathematician stretches one side of the triangle and obtains two adjacent angles, which together equal two right angles. In the end, there is a fully evident and universally valid solution to the problem.

There is, however, a danger lurking behind such success. Reason needs discipline, lest it takes its achievement in mathematics to promise comparable knowledge in metaphysics. The philosopher and the mathematician both employ reason, but the former purely by way of concepts, whereas the latter by way of intuitions with which to exhibit a priori those objects that exemplify the concepts. Although philosophy and mathematics have a common object, the mode in which reason handles that object is wholly different in philosophy and in mathematics. Philosophy confines itself to universal concepts; mathematics can achieve nothing by way of concepts. It must proceed to an intuition by which it considers the concept *in concreto*. The intuition, though presented a priori in the concrete individual instance, must nonetheless be universally valid.

The Pythagorean theorem, for example, is satisfied by every and any right-angle triangle. In like manner, the geometer constructs her own concepts, but these are then precisely mapped on to and realized in the external world. This world is cognized by way of synthetic propositions whose validity is nonetheless established a priori. The geometer constructs a triangle by representing the object that corresponds to the concept. This is all worked out a priori without benefit of any experience. Indeed, the geometer may never have seen the very object now derived from the concept itself. The figure thus drawn is empirical, yet it expresses the universal concept "triangle."

The empiricists would have perception a passive process in which the percipient contributes nothing but some physiological apparatus making stimulation possible. As on this account one does not experience objects directly, but only by way of some sort of mediated mental representation; the resulting experience might well be the product of a dream. Knowledge claims arising from such a process can never be self-justifying. To the extent that all knowledge arises from just such experiences there must be a vicious circularity in every attempt to tie knowledge to anything firmer than particular habits and tendencies of mental life.

What leads to a vexing skepticism in such an account is the mediated nature of experience itself. If the content of synthetic propositions is experiential, and if the sole means by which to establish the truth of such propositions is also experiential, then the entire enterprise is but psychology by another name. The grounds on which one might avoid the dream-state option will be pragmatic and utilitarian: Getting on with what one takes to be important simply leaves no room for a skepticism otherwise validated by philosophy.

Again, as noted earlier in this chapter, suppose the very properties of the objects of knowledge are not passively processed but actually conferred by the conditions of sensibility and the categorical framework of human understanding. In that case, it would be possible to anticipate such knowledge as can be gleaned by way of experience. Granting the empiricist's claim that all knowledge arises from experience, it would nonetheless be shown that experience itself requires a grounding. Enter *the pure intuitions of time and space.*

Kant claims that time possesses both "empirical reality" and "transcendental ideality" (A35–6/B52), terms that prove difficult to keep properly partitioned. He also offers arguments to establish that time is an a priori form of inner sense. Consider again the three arguments defending the apriority of time as outlined in the preceding chapter.

The first argument asserts that time is not an objective property of things but "the immediate condition of the inner intuition . . . [and] the mediate condition of outer appearances" (A32–4/B49–51). Thus, it is by way of this a priori form of sensibility that several things be represented either as simultaneous or successive in experience. The simultaneity or succession of events does not convey but presupposes time as the form of inner sense (A30/B46). In *Kant's Transcendental Idealism* Henry Allison makes the same point about space: There would be no means by which to distinguish ourselves

from the items of experience were there no a priori spatiotemporal framework. Only by way of the spatial "outer" is it possible for
objects to be cognized as distinct from oneself. Absent this "outer,"
the percipient would be driven to solipsism. All items and occur-
rences normally perceived as "out there" would be ordered in time
but on some inner purely subjective screen of consciousness. Worse,
the experiences would not be anyone's, for absent this same "outer"
sense the division between "I" and "That" would be eliminated. In
some odd way, there could be experiences, but not *one's own* experiences. Against the common criticism that Kant might just as well
have regarded time as a fact of reality, such that both the observer
and the observed are "in" time together, Kant's reply would surely
be that nothing in the bald fact of events conveys time, for every
"change" is a change only with respect to time itself.

In his second argument he contends that time is comprehensible
even in the absence of actual items, but there can be no sensible
awareness of an item except *in time*. Asserted here is not a "logical"
an ontological necessity if there are to be appearances at all. Allison
properly rejects the Kemp Smith reading that finds Kant making a
(merely) "psychological" claim about how appearances come to be
formed. Were this reading correct, then there might just as well be
non-Kantian "appearances" that are not spatiotemporal.

Finally, if time were an empirical given, simultaneity and succession would be neither necessary nor universal conditions of sensibility but merely contingent features of it, unable to establish *how
matters must stand*. Time is not a "concept" as such, for

> The proposition that different times cannot be simultaneous . . .
> is synthetic, and cannot have its origin in concepts alone. (A32)

Time is infinite such that any measure of time is a limitation
imposed on the totality. Thus,

> the original representation, *time,* must therefore be given as
> unlimited. But . . . an object . . . so given . . . cannot be given
> through concepts, since they [concepts] contain only partial rep-
> resentations. (B48)

How, in light of this, should Kant be understood when he claims
that time is "the immediate condition of the inner intuition . . . [and]

the mediate condition of outer appearances"? The pure intuitions comprise the necessary conditions for all sensibility. Indeed, sensibility is to be understood as the very capacity by which representations become possible. Such representations include a sensibility to objects and events distinguishable from the observer as well as representations of objects and events internal to the observer. All formal representations are of necessity spatial. Only this way is it possible to distinguish objects from thoughts about objects. Inner intuition, then, refers to thoughts, feelings, and experiences in general. The separation and distinction of each of these from any other presupposes time as a necessary condition. This is the sense in which inner intuition is *immediate.* Similarly, there must be a necessary condition by which inner (mental) intuitions are distinguishable from objects of perception. It is by way of the pure intuition of *space* that such distinctions are possible. All inner representations are in time. The representations of objects distinct from one's mental states are in space. Neither time nor space is given by properties of the stimulus and thus are not given by experience as such. They are *pure* (nonempirical).

Kant argues further that concepts contain only partial representations. The concept "dog" represents no specific dog, and therefore, a given object is not, as it were, delivered by concepts alone. Different events, if they are to be comprehended as different, must be distinguishable from each other. But there is nothing in an object as such that conveys *here* and *now*, contrasted with *there* and *then*. Moreover, if in some way, the spatiotemporal character of a given representation were itself empirical, then it would be merely a contingent fact of experience that it somehow includes space and time. The spatiotemporal properties of an object would be no different from its color or hardness.

Kant, of course, was not the first to develop arguments along these lines, nor have such arguments been spared very severe challenges. As for the arguments, it would not be stretching the point to trace the line of reasoning to Plato. Descartes in particular anticipates the basis on which Kant declared mathematical truths to be in the form of synthetic propositions known to be true a priori. Descartes put the matter this way in the Fifth Meditation:

And what I here find of most importance is, that I discover in my mind innumerable ideas of certain objects which . . . possess true and immutable natures of their own. As, for example, when I imagine a triangle, although there is not perhaps and never was in any place in the universe apart from my thought one such figure, it remains true nevertheless that this figure possesses a certain determinate nature, form, or essence, which is immutable and eternal, and not framed by me, nor in any degree dependent on my thought; as appears from the circumstance, that diverse properties of the triangle may be demonstrated, viz., that its three angles are equal to two right, that its greatest side is subtended by its greatest angle, and the like. . . . It cannot be supposed that they were ever objects of sense. I recollect that even when I still strongly adhered to the objects of sense, I reckoned among the number of the most certain truths those I clearly conceived relating to figures, numbers, and other matters that pertain to arithmetic and geometry, and in general to the pure mathematics.[14]

Similarly, the concept of time has received close philosophical inspection since the time of Aristotle. In his treatise on *physics* he relates time and motion, specifically celestial motion. If such motion did not exist there would be no "time" as such.[15] Aristotle's reasoning opposes the Newtonian conception of absolute time and stands in close relation to Leibniz's view.

In the matter of criticism, more than one student of the *Critique* has found the presumed synthetic nature and a priori status of mathematical propositions to be problematical, even question begging. Is Kant saying that "X" cannot be represented unless there is some sort of a priori "X" it matches? Against this Sebastian Gardiner offers a reading of the text that is surely closer to the argument Kant adduces in support of his conclusions regarding mathematical propositions. Gardner writes,

If the representation of space were not *a priori*, then it would be empirical; but if it were formed empirically, then it would be obtained from experience of outer objects. But this is impossible, since outer experience is impossible without the representation of space. So the representation of space must be *a priori*. In sum, because the representation of space is invoked in the very act of representing the world of outer objects, it cannot be based on experience of outer objects.[16]

How good these and related arguments are is a question that still divides scholars. Other criticisms understand "time" as better explained either in psychological or in logical terms. Is it, for example, "analytic" that all appearances presuppose a temporal framework not itself given in the experience? Contemporary philosophy offers a varied and intriguing set of conjectures on the nature and structure of time, much of it seemingly indifferent to Kant's analysis. After all, with the advent of relativity theory the concept of time was radically transformed in ways that Kant presumably could not have anticipated.

On closer inspection, however, even or perhaps especially the more avant garde contributions draw from the considerations developed by Kant. It is received doctrine in Einstein's version of relativity theory that the temporal reality of simultaneity is determined by the motion of the observer. Kant would add to this discovery by noting that "motion" itself presupposes change *with respect to time* and, to this extent, attempts to dissolve time as a construct arising from matter-energy succeed only to the extent that time is presupposed in all assessments of change. In this connection, Mauro Dorato has observed that no less a figure than Kurt Gödel understood the compatibility. He offers this passage from one of Gödel's unpublished manuscripts:

> The agreement described between certain consequences of modern physics and a doctrine that Kant set up 150 years ago in contradiction both to common sense and to the physicists and philosophers of his time, is greatly surprising, and it is hard to understand why so little attention is being paid to it in philosophical discussion of relativity theory.[17]

There is yet another question, again in light of relativity theory, of whether Kant was right about geometry, namely, that our representation of space is necessarily Euclidean. This is but a part of the larger question of whether Kant was right about space itself. There is a robust secondary literature devoted to both of these questions. A "Google" search containing the terms, "Kant Geometry," turns up more than 200,000 items. Narrowing the search to Euclidean geometry, one still must deal with more than 20,000 items. Interest here arises in large measure from Kant's controversial claim that the propositions in Euclidean geometry are synthetic, that their truth can be established a priori, and that our mode of spatial representation is *necessarily* Euclidean.

As noted, for both time and space, Kant provides both a *metaphysical* and a *transcendental* exposition of the concepts. The former establishes the nonempirical grounding of the concepts, and the transcendental exposition establishes their necessity. Outer sense—which he calls a property of the mind—is the basis on which objects are represented as outside oneself and without exception in space (A22/B37). Properly understood, space itself is not an empirical concept for space is not "given" by material impingements. It is not the result of a sensation. To perceive the location or separation of objects, and to perceive such objects as distinct from oneself, the nonempirical "pure" intuition of space must be presupposed. It cannot arise from the set of appearances. Rather, it constitutes the necessary framework for these very appearances. This much said, it is here for the first time in the *Critique* that Kant takes up the question of geometry (A25/B40). He says,

> Geometry is the science which determines the properties of space synthetically, and yet, what, then, must be our representation of space, in order that such knowledge of it may be possible? It must in its origin be intuition; for from a mere concept no propositions can be obtained which go beyond the concept—as happens in geometry. Further, this intuition must be a priori, that is it must be found in us prior to any perception of an object and must therefore be pure, not an empirical intuition. For geometrical propositions are one and all . . . bound up with the consciousness of their necessity; for instance, that space has only three dimensions. Such propositions cannot be empirical or, in other words, judgments of experience, nor can they be derived from any such judgments. (B41)

What, then, of Kant's contention that the representation of the external world is *necessarily* Euclidian? The philosopher and mathematician exemplify different modes of knowing, but surely one person can live both of these lives. Through purely philosophical modes of knowing, one is engaged chiefly in the analysis and valid deployment of concepts. With geometrical constructions, however, that manifold that belongs to the *schema* of the triangle in general is combined in a pure intuition, the result being a universal *synthetic* propositions the truth of which is established a priori (A718/B746). In light of this, the worry—both ancient and contemporary—that the principles of geometry do not match up with natural phenomena was entirely misplaced. The worry disappears once one recognizes that the spatiality of entities in the external world necessarily conform to space as the geometer considers it. Objects in space are known only by way of representations, and this same mode of representations is the basis on which the geometer constructs those objects that answer to such concepts as "triangle," "square," and so on. The space that is "thought" by the geometer is itself a form of sensible representation and thus must conform to the same pure intuitions as those that permit the construction of forms in the first place.

The process does not result in mere subjectivity, however. Kant makes this clear in the *Prolegomena* (note 1):

> The propositions of geometry aren't mere fantasies that might have nothing to do with real objects. Pure mathematics, and in particular pure geometry, is objectively valid, but only in application to objects of the senses. . . . Outer appearances must conform to what geometry says about them. . . . All outer objects of the world of the senses must agree exactly with the propositions of geometry.

These assurances duly noted, Kant's entire analysis has not been immune to serious and sustained criticism. Gary Hatfield's assessment represents what is now close to a consensus:

> The single most important event for the evaluation of Kant's theory of space was the discovery of non-Euclidean geometries in the nineteenth century and the subsequent conclusion that physical space-time is non-Euclidean in the twentieth. Kant had contended not merely that the space of experience is Euclidean and grounds Euclidean demonstrations, but that (owing to transcendental idealism) we can therefore know *a priori* that physical space and physical objects are described by Euclid's geometry with apodictic certainty. In Kant's view, Euclid's description of spatial structure provides universal and necessary principles of the structure of physical space and physical objects.[18]

Was Kant simply overtaken by history? Kant might find difficulty with the passage above that begins, "not merely the space of experience." For Kant, that actually is the only space that is knowable. To the extent that there is a *knowable* physical space with physical objects in it, this is the *cognized* reality arising from the application of the sensuous intuitions to appearances and then the subsumption of these under the relevant categories. Recall again Kant's claim that

> Pure geometry . . . is objectively valid, but only in application to objects of the senses.

Objects of the senses are, of course, objects only in so far as sensations have been transformed into appearances again by way of sensuous intuition. So, was Kant finally right about geometry? Frege seems to have thought so, though such matters are never settled by a show of hands.[19] Perhaps it is sufficient to say that Kant's argument presupposes creatures such as ourselves whose forms of sensuous intuition control the manner in which outer objects are amendable to representation. This is at least arguably "Euclidian," no matter how many other systems of geometry are contrived by mathematicians.

The Kantian "necessities" in this connection include the one that finds us aware that space has only three dimensions. Clearly, if Kant conceived of space as an external and mind-independent reality, he would be legislating necessity where no more than contingency would obtain. But space, as we have seen, is a pure intuition, neither empirically derived nor subject to empirical verification. Indeed, it is a necessary condition for the very possibility of empirical verification. And it is this whole line of thinking that raises again the allegedly unbridgeable divide between the *noumenal* and the *phenomenal.* Is Kant saying that necessarily space has only three dimensions *for us*, or that necessarily space has only three dimensions?

Some contend that such distinctions render Kant's ontology dualistic, one sort of thing, which is the thing in itself, and another ontologically distinct entity, which is the thing as thought. Others contend that there is no such cluttered ontology but rather a *dual-aspect* thesis.

Each interpretation has been cogently defended by Paul Guyer and Henry Allison, respectively.[20] It is Guyer's thesis that spatio-temporality is the necessary condition of all that can be represented in experience. The "thing in itself"—the *noumenal* entity—is not representable, which would seem to entail that it lacks spatiotemporal properties. Accordingly, there is a dual *ontology* rather than a merely *dual aspect*. Guyer favors the dual ontology interpretation on the plausible grounds that Kant would not have stressed spatiotemporality in relation to our *representations*, spatiotemporality as an *epistemic* condition. Space and time are not conditions that figure in Kant's discussion of "things in themselves." Moreover, if "things in themselves" actually did have spatial and temporal properties, these would be merely contingent attributes and the necessity attaching to formal mathematics would thereby be undermined.

Against the "two-world" view endorsed by Guyer there is the dual-aspect thesis defended by Allison and adopted here. Central to the defense is a distinction between *epistemic* enabling conditions and ontologically distinct *kinds* of things. Objects as *experienced* are possible owing to the conditions that enable all sensibility. These same objects can be considered abstractly, devoid of sensible features. Although one may comprehend an object either as sensible or as an entity independent of the very conditions by which it is, in fact, sensible, it is the same object. These two aspects are distinct in the epistemic and not the ontological respect.

What does Kant say? First, he dismisses the very prospect of our knowing things noumenally. He makes his position clear in the *Amphiboly of Concepts of Reflection* where he says:

> If by the complaints—that we have no insight into the intrinsic nature of things—it be meant that we cannot conceive by the pure understanding what the things which appear to us may be in themselves . . . (the complaints) are entirely illegitimate and unreasonable. For what is demanded is that we should . . . not be humans. (A277–8/B333–4)

The phrasing here is important. He says, if "it be meant that we cannot conceive by the pure understanding what the things which appear to us may be in themselves. . . ." Clearly at issue is the extent to which by pure understanding alone we are able to reach that ultimate reality of things in themselves. Nothing in the passage (and there are many such passages) suggests a dual *ontology*. In referring to "what the things which appear to us may be in themselves" he is including under the same cognitive roof something that (a) appears to us and (b) is as itself. It is the former aspect that renders it knowable; the latter aspect is only *thinkable*. A concise statement of the position adopted here was given some years ago by Leslie Stevenson:

> It is clear from many pronouncements that (Kant) is not denying either meaning or truth-value to statements about how things are in themselves; he is only denying that we can know their truth-value. It is vital to his "practical" defence of belief in God, freedom, and immortality that we be able to think of them (Bxxvi), that is to entertain meaningful non-contradictory propositions, even though "objective" validity, that is, "real possibility" is lacking here. . . . It is clear . . . that Kant thinks there are truths, facts of the matter, about how things are in themselves, which we can never know.[21]

A relevant passage speaks of appearances in two ways: First, as they are "thought as objects according to the unity of the categories" and are, in this sense, *phenomena*; but also as "objects of the understanding and which, nevertheless, can be given as such to an intuition." He states explicitly that, in this latter sense, what is available to *us* is not available owing to our power of sensibility. What is available is so *"coram intuitu intellectuali"*—in the presence of an intellectual intuition. "Such things would be entitled *noumena (intelligibilia)*." He does not say that they would *be* different entities, *entitled—called*—something different from *phenomena*.

He goes on to acknowledge that, although our mode of representation is sensible, limited by spatiotemporal intuition, this does not establish that such is the only possible intuition; it is only such *for us* (A252). Clearly, the implication is not that there are multiple realities (a dualistic ontology) but potentially multiple modes of representing the objectively real (a dual-aspect epistemology). The point is made again at A258/B314 and elsewhere. Scholars well familiar with these passages have nonetheless reached different conclusions but, again, it would seem that if he meant the phenomenon–noumenon distinction to refer to nothing less than two ontologically distinct realms of real existence, Kant would surely have said so straightaway.[22]

A word more on this point may be drawn from Kant's *Critique of Judgment*, which is considered in greater detail in Chapter 7. Under the heading, "Analytic of Beauty," he says,

> The judgment of taste, therefore, is not a cognitive judgment, is not logical, but is *aesthetic*—which means that it is one whose determining ground cannot be other than subjective. Every reference of representations is capable of being objective, even that of sensations (in which case it signifies the real in an empirical representation).[23]

There is, even in sensations, content referring to what is "real" and not itself dependent on the peculiarities of perceptual-cognitive processes. This passage is surely not decisive in settling the question of Kant's final position as regards two worlds versus two aspects, but it adds some evidence favoring the latter. Additional evidence can be found in Kant's correspondence but, again, not decisively so. For example, writing to Moses Mendelssohn (whose resistance to a thorough and critical reading of the *Critique* was based on Mendelssohn's admission that he was "dead to metaphysics") Kant makes clear that experience cannot "encompass all things in themselves," there being "other objects in addition to objects of possible experience. . . ."[24] There is no intimation of another world in any of this; only perceptually inaccessible reaches of the one world in which experience finds its contents.

To repeat, spirited controversy aside, the text never claims that there are two *ontologically* distinct realms, only an *epistemically* distinct domain in which all legitimate knowledge claims are grounded. Again, if sides must be chosen, I am in the one-world, dual-aspect camp, but with due respect for the thesis defended by Paul Guyer and others. In this same connection, Kant's contention is sometimes referred to as his "restriction thesis," which would restrict our knowledge to *phenomena*. As already discussed, there are no convincing arguments to the effect that the "restriction thesis" generates a dualistic ontology. What it does require is that all sensible representations are made possible by the pure intuitions of time and space. Kant's argument for this is developed in several ways. One may ask why there must be *both* spatial and temporal intuitions if there is to be sensibility. More than one commentator has raised this question and has found Kant's answer to be less than convincing. In *The Bounds of Sense,* Peter Strawson offered a thought experiment featuring a world experienced only by way of audition. We will consider the experiment in Chapter 8, but it is worth noting here to underscore the many points of contention raised by what Kant takes to be the universal and necessary foundations of sensibility and understanding.

Noted is that substantial literature spawned by Kant's reflections on space and his counterintuitive claim that the truths of mathematical propositions are at once a priori and synthetic. Clearly, the world of both outer and inner sense presents a welter of changing entities beyond the ambit of human knowledge. Their effect initially is by way of *appearances.* The manifold of representations arising from the manifold of inner and outer events is, on Kant's account, necessarily within a spatiotemporal framework. If, however, such a manifold is to be *known*—as a "this" or a "that"—it is necessary that it be unified. Having no access to noumenal entities, it must be within consciousness itself that the unification takes place. Unity as such is not "given" in the physical impingements themselves, so it must arise within consciousness. As space and time are the necessary ("transcendental") conditions of all sensibility, so the unity of consciousness is the necessary ("transcendental") condition of all concepts. Nothing is a "this" or a "that" except in so far as it is conceptualized. To have knowledge of anything is to have a concept to which it is answerable. Any concept of a "this" or a "that" requires stability in the object of which there is the concept. Accordingly, the concept must be held within a field that is itself stable and unified. Kant puts it this way:

> The pure, original, unchangeable consciousness I shall name *transcendental apperception.* . . . The numerical unity of this apperception is thus the *a priori* ground of all concepts. (A107)

Here the argument approaches the metaphysical mine field of dread "Cartesianism." Whatever position one is inclined to take on Descartes's *Cogito,* there must be a coherent basis on which to identify any concept as *someone's.* To the question, "Why must there be both spatial and temporal intuitions?," another is added, "What is the basis on which the unification of the manifold is an achievement within the framework of *my* consciousness?" These and related questions are taken up in Chapter 8.

Finally, what of Kant's vaunted "transcendental" mode of argument? As it is central to the entire metaphysical project, it is important to consider criticisms arrayed against the very notion of a "transcendental proof." One of the more successful of these was advanced again by Barry Stroud and has been influential among critics of Kant.[25] Kant seems to require of a transcendental argument that certain conditions are *necessary* for a given cognitive or perceptual event. Stroud, however, notes that the skeptic might contend that such conditions only *seem* to be the case or are based on no more than firm convictions and beliefs. There is, after all, a great difference between a condition being necessary and a condition being no more than *apparently* necessary. In the end, the confirmed Kantian must rely on one or another verificationist procedure and, thus, must finally be open to the very conventionalism that the transcendental method was to replace.

But surely Kant was mindful of a difference as elementary as that between knowledge and mere conviction. In the face of a Stroud-like criticism, he would wish to know just how "verification" is to be understood. If the procedure (whatever its logical structure) is pivotally dependent on observation, then verificationism itself would be shown to be necessarily absorbed into that part of the transcendental argument pertaining to perception, experience, causal concepts, and so on.

Regarding "conventionalism," it is to be understood in two different ways, one of them reducible to the democratizing of epistemology. This can be safely ignored, for whether or not a transcendental argument succeeds cannot be settled by a show of hands. However, Kant is at pains in the *Critique* to make clear that the overall argument does, indeed, pertain to creatures of a certain kind, to *human beings*. For example, in replying to those who demand a metaphysics that guarantees human access to reality as in itself it really is—unaffected by the processes and limitations of perception—he famously answers that ". . . what is demanded is that we should . . . not be humans . . ." (A277–8/B333–4). Understood this way, the success of a transcendental argument would be unaffected just in case the modal requirement of necessity were replaced with "necessity within the capacities of human sense and reason." That is the only framework in which any statement could be meaningful to us at all.

Stroud and others anticipate such a rejoinder and are prepared to accept a limited version of transcendental modes of proof.[26] Kant's apparatus thus conceived may be taken to be indispensable as human beings go about the task of forming and applying concepts, but none of this has legislative or logical force vis-a-vis what is or isn't a *necessary* state of affairs. The point is that, in establishing the necessity of a state of affairs for one sort of creature, nothing follows as to whether such a state of affairs is itself necessary. Again, though acknowledging the force and acuteness of such critical appraisals (not to mention the frequency with which they are repeated), they appear to be directed toward a thesis that does not deny their validity. Kant makes clear throughout the *Critique* that it is to be *transcendental logic*, not *formal logic* that is applicable to the issues at hand. The overall argument is akin to a legal brief designed to persuade the fair-minded juror, not a syllogistic argument whose conclusions can be doubted only at the cost of contradiction.[27] If, therefore, the conditions taken to be necessary prove (somehow) instead to be merely indispensable (!), that will be sufficient.

CHAPTER 5

IDEALISMS AND THEIR REFUTATION

In the second edition of *Critique* Kant reminds readers yet again that

> The proper problem of pure reason is contained in the question: How are *a priori* synthetic judgments possible? (B19)

The focus, of course, is on synthetic judgments—those that reach the objective facts of the world. Failure here sets a path to skepticism. Locke attempted to avoid this by way of the distinction between primary and secondary qualities. On Locke's account one has direct and veridical perceptions of the solidity, extension, motion, number, and figure of physical stimuli, but colors, tastes, odors, and sounds are perceived only indirectly and through the mediation of organs and processes whose filtering and transforming effects cannot be known. The mind is, indeed, furnished by experience, but there is an unbridgeable gap between such experiences and that Newtonian corpuscular world of invisible matter.

As noted in previous pages, Kant recognizes that once the authority of experience is taken to be total, the door is open to various skeptical arguments, whatever the intentions of defenders might be. The skepticism presents itself in two different forms of *idealism*, one espoused by Descartes and another by Berkeley. He identifies each as subscribing to a theory

> which declares the existence of objects in space outside us to be merely doubtful and indemonstrable or to be false and impossible. The former is the problematic idealism of Descartes. . . . The latter is the dogmatic idealism of Berkeley. (B274)

As Kant rejects both, he cannot plausibly be charged with either of these forms of idealism. Berkeley famously dissolved the distinction between primary and secondary qualities on the grounds that all experience is mediated. Accordingly he reached the conclusion that the notion of a mind-independent material world was incoherent. *To be is to be perceived* was the resulting motto. The reality of a thing is exhausted by its properties, and properties by their very nature presuppose a percipient. The realm of reality is thus the realm of "idea." Here, then, is one source of that abiding "scandal." Whatever evidence might be adduced to support the claim that there is an external world will be in the form of perceptions by which the mind becomes stocked with ideas. And, as an idea can be like nothing but another idea, all such evidence is finally ideational.

Descartes, on the other hand, advanced what Kant dubbed *problematic idealism*, contrasting this with Berkeley's *dogmatic idealism* (B274) *Problematic* or *skeptical idealism* is based on the uncertainty that attaches to all empirical claims, except one, namely, Descartes's *Cogito.* Certain only that he is a "thinking thing," Descartes was left with the conclusion that all other merely empirical contents of consciousness are subject to manipulation by the evil demon. Descartes's knowledge of the external world, supplied by the contents of thought—by his "ideas"—would lack the resources with which to test the veridicality of such mental representations. Having no direct access to this merely possible world, he becomes hostage to representations bearing an unknowable relation to the (assumed) reality thus represented. Hence, a *problematic idealism*.

Dogmatic idealism, by way of Berkeley, maintains that space is something that in itself is impossible, forcing the conclusion (dogmatically) that those things we locate in space must finally subsist in the mind. As there can be no mind-independent external reality, it is by way of perception and mental representation that reality subsists in the minds of percipients. Add to this Leibniz's reliance on the principle of sufficient reason in rejecting the absolute space of Newton, and even the metaphysical coherence of the very concept space. All in all, both rationalists and empiricists offered daunting challenges to what Kant would defend as the objective scientific image of the world, the "world" understood as nothing less than "the absolute totality of all existing things" (A420).

In his *Meditations* Descartes acknowledges that he knows from experience that the effects he feels are not willed by him. He says in the third meditation that he feels heat whether he chooses to or not, concluding from this that sensations and ideas come to him from sources other than himself. But then, as noted in the previous chapter, dread skepticism sets in forthwith:

> although these [apparently adventitious] ideas do not depend on my will, it does not follow that they must come from things located outside me. Just as the impulses which I was speaking of a moment ago seem opposed to my will even though they are within me, so there may be some other faculty not yet fully known to me, which produces these ideas without any assistance from external things; this is, after all, just how I have always thought ideas are produced in me when I am dreaming. (*Mediation* 3, AT 7:39)

What Descartes and Berkeley share metaphysically is the supposition that nothing in consciousness per se can establish the objective reality of an external world. Such a world rises no higher than an inference drawn from inner experience. The thesis that Kant advances against this claim is at once direct and bold:

> The mere, but empirically determined, consciousness of my own existence proves the existence of objects in space outside me. (B275)

But examining the argument for this, Hume must be revisited, for it is likely that his *Enquiry* was significant in Kant's fuller abandonment of Leibnizian rationalism. Hume's *Treatise* of 1739 was not translated into German in Kant's lifetime, but a German edition of the *Enquiry* of 1748 appeared in 1754–6. In that work, and after commiserating with the academical skeptics of old—so roundly criticized and even despised—Hume illustrates the utter impoverishment of reason in relation to the knowable world and, in so many words, legislates against any attempt to derive or deduce the truth of synthetic propositions a priori:

> Suppose a person, though endowed with the strongest faculties of reason and reflection, to be brought on a sudden into this

world; he would, indeed, immediately observe a continual succession of objects, and one event following another; but he would not be able to discover anything farther. He would not, at first, by any reasoning, be able to reach the idea of cause and effect; since the particular powers, by which all natural operations are performed, never appear to the senses. . . . Such a person, without more experience, could never employ his conjecture or reasoning concerning any matter of fact, or be assured of anything beyond what was immediately present to his memory and senses. (section 5, part 1)

It is worth noting here the passage in the foregoing where Hume claims that "the particular powers, by which all natural operations are performed, never appear to the senses." Controversy still abounds in the matter of Hume's skepticism about causation.[1] Passages such as this strongly suggest a realist position regarding causation, but a skeptical position regarding either rational or perceptual means of discovery.

Later, in the same section, he considers the possibility of establishing knowledge of the external world by way of reason alone and simply throws up his hands:

By what argument can it be proved, that the perceptions of the mind must be caused by external objects . . . and could not arise either from the energy of the mind itself . . . or from some other cause still more unknown to us? It is acknowledged, that, in fact, many of these perceptions arise not from anything external, as in dreams, madness, and other diseases. . . . It is a question of fact, whether the perceptions of the senses be produced by external objects. . . . But here experience is, and must be entirely silent. The mind has never anything present to it but the perceptions, and cannot possibly reach any experience of their connection with objects. The supposition of such a connection is, therefore, without any foundation in reasoning.[2]

For Kant, the Humean account is less incorrect than incomplete. In the *Transcendental Aesthetic* he examines those conditions of possibility by which perceptions relate to objects and thereby enter into a scientific comprehension of reality. For this to take place, there must be a *readiness*—what might be thought of as an a priori "tuning"—such that cognition can make use of appearances. To make use of appearances is to subsume them under general concepts, this being a necessary condition for thought itself. To think is to think of something.

If the process is to be understood as a species of idealism, then it is what Kant called *transcendental idealism*:

> By *transcendental idealism*, I mean the doctrine that appearances are to be regarded as being, one and all, representations only, not things in themselves, and that time and space are therefore only sensible forms of our intuition, not . . . conditions of objects viewed as things in themselves. (A369)

Transcendental is not to suggest anything "transcendent." The latter refers to what is not a possible object of experience and, thus, is not a possible object of knowledge. As all perceptual representations are spatiotemporal and as neither space nor time is "given" in the array of impinging stimuli, the only explanation for the ubiquity of spatiotemporal representations is that the framework itself is a priori and nonempirical. An "idealism" generated by this form of analysis is "transcendental," not skeptical or dogmatic. This becomes clearer when recalling how Kant would have knowledge itself understood. It is an amalgam of *sensibility* and *understanding* such that what cannot in principle enter into experience cannot in principle be known.

He states clearly how his use of "transcendental" is to be understood in this regard and cautions the reader to bear it in mind,

> as it extends its influence over all that follows. Not every kind of knowledge *a priori* should be called transcendental, but that only by which we know that—and know how—certain representations (intuitions or concepts) can be employed, or are possible purely *a priori*. (A56)

If *appearances* are the sole source of the contents of perception, does this not lead directly to Berkeley's idealism? In part 2 of the *Prolegomena* at section 36 and following Kant leaves himself open to such interpretations when declaring that nature in the material sense is known by means of the constitution of our sensibility, according to which it is in its own way affected by objects which are in themselves unknown to it and totally distinct from those appearances.

Here is the well-known distinction between *noumena* and *phenomena*, where knowledge is confined to the latter. Moreover, Kant seems comparably the idealist when he goes beyond sensibility and states that appearances are brought under those rules that permit them to be *thought* only

by means of the constitution of our understanding by which the peculiar way in which we think (namely, by rules) and hence experiences also are possible. (B318–19)

There is symmetry here between the pure intuitions by which appearances become possible and the pure categories by which experiences become integrated into thought itself. Is this all not "psychology"? Is this not all leading up to a subjectivity one step removed from skepticism? These possibilities, duly noted by commentators on the first edition of the *Critique*, required Kant to consider the matter systematically in the second edition in a new section titled *Refutation of Idealism*. The detailed argument developed there can be summarized neatly, but it is suffused with subtle and arguable elements. It has spawned an extensive, conflicting, and unsettled literature featuring veritable "schools" of Kantian idealism interpreters. In light of the conflicts, all the commentators cannot be right, and choosing sides is difficult. Karl Ameriks, a leading Kant scholar, offers a detailed examination of these competing views in his *Interpreting Kant's Critiques*.[3] He finds that the emphasis of modern commentators has varied from the 1970s to the 1980s, the earlier works giving pride of place to Kant meeting the challenge of skepticism, with later works focusing on the realism–antirealism tension.[4] A similar division among commentators can be found during Kant's lifetime.

This much should be clear, whatever theory captures one's loyalty: First, the *Refutation of Idealism* is the one really new argument in the second edition of the *Critique*, important enough for Kant to discuss it in the introduction to that edition. Second, Kant has no need to participate in a realist–antirealist debate, for, as will become clear in Chapter 9, his discussion of the antinomies and paralogisms locates much of that debate in the thickets of metaphysical muddle. The question Kant recognizes as *the* question is just how it is that our *representations* of objects match up with the objects themselves. As for the "objects," Kant is under no illusion as to prospects for reaching their putative "real essence." What is available to a creature with sensibility is an ensemble of properties to which that creature's capacities are suited. One doesn't know what it is like to hear what the bat hears, in part because human beings are insensitive in the frequency region of bat "sonar." Nonetheless—and here a contemporary scientific triumph is not out of place—human beings did successfully fly to the moon and back, carried samples of its dust, and took photographs of the Earth. Accordingly, there are good reasons to accept the proposition that the cognitive "representations" of objects in the external world are sufficiently trustworthy (veridical?) to accomplish such feats.

What formulation of the right metaphysical method renders it compatible with just such feats? How best to explain the otherwise startling agreement between the perceptual-cognitive representations and these external things in light of the what is otherwise a turbulent ocean of impinging stimuli?

Idealists, one and all, limit knowledge to what is present in the mind or consciousness. It is then by way of logically specious inferences that we make claims regarding an external reality. The one certain bit of knowledge is one's own thought—Descartes's *Cogito* serving as the motto. In claiming to turn such idealisms against themselves, Kant sets out to establish that the very possibility of self-awareness (an "inner sense" with content) requires an awareness of an external world by way of "outer sense" (B274). Only through awareness of stable elements in the external world is self-consciousness possible. The argument develops in tightly connected steps[5]:

1. One is conscious of one's existence as determined in time.
2. All determination of time presupposes something *permanent* in perception.
3. The permanent is not within the conscious percipient, for that very consciousness requires something permanent outside oneself.
4. Only through perception of an objective "thing" outside oneself can there be consciousness of an enduring "self."

5. To be conscious of one's enduring existence in time there must be among the objects of perception an objective and permanent "thing" outside oneself.

Kant contends that self-consciousness requires perceptual awareness of objects external to oneself. This runs counter to the idealist claim that the mind has direct access only to its own internal states and processes. There could be such an idealized mind, but it could not be anyone's, for it would lack the conditions necessary for self-consciousness. This is so because self-consciousness requires conditions whereby the mind's own operations can be determined in time. That is, self-consciousness requires an *enduring* substance in which modifications take place. But for anything to be thus set or determined "in time" requires stable and permanent conditions external to it. That is, one is aware of the stream of one's experiences only insofar as this unfolding takes place against a perceived background of permanence. An enduring self cannot be cobbled together from the flotsam of inner sense. Kant is clear on this:

> For in what we entitle "soul" [namely, myself as an appearance of inner sense], everything is in continual flux, and there is nothing abiding except (if we may so express ourselves) the "I." (A381)

This "I," however, is but an intellectualized subject term, something of an indexical that locates the position of the continual flux. It is not easy to extract clarity from Kant on this point. Perhaps he is taking a page from Hume and accepting that a mere stream of sensations (Hume's "bundle of perceptions") cannot rise to the level of *self*-awareness. It is surely conceivable that a creature could be the subject of sensations and not absorb them into *self*-awareness. Any number of neurological and psychiatric conditions provide evidence of this, for example, out-of-body experiences, phantom limb, "blind sight," and so on.

Awareness of sensations or "representations" requires that they inhere in or are possessed by an enduring or persistent entity. For a representation to have duration it must take place within a temporal framework where the temporal packets are connected within the same consciousness. Awareness of oneself persisting in time calls for something permanent; that is, the inner and dynamic representations must unfold against the background of an enduring state of affairs. Existing in time presupposes something permanent, but the permanence must be external to the self, for it is the necessary precondition for self-awareness. This permanence cannot be in the self, since it is only through the permanence that one's existence in time can itself be determined. All this is to challenge the idealist's claim that one is directly aware only of the modifications of one's own mental representations.

Kant's refutation is in the form of a transcendental argument: The thesis that must be defended asserts that

> The mere, but empirically determined, consciousness of my own existence proves the existence of objects in space outside me. (B275)

Confirmation will establish that there is an objective external world that cannot be reduced to patterns of representation within consciousness. Where idealism is committed to the proposition that only inner experience is directly known—an outer world being merely an inference from this—Kant sets out to prove that it is outer experience that is immediate and the necessary precondition for there to be self-conscious inner experience. The proof is intricate. When Kant says he is conscious of his own existence as determined in time, he acknowledges that every conscious experience carries with it the representation "I am." As he says,

> It must be possible for the "I think" to accompany all my representations; for otherwise something would be represented in me which could not be thought at all, and that is equivalent to saying that the representation would be impossible, or at least would be nothing to me. (B131–2)

Indeed, thought itself carries this, as Descartes's *Cogito* presumed to show. However, although the very fact of an experience includes the existence of a subject, ". . . it does not so include any *knowledge* of that subject" (B277). To be conscious of one's own existence is to be in possession of knowledge. Thus, there must be empirical content. But this requires the spatiotemporal framework of the pure intuitions. Thus, consciousness of one's own existence is temporally determined, but then

> All determination of time presupposes something *permanent* in perception.

Kant amplifies this in a note. He states that it is impossible to perceive what is determined in time except by way of a "change in outer relations (motion) relatively to the permanent in space" (B277).

Consider the apparent motion of the sun in the course of a day. One perceives the sun's *motion* only insofar as its position changes relative to the apparently permanent (stationary) objects on Earth. The analogy fully describes the conditions that must obtain if one is to be conscious of one's own existence as determined in time. There must be something permanent in perception against which the sequence of representations flows.

> This permanent cannot, however, be something in me, since it is only through this permanent that my existence in time can itself be determined.

With this Kant seeks to make clear that the permanent cannot be an intuition supplied by inner sense. The changes taking place in one's representations require something permanent that is distinct from the representations themselves. One knows oneself as existing *in time* by way of changes relative to what is permanent. Were this a feature of inner sense, there would be no grounds on which to be aware of oneself as existing in time. Therefore,

> The perception of this permanent is possible only through a *thing* outside me, and not through the mere *representation* of a thing outside me. (B276)

There is still at least a hint of subjectivism here. It is only when by returning to Kant's treatment of the pure intuitions that this unwanted subjectivity gives way to what is a priori, universal, and necessary. Thus,

> We shall understand by *a priori* knowledge, not knowledge independent of this or that experience, but knowledge absolutely independent of all experience. Opposed to it is empirical knowledge, which is knowledge possible only *a posteriori,* that is, through experience. . . . [But] experience never confers on its judgments true or strict *universality.* . . . If, then, a judgment is thought with strict universality, that is, in such a manner that no exception is

allowed as possible, it is not derived from experience, but is valid absolutely *a priori*. (B2–4)

The two are inseparable from one another; what is strictly necessary is strictly universal, where "strictly" is contrasted with the "relative" universality of inductive inferences and generalizations. Generalizations from experience rise no higher than the level of "subjective necessity," such as what Hume would explain in terms of "constant conjunctions." But even in its ordinary employment, human knowledge includes judgments based on what is strictly necessary and universal; for example, "every alteration must have a cause" (B5).

Kant summarizes his conclusion in the famous passage (B74–6),

Without sensibility no object would be given to us, without understanding no object would be thought. Thoughts without content are empty, intuitions without concepts are blind.

This is not to be understood as a species of *cognitive relativism*. This part of Kant's argument, with appropriate reservations, may be taken to be a chapter in the anthropology of thought but not as a species of psychologism. The manner in which the external world is objectified is according to rules at once universal and necessary within the community of rational and human beings. It is conceivable that a different kind of creature might subsume appearances under different rules. That, of course, is not only something not known but something unknowable by human creatures. The emphasis here is on what is knowable in principle.

In the end, is Kant not some sort of "idealist"? As noted, the question has spawned a substantial secondary literature with no end in sight. Disagreements among commentators arise not only from the complexity of the text itself but also from certain presuppositions that often remove Kant from the philosophical and intellectual context within which his own thought developed. On the central problem posed by the idealists, if Kant is to be numbered among the defenders it is over his own explicit objections. He was at pains to trace the rationale that would find even "good Berkeley . . . degrading bodies to mere illusion" (B71). It was in the *Prolegomena* that he had hoped to put to rest such systematic misunderstandings that would cast him as an idealist. His most succinct statement on the matter is given there:

Idealism consists in the assertion, that there are none but thinking beings, all other things, which we think are perceived in intuition, being nothing but representations in the thinking beings, to which no object external to them corresponds in fact. Whereas I say that things as objects of our senses existing outside us are given, but we know nothing of what they may be in themselves, knowing only their appearances, i.e., the representations which they cause in us by affecting our senses. Consequently I grant by all means that there are bodies without us, that is, things which, thought quite unknown to us as to what they are in themselves, yet we know by the representations which their influence on our sensibility procures us, and which we call bodies, a term signifying merely the appearance of the thing which is unknown to us, but not therefore less actual. Can this be termed idealism? It is the very contrary. (289)

In light of the "Refutation of Idealism," why would he be cast as an idealist at all? And how did Kant himself understand "idealism"? He recognized different forms of the ism, each with its own portents, each with its special defects. The one form to which he expressly committed himself is *transcendental idealism*:

By *transcendental idealism*, I mean the doctrine that appearances are to be regarded as being, one and all, representations only, not things in themselves, and that time and space are therefore only sensible forms of our intuition, not . . . conditions of objects viewed as things in themselves. (A369)

Here again are those necessary and universal forms of sensibility that, obviously, are neither "given" in experience nor confirmed by it. In opposition to this is what Kant calls *transcendental realism*, which ". . . regards time and space at something given in themselves, independently of our sensibility. The transcendental realist thus interprets outer appearances (their reality taken as granted), as things in themselves, which exist independently of us and of our sensibility, and which are therefore outside us. . ." (A369).

It is this *transcendental realism* that grounds that form of idealism Kant dubs empirical idealism of the Cartesian sort. The sequence is winding but inevitable: First, the transcendental realist accepts outer appearances as real and as independent of the percipient, including the spatial location of what is perceived. Thus does he confuse appearances with things in themselves. But, as the percipient has direct access only to the contents of his own mind, his own representations, the percipient must deal with some sort of epistemic gap separating the outer world of spatial objects from the immediately known world of his mental representations. Enter Cartesian skepticism. However, once it is granted that "space" is the very form of sensibility and is provided by the percipient, there is no gap at all between the perception of objects "in space" and the representation of this in experience. Kant concludes,

> If we treat outer objects as things in themselves, it is quite impossible to understand how we could arrive at a knowledge of their reality outside us, since we have to rely merely on the representation which is in us. For we cannot be sentient of what is outside ourselves, but only of what is in us, and the whole of our self-consciousness therefore yields nothing save . . . our own determinations. (A378)

On such an account, the metaphysical scandal is fully restored and skepticism regarding the external world is again secure, with idealism triumphant. Kant will have none of this.

Clearly, casting Kant as an idealist is based on confusions and conflations of his distinction between empirical and transcendental forms of "ideality." Kant says of himself that he is an *empirical realist* but not an *empirical idealist*. How is this to be understood? The basic distinction between ideality and reality is the distinction between what is in us ("*in uns*") and what is outside us (*ausser uns*). The former is mind dependent, and the latter is not. For Kant, the term *empirical idealist* is attached to the notion of reality as confined to the individual perceiver, the individual mind, a clear version of subjectivism. By contrast, *empirical realism*, as Henry Allison puts it, "refers to the intersubjectively accessible, spatiotemporally ordered realm of objects of human experience"[6] and is therefore universal. Kant now has the required framework for attacking the idealism of a Berkeley or a Descartes and the skepticism fostered by each. He is in a position to claim that

> We have experience, and not merely an imagination of outer things. (B274)

He is not skeptical about the external world or its spatiotemporal features. Rather, he is at pains to establish the grounds on which such a world *can* be apprehended by creatures such as ourselves. Moreover, as argued earlier, this real, objective external world is necessary if the percipient is to be the knowing, self-conscious bearer of experience.

Finally, there are those who regard the *Critique* as grudgingly but transparently Berkeleian. Their reading of the text leads them to the conclusion that Kant can postulate objects in the external world solely as objects of perception. Interpreted this way, the text is compatible with the Berkeleian maxim: *To be is to be perceived.* There are comparably authoritative commentaries that spare Kant the burdens of such an idealism, finding a very different line of argument in the *Critique.* In establishing the necessary conditions for knowledge of the external world, Kant read in a different light is not "psychologizing" the objective world but providing an account of how it is known by creatures constituted a certain way.

Opposed to *transcendental idealism* is *transcendental realism,* which, says Kant, ". . . regards time and space at something given in themselves, independently of our sensibility. The transcendental realist thus interprets outer appearances (their reality taken as granted), as things in themselves, which exist independently of us and of our sensibility, and which are therefore outside us . . ." (A369).

This leads to the "empirical idealism" of the Cartesian sort. The sequence again is winding but inevitable. The transcendental realist begins by regarding outer appearances as real and independent of any percipient. Here then is a confusion of appearances with things in themselves. But, as the percipient has direct access only to the contents of his or her own mind, his or her own representations, he or she now must deal with some sort of epistemic gap separating the outer world of spatial objects from the immediately known world of his or her own mental representations. Enter Cartesian skepticism.

However, once it is granted that "space" is the very form of sensibility and is provided by the percipient, there is no gap at all between the perception of objects "in space" and the representation of this in experience. Otherwise,

> If we treat outer objects as things in themselves, it is quite impossible to understand how we could arrive at a knowledge of their reality outside us, since we have to rely merely on the representation which is in us. For we cannot be sentient of what is outside ourselves, but only of what is in us, and the whole of our self-consciousness therefore yields nothing save . . . our own determinations. (A378)

In all, perhaps matters are rather less complicated than the secondary literature would have one believe. There is an item in the external world that the visually normal percipient will refer to as a yellow flower. The item in question absorbs certain wavelengths and reflects others. The observer has receptor cells in the retina containing photo pigments. In daylight, the observer is most sensitive to wavelengths in the region of 550 mμ. The name assigned to such radiation is yellow. The honeybee has antennae by which to recognize the same object. But the honeybee's greatest sensitivity is to wavelengths in the ultraviolet region of the spectrum. It is quite clear that a human observer and the honeybee don't see things the same way. But that there is a physical object capable of generating appearances in both instances there is no doubt. Neither the observer nor the bee would have any warrant for claiming to know the object "as in itself it really is." Each, however, is the subject of appearances, and perhaps at this point the comparisons come to an end. The human observer, owing to the pure intuitions of time and space, will have appearances arising from the resulting sensations. Subsuming these under general categories, the human observer will have bona fide experiences. Then, by way of the pure categories of the understanding, and by way of those rules that determine where within that categorical framework experiences are properly placed, the observer now knows it is a yellow flower that is the object of regard. To know the object as a flower is not to know all of the subparticle and particle physics generative of every potential source of appearances. However, it is only because the physics of the situation can in fact result in the ensemble of experiences that there can be knowledge. It is not illusory, nor are flowers mere ideas.

By way of summing up, it is instructive to address the question of whether there still remains a gap, even a fatal gap, in Kant's attempts to refute idealism. The possibility has been the subject of scholarly interest and debate and warrants attention here. Amidst the complexities of the *Critique*, it is after all the *Refutation of Idealism* that has attracted the most detailed commentaries.[7] Some scholars locate a significant *lacuna* in Kant's argument even as others deny or attempt to fill it. The alleged problem is identified by Jonathan Vogel with commendable economy:

> A step necessary to the completion of the Refutation appears to be missing altogether. If the self can be directly known to persist through change, the Refutation fails, yet Kant seems not to address such a possibility.[8]

The matter becomes even more confused when we recall Kant's insistence that all cognition is "combined in one single self-consciousness" (A117/B136). Of course, if the self (soul) were directly known to persist through change, the self would be directly known to be a *substance*, and this is explicitly ruled out by the First Paralogism (A349–51). Kant says as much.

Indeed, if the self *could* be directly known to persist through change, the Refutation would fail. Contrary to such a reading, however, it would appear that Kant not only addressed such a possibility but also established that it must be ruled out on both transcendental and epistemic grounds. He takes up the question as early as the Preface to the second edition, framing the possibilities this way:

> If, with the *intellectual consciousness* of my existence, in the representation "I am". . . I could at the same time connect a determination of my existence through *intellectual intuition*, the consciousness of a relation to something outside me would not be required. (Bxlii)

Intellectual intuition, as Kant would have it understood, would be a cognitive power granting direct access to the things of the world without meditational processes. This, alas, is not a human power. Kant requires of any and every knowledge claim that it have empirical content. Thus, if there is to be knowledge of an enduring self-consciousness it must be by way of representations. This is established by Kant's transcendental idealism, which he defines as

> the doctrine that appearances are to be regarded as being, one and all, representations only, not things in themselves. (A369)

On this point, Vogel is right, but for an utterly fundamental reason different from the one he advances: Such direct knowledge—such an "intellectual intuition," independent of representations, whether inner or outer, would ultimately ground a form of solipsism.

In his Preface to the second edition (where the Refutation appears for the first time), Kant states that his attempt here is the only really new addition to the work itself. What he promises "is the new refutation of psychological *idealism* . . . and a strict (also as I believe, the only possible) proof of the objective reality of outer intuition."[9] There is no question, then, about the absolute centrality of this addition to the larger project. It should be noted that this, contrary to the view of some, is certainly no mere extension of the transcendental deduction.[10] Indeed, if that had been Kant's intention, he surely would have located the argument somewhere in chapter 2 of the *Analytic of Concepts*. Moreover, in light of the sustained attention given to the challenge of idealism in the Fourth Paralogism[11] and elsewhere, there is added reason to accept his claim that the treatment in the second edition is necessary, unique, and original.

It has also been suggested that the Refutation is directed at Hume's argument against a putative continuing self.[12] This, too, seems unconvincing. The philosophers actually named by Kant are Berkeley and Descartes, and there is no evidence in the *Critique* of Kant's reluctance to name Hume where Hume is actually the subject of criticism. Moreover, Hume's sustained discussion of the continuity of self appears in his *Treatise*, which was not translated into German in time to be available to Kant. The German edition of Hume's *Enquiry* was owned by Kant, but that work contains no such analysis of the continuity of personal identity. There is, to be sure, ample room for interpretation on any close reading of the *Critique*, but on a matter of this importance it is prudent to assume that Kant added and drew attention to an entirely new section for the reasons he himself provides. And, in light of his declaring his analysis to be the only possible proof of the objective reality of outer intuition, one should be further inclined to take him at his word and assume that any apparent "gap" is more likely to be in the reading than in the writing.

Back, then, to the Preface to the second edition, where Kant goes so far as to edit in advance the treatment he will provide in the body of the work itself. Here again he refers to that

> scandal to philosophy and to human reason in general that the existence of things outside us (from which we derive the whole material of knowledge, even for our inner sense) must be accepted merely on *faith*.[13]

Not only is knowledge of the external world dependent on the functions of outer intuition, but so too is inner sense. There is in this an anticipation of the discussion of space in the *Transcendental Aesthetic* where he argues that

> For in order that certain sensations may relate to something outside me the representation of space must already exist as a foundation.[14]

To repeat the specific thesis that is to be proved by way of a transcendental argument:

> The mere, but empirically determined, consciousness of my own existence proves the existence of objects in space outside me. (B275)

Regarding the proof, it should be clear that the Second Analogy is sufficient to do much of the work. All alterations take place in conformity with the law of the connection of cause and effect. It is a fact of consciousness that events occur in time and succeed each other in time. Thus, the empirical grounding of being conscious of one's existence is just such temporal sequences.

The proof's second step asserts that "All determination of time presupposes something *permanent* in perception." The work to be done here is provided chiefly by the First Analogy according to which, "In all change of appearances substance is permanent . . ." (A182–9/B224–32). All appearances are in time, for all appearances have duration. Time itself is not given in the appearance; rather, it is one of the forms of sensibility. It is a necessary condition for the representation of succession or coexistence (Second Analogy). For there to be the appearance of change, however, there must be some unchanging substrate amenable to alteration. Thus, it must be a permanent substance whose various properties are subject to alteration. Thus, consciousness of one's own existence as determined in time entails something permanent.[15] However, "This permanent cannot . . . be something in me, since it is only through this permanent that my existence in time can itself be determined." The explanation Kant provides in the text is actually modified in his Preface to the second edition. It is in the Preface that he would have the reader insert these lines to qualify what is offered as follows:

But this permanent cannot be an intuition in me. For all grounds of determination of my existence which are to be met within me are representations; and as representations themselves require a permanent distinct from them, in relation to which their change and so my existence in the time wherein a change, may be determined. (B276/Bxi)

The German for "grounds of determination" is *Bestimmungsgründe*. This is rather awkward. Speaking more plainly, one might say that the required permanence is not given by way of an intuition and that whatever it is within one that is foundational for self-consciousness, it must be in the form of representations. The verb *angetroffen* in the German text translates readily as *to come across, to meet with*. Thus, whatever it is that one might come across within oneself that might be foundational for self-consciousness, it must be in the form of representations. After all, if self-consciousness is to be something more definite than an abstract postulate, it must be some sort of empirically represented entity. But, for something, including existence, to be represented at all, the same permanence is required in that which undergoes modification. There must be something permanent against which there may be the time-ordered changes (i.e., representations) of one's existence. As noted, the work here is done by the First Analogy. The next step in the proof is the claim that ". . . perception of this permanent is possible only through a thing outside me and not through the mere representation of the thing outside me. . . ." What one comes across by way of inner sense are representations. These depend on but do not provide the requisite permanence, ". . . and consequently the determination of my existence in time is possible only through the existence of actual things which I perceive outside me." The conclusion that follows is that "consciousness of my existence is at the same time an immediate consciousness of the existence of other things outside me."

In the note Kant adds to this proof he boasts that in a game played against idealism he has turned it against itself (B276). The proof is more fully comprehended by way of this strategy. The idealism he has in mind applies if not equally then generously to Descartes, Berkeley, Locke, and Hume. In their respective ways, each embraces what Thomas Reid would dub the "ideal theory."[16] The only domain to which the mind has direct access is what is featured in its own consciousness. Accordingly, judgments regarding any domain external to consciousness must be by way of inference. In another of his "Copernican" perspectival shifts, Kant turns this around, arguing that outer experience is *immediate* and that it is the only means by which his existence in time can be determined (B277).

But a subtle distinction is called for here. There is a version of the *Cogito* that Kant is found endorsing, but not in the manner intended by Descartes. Kant says that

> It must be possible for the "I think" to accompany all my representations, otherwise, something would be represented in me which could not be thought at all, and that is equivalent to saying that the representation would be impossible, or at least would be nothing to me. (B132)

Thus, the "I think" is a necessary condition if an object is to be thought at all. It is not a Cartesian device designed to defeat total skepticism. Consciousness accompanies all thought, of course, and

> immediately includes in itself the existence of the subject; but it does not so include any *knowledge* of that subject, and therefore also no empirical knowledge, that is, no experience of it. (B277)

That a particular condition or state of affairs is necessary for some other condition or state of affairs can be established by way of the transcendental argument. This, however, is quite different from an epistemic state of affairs in which something is actually an item of knowledge. The latter always requires empirical content, and for this there must be the intuitive framework. For there to be knowledge of that subject possessing consciousness it must be by way of an inner intuition. All such inner intuitions are ordered—are determined—in time. However, as the proof makes clear, time is not given in the manifold of experience and must, therefore, be derived from what is permanent. Hence,

> outer objects are quite indispensable; and it therefore follows that inner experience is itself possible only mediately, and only through outer experience. (B277)

Referring to this perspectival shift as Copernican is warranted by the example Kant offers in note 2 in this section. Setting aside the (transcendentally) necessary conditions for a given process, there is the question of what is actually possible as a perception. Time, of course, is not perceived. If one is to perceive determinations in time, this must be by way of alterations in the outer relations among things. These alterations, however, are relative to what is permanent in space. As noted, the example Kant offers is that of the motion of the sun relative to objects on Earth.

The mistake made by Descartes and other rationalists, in the matter of "I" and the proof of its existence, was in thinking that existence can be an object of knowledge based on mere concepts. But for any object to be known it must be accessible at the level of perception and subsumed under the universal rules of experience (A227). Moreover, to the extent that something is an object of knowledge it cannot be established as a necessity. This is the burden of Kant's claim that

> it is not, therefore the existence of things (substances) that we can know to be necessary, but only of the existence of their state; and this necessity of the existence of their state we can know only from other states, which are given in perception, in accordance with empirical laws of causality. It therefore follows that the criterion of necessity lies solely in the law of possible experience, the law that everything which happens is

determined *a priori* through its cause in the field of appearance. (A227–8/B279–81)

This sets a fairly tight limit on what can be known.[17] The necessity imposed on sequential events as perceived makes possible the integration of the manifold into one coherent experience. This is a form of hypothetical necessity

> which subordinates alteration in the world to a law, that is, to a rule of necessary existence, without which there would be nothing that could be entitled nature. (A228–9/B280–2)

According to Kant, "nature" is

> the connection of appearances as regards their existence according to necessary rules, that is, according to laws. There are certain laws which first make a nature possible, and these laws are *a priori*. (A216/B263)

Considering the existence of "I" in this connection, it is clear that it cannot be *known* to be necessary. In fact, to the extent that it stands as a *substance*, it cannot be perceived as the effect of some antecedent cause.

Returning to the Preface to the second edition, it is clear just what resources would be required in order to obviate the need for something permanent and external. As stated earlier, what would be required is a species of *intellectual intuition* granting direct (unmediated) access to things as they are in themselves, but this is ruled out entirely.

The central question, however, has to do with what can be known. In being conscious of one's existence, there is within one a concurrent consciousness of standing in relation to things external to oneself. This is an experience and not a mere product of fancy or invention. Kant says it refers to sense and not imagination. This outer sense presupposes spatial intuition as the form of sensibility, and some actual material entity as the source of empirical content. Again, the reference is to something actually outside the percipient and not to a figment of the imagination.

Even granting such an *intellectual* consciousness, actual knowledge still requires that inner intuition that renders sensibility possible. It is only in this way that there can be inner experience. However, this very set of time-varying events,

> and therefore the inner experience itself, depends upon something permanent which is not in me, and consequently can only be in something outside me, to which I must regard myself as standing in relation. The reality of outer sense is thus necessarily bound up with inner sense, if experience in general is to be possible at all. (Bxlii)

The self certainly cannot have direct knowledge of its persistence through change, for it cannot have direct knowledge of any substance. It cannot even know itself as having a necessary existence or even as the merely possible subject of experience. Thus, one gap is filled.

But might there not be another? Is it the case, as has been suggested, that Kant's success in the refutation is limited and that the overall argument cannot even rule out "brains in vats"?[18] It is conceivable that the brain in a vat could be stimulated in ways that mimic the order of events ordinarily occurring as percipients experience the succession of inner and outer states. On the assumption that the categorical and schematic structure of experience is properly preserved under such conditions, the vatted brain would have a cognized reality of its own offering no proof of objects external to itself. But then it would lack any means by which to assess the objectivity of its possessions, for it would lack the support of intersubjective agreement. Of course, if the thought experiment grants to the vatted brain all that goes into the process of distinguishing between subjective states and objective knowledge, then the unsurprising outcome is simply, $a = a$, and there is no gap to fill. If Kant in all of this was mistaken, it was surely not the result of oversight.

CHAPTER 6

CONCEPTS

Led by Locke and then Hume, the British empiricists opposed
rationalism by offering an associationistic theory to account for
the complexities of cognition. On the empiricist account, the initial
event of consequence is stimulation and the response of the senses
to it. The resulting elementary sensations are then merged with
others, through an associative process, to produce a more complex
compound or composite. Locke expressed it this way;

> There is another Connexion of Ideas wholly owing to Chance or
> Custom; Ideas that in themselves are not at all of kin, come to be
> so united in Mens Minds, that 'tis very hard to separate them . . .
> and the one no sooner at any time comes into the Understanding
> but its Associate appears with it.[1]

Hume gives a comparable account:

> There is a secret tie or union among particular ideas, which
> causes the mind to conjoin them more frequently together, and
> makes the one, upon its appearance, introduce the other.[2]

Concepts, no matter how complex, are ultimately reducible, at
least in principle, to their atomic substrate, for the complex idea
is but a collection of such atomic particles joined in various ways.
Hume's "matters of fact" arise entirely from this presumed process.
His "relations of ideas" are different, but these rise no higher than
logical or verbal truths, which, if they are meaningful at all, refer
to identity relations between items gleaned by experience. Even in
the matter of relations of ideas, therefore, if the very terms have

meaning, there must be some idea to which they are answerable, and that idea itself has its source in experience. In the *Enquiry*, Hume instructs the reader who would understand the meaning of a concept or idea. The first step is to

> enquire, *from what impression is that supposed idea derived?* And if it be impossible to assign any, this will serve to confirm our suspicion. By bringing ideas into so clear a light we may reasonably hope to remove all dispute, which may arise, concerning their nature and reality.[3]

Perhaps the first distinction to draw between Hume and Kant in the matter of concepts is this: On the empiricist account, concepts (complex ideas) arise passively from the processes by which mental contents come to be associated. The rules are essentially mechanical. Associations form as a result of the frequency with which objects are perceived. The strength of such associations is greater the closer are the events in time and location and the degree to which they share similar properties. Frequency, contiguity, and resemblance are the factors responsible for the association between and among ideas. Once formed, the associations stand as habitual tendencies of the mind to expect or anticipate a "Y" when the associated "X" occurs.

On Kant's radically different understanding, the conceptual framework is not formed but is already in place. Concepts reflect an active mode of representation, governed by the rules by which sensual representations are assigned within the pure categories of the understanding. He develops the argument for this systematically, beginning with the first part of the *Transcendental Doctrine of Elements*. The *Transcendental Aesthetic* sets the a priori conditions of all sensibility. This is then followed by the *Transcendental Logic*, which addresses the conditions necessary if what is given by way of sensuous representation is to be present in *thought*. The process cannot be willy-nilly or be the mere byproduct of passive associations. The required move is from receptivity to "the power of knowing an object through these representations" (A50). All knowledge, Kant insists, requires both intuition and concepts. Neither without the other can rise to the level of knowledge. Against the settled position of the empiricists, Kant then introduces *pure concepts* of the understanding that owe nothing to experience but nonetheless reach objective reality. To make the case for this, Kant finds no help from formal logic. Something different is called for, namely, a *transcendental logic*. Formal logic, traced respectfully to Aristotle, contains "the absolutely necessary rules of thought" if there is to be any understanding whatever (A52). As a formal system, however, it is abstract, aloof to facts as such, and designed to regulate the very form of thought. Kant says of it that it "considers only the logical form in the relation of any knowledge to other knowledge" (A55). Thus, if X is greater than Y, and Y is greater than Z, general logic establishes that X is greater than Z. The relations here are among knowledge claims that may be abstract (X, Y, Z) or concrete (loaves of bread). Following the course he employed in developing the *Transcendental Aesthetic*, he makes a distinction between *pure* and *empirical* thoughts of objects. The Locke–Hume scheme addresses only the latter; thought as arising from empirical engagement with the contents of experience. However, just as the *Transcendental Aesthetic* established the *pure* intuitions of time and space as the necessary mode of sensuous representation, so the *Transcendental Logic* has as its aim unearthing "the rules of the pure thought of an object" (B80). What is to be delineated here are the very modes of understanding itself; the rules by which a given sensuous representation is subsumed under the right categories of the understanding such that the representation now is something *known*.

"In a transcendental logic, we isolate the understanding—as above, in the Transcendental Aesthetic, the sensibility—separating out from our knowledge that part of thought which has its origins solely in the understanding" (B87). Thus separated out, that part of thought grounded in the understanding itself now must be analyzed to identify its determining conditions. If the pure intuitions of time and space are the universal and necessary forms of receptivity—the forms by which anything may be "given" to the percipient—what comparable powers or conditions must be in place for the object now to be *known* and not simply perceived? Kant answers this question in the *Transcendental Analytic*, beginning with the *Analytic of Concepts*:

> By "analytic of concepts" I do not undertake their analysis, or the procedure usual in philosophical investigations, that of dissecting the content of such concepts as may present themselves, and so of rendering them more distinct; but the hitherto rarely

attempted *dissection of the faculty of the understanding* itself, in order to investigate the possibility of concepts *a priori* by looking for them in the understanding alone as their birthplace, and by analysing the pure use of this faculty. (B90)

As noted earlier, the *Critique* is not merely or primarily an exercise in "conceptual analysis." If such was his aim in the *Prize Essay*, Kant would soon judge conceptual analysis to be a chapter from the older metaphysics. One need not look far to identify those who had adopted methods classified by Kant as "usual" in philosophy; those who dissect concepts to find more elementary components. Credit may be given to Locke for initiating a mode of analysis with which to dissect *empirical* concepts. But what the empiricists neglected was the possibility that a nonempirical framework must be in place a priori if perceptions are ever to be integrated into coherent experiences.

But traditional rationalism suffers from its own liabilities that lead to empty and misleading conjectures. It is reason that is supposed to guide and correct the senses, but reason itself has never been subjected to critical analysis. Kant must, therefore, test the limits of pure reason—what it can establish through its own resources without the benefit of experience. If, as he says, reason is to be its own student, concepts, as such, are not the central focus. Rather, it is their *grounding* and the preconditions that render them even possible. The recognition of this as the central issue in metaphysics was conveyed in Kant's letter of 1772 to Marcus Herz:

I still lacked something essential something that in my long metaphysical studies I, as well as others, failed to consider and which in fact constitutes the key to the whole secret of metaphysics. . . . I asked myself this question: What is the ground of the relation of that in us which we call "representation" to the object?[4]

He then weighs the two obvious possibilities to answer this most significant of metaphysical questions. The mental representation is nothing but the effect causally brought about by an object, or the mental representation actually determines the object itself as known and knowable. Traditionally, philosophy has hosted two radically different positions on the matter: Either the mind is the passive *intellectus ectypus* of the empiricist or, as with the divine mind, a creative and active *intellectus archetypus* of the dogmatic idealist. Roughly speaking, the *archetypus* is an original, the *ectypus* a copy. He dismisses Plato's theory that takes ideas to be the actual archetypes of the material objects (A313/B370). Such a thesis reserves real being to the "true form" of an entity rather than its merely empirical features. The empiricist would have the *ectypus* provide the totality of what can be known, the rationalist the *archetypus.* Kant tells Herz that he will reject both alternatives. An utterly passive mind could never reach beyond the effects brought about through the senses from the effects themselves. One would again be in the position of the skeptic, uncertain as to the existence of anything outside the mind itself. As for an *intellectus archetypus*, it finally leads back first to Berkeley and finally to Plato. There are, to be sure, active inner mental processes, but ". . . whence comes the agreement they are supposed to have with objects?"[5]

The question calls for a method previously not considered, but one so successfully applied in disciplines that, unlike metaphysics, actually have enjoyed great progress and refinement. Kant announces his new methodology in the Introduction to the B edition. It is worth repeating the quotation given earlier in Chapter 2:

> This attempt to alter the procedure which has hitherto prevailed in metaphysics, by completely revolutionizing it in accordance with the example set by the geometers and physicists, forms indeed, the main purpose of this critique of pure speculative reason. It is a treatise on the method, not a system of science itself. (Bxxi)

Consider again the question itself. Sitting at a large desk and facing a computer monitor, I notice to the left of the screen two small bottles of ink. The contents appear black, the surfaces feel smooth, and one is shorter than the other. Is the smoothness a property of the bottles? Or of the mind in which smoothness is (somehow) represented? Is there a direct relationship between each and every physical property of these bottles and the associated "representations"?

Now consider a more difficult case. In the garden at the rear of the house there are red roses growing within a row of other plantings. Honey bees hover above the roses, some settling in the very center of the flowers. The bees do not see "red." Even human beings suffering from color blindness will not see the redness, and no human being will see whatever the bees see. For the given percipient, what is it that is seen? Is it the red rose or the "representation" of the red rose? If all, in the end, is but a congeries of mental representations, on what basis can science claim to establish the systematic laws accounting for events in the world external to mere representations? Phrased economically, what is the epistemic standing of concepts regarding the external world?

It is Hume who must be dealt with here more than any other philosopher. His formidable arguments had attracted close attention and criticism at home before translations became available in Germany. Thomas Reid's *An Inquiry into the Human Mind* was by far the most successful of the contemporary criticisms. There is good if circumstantial evidence that Kant had read either a redaction of Reid's *Inquiry* or even a full translation of the work.[6] And, notwithstanding Kant's "politically correct" rejection of "commonsense" philosophy, any number of Kantian arguments are "Reidian." There is good reason then to rehearse the Reidian version, if only briefly.

The Cartesian and Humean accounts, along with those of many other philosophers both ancient and modern, are what Reid referred to collectively as "the ideal theory." Its various forms amount to the same conclusion: We do not have access to the real world directly, but solely to the contents of our own consciousness (i.e., "ideas"), a view often referred to as *phenomenalism*. Accordingly, referential statements regarding what is putatively a feature of the external world are actually statements about one's "ideas" or mental contents. Against this, Reid advanced an argument for "direct realism" and rejected as mere conjecture the notion that the facts of the external world are inaccessible as such. Even caterpillars could not survive under such a regimen! In the section Reid titles, "The Geometry of Visibles," he argues that we, too, are not under its sway.

The "Geometry of Visibles" has attracted considerable attention but warrants no more than a sketch here.[7] Draw with care, using a straightedge, a right-angle triangle. Look at it. But consider the manner in which it comes to be represented. Light rays must be projected on to a spherically shaped cornea; some of the rays are then dispersed in their journey through the aqueous humor of the eye's anterior chamber. Next there is the lens, whose anterior surface will reflect some of the rays back toward the external world. Behind the lens is the pool of vitreous humor, also optically dispersive. Finally, incident light will reach the curved surface of the retina. It is clear that the *perceived* straight lines of the drawn triangle differ markedly from how such lines are projected on a spherical surface. Reid referred to the physical and physiological responses to the light as "natural signs" and concluded, from the very facts of the matter, that, by a process still not understood, the mind is able to move from the natural signs to the things actually signified. What is seen is what in fact is *out there*, not some (Humean) "copy" of what is out there.

Kant moves in a similar way against versions of subjectivism. In the *Transcendental Aesthetic* he analyzed those conditions by which perceptions are at once possible and are also able to relate to objects, thus entering into a scientific account of reality. For this to take place, there must be a *readiness*—some sort of a priori "tuning"—such that cognition can make proper use of appearances. However, it is always *appearances* that are the source of the content of perception. Against direct realism, Kant insists that we do not apprehend things as in themselves they really are but only in the form of perceptions, this being the distinction between *noumena* and *phenomena.*

At first blush, the claim looks very much like Berkeley's idealism and, as discussed in the previous chapter, Kant is still charged by some with being closer to Berkeley than he would wish to be. In part 2 of the *Prolegomena* at section 36 and following he leaves himself open to such interpretations when declaring that nature in the material sense is known

> by means of the constitution of our sensibility, according to which it is in its own way affected by objects which are in themselves unknown to it and totally distinct from those appearances.

Moreover, Kant seems comparably the "idealist" when he goes beyond sensibility and states that we are able to bring appearances under those rules that permit them to be *thought* only

> by means of the constitution of our understanding by which the peculiar way in which we think (namely, by rules) and hence experiences also are possible. (B318–19)

There is symmetry here between the pure intuitions by which appearances become possible, and now what will be the pure categories of the understanding by which experiences become integrated into thought itself. Is this not all "psychology" at most one step removed from phenomenalism? Reflecting back on his treatment of the pure intuitions, however, it is clear that this worrisome element of subjectivity gives way to what is a priori, universal and necessary. Thus,

> We shall understand by *a priori* knowledge, not knowledge independent of this or that experience, but knowledge absolutely independent of all experience. Opposed to it is empirical knowledge, which is knowledge possible only *a posteriori,* that is, through experience. (B2–B3)

Or again,

> experience never confers on its judgments true or strict . . . *universality. . . .* If, then, a judgment is thought with strict universality, that is, in such a manner that no exception is allowed as possible, it is not derived from experience, but is valid absolutely *a priori.* (B4)

In the famous passage that integrates the intuitions and the pure concepts of the understanding (B74–6) absence of the latter makes it impossible even to think and object. Concepts are the "seeing" elements of experience. Without them, no more than a parade of sensations takes place, never rising to the level of a "this" or a "that."

What, then, is "knowledge" in the Kantian scheme? It is an amalgam, as it were, of *sensibility* and *understanding* such that what cannot in principle enter into experience cannot in principle be known. To be known, however, the object goes beyond an element of experience and is located within a *conceptual* framework, the framework of *the pure concepts of the understanding.* Required now is an argument establishing the necessity and universality of the pure concepts; required is what Kant refers to as *the transcendental deduction of the categories.*

If this phase of the project is to be understood clearly, Kant's use of "transcendental" must be kept in mind.

> Not every kind of knowledge *a priori* should be called transcendental, but that only by which we know that—and know how—certain representations (intuitions or concepts) can be employed, or are possible purely *a priori.* (A56)

Recall again how the "transcendental aesthetic" pertains to the forms of sensibility—the latter is defined as

> The capacity (receptivity) for receiving representations through the mode in which we are affected by objects. (A19)

With this in mind, we can turn to the "transcendental deduction," the argument designed to establish the necessity of the pure concepts of the understanding.

The place to begin an examination of this pivotal point in the *Critique* is with a set of interrelated questions: How do the most rudimentary sensations into the formation of concepts? How is it that the concepts are "mine"? How does the manifold of otherwise disparate appearances become an experience unified in a given consciousness? These are the questions Kant addresses in the sections devoted to the *Synthetic Unity of Apperception* and the *Pure Concepts of the Understanding.* First, he must establish the basis on which mere sensations rise to the level of a bona fide experience. Kant uses both *Urteil* ("judgment") and *Erkenntnis* ("knowledge") in discussions of experience, thereby making clear that he intends experience to include something beyond and different from feelings and appearances. An experience is of a "something," not merely a parade of disconnected sensations. There must be a means, not contained in the sensations themselves, by which experiences are forged.

In addressing the question of how synthetic unity is achieved, Kant presents two "Supreme Principles": The first is the supreme principle in relation to *sensibility.* It states that the manifold of intuition "should be subject to the formal conditions of space and time." The supreme principle in relation to *understanding* is that "all the manifold of intuition should be subject to conditions of the original synthetic unity of apperception" (B136). These are the principles that enter into the *transcendental deduction*, the aim of which is to uncover the necessary conditions of all knowledge and, in the process, to give metaphysical credibility to science.

Kant introduces the notion of the deduction as he wishes it to be understood:

> Jurists, when they speak of entitlements and claims, distinguish in a legal matter between the question concerning what is lawful

(quid juris) and that which concerns the fact (quid facti), and since they demand proof of both, they call the first, that which is to establish the entitlement or the legal claim, the deduction. (A84/B116)

Kant had experience with what in the German-speaking world were known as *Deduktion Schriften*. These were legal briefs presenting arguments to settle various legal claims. Intrinsic to such arguments were issues of priority, history, pedigree—how a state of affairs had come about and the claims arising from an essentially genetic analysis. Thus, a *Deduktion* in this context is not a logical but a juridical concept. At issue is not the particular facts but what the law requires to establish an *entitlement*, given the facts. The question at issue is whether Kant has made his case for *the transcendental deduction of the categories*.

Now, the task of the transcendental deduction is to answer the question, "How do we come to have knowledge of objects?" More precisely, the task is to establish the warrant or justification of any knowledge claim to be a claim objectively tied to reality. Kant's approach unfolds through a series of steps from sensations to appearances to concepts and then to one's *own* concepts. The process begins with sensation, a response, or reaction of sensory organs to stimulation. Then, by way of the pure intuitions of time and space, sensations are transformed into appearances. Only when these are subsumed under the *pure categories of the understanding* is there an *experience* of what is present in the external world. He says that the necessary conditions by which there is the very possibility of experience are the pure concepts of the understanding (B161). A creature without the a priori categories could have the same sensations and appearances as we do, but not the same experiences. As previously noted, such a creature sees a tree, but it does not "experience" it as a tree as such.

Appearances are comprised of a manifold of various and time-varying properties. If there is to be the objective experience of a determinate "something," there must be a mode of unification such that the manifold is integrated in such a way as to constitute a "something." Thus, *the transcendental unity of apperception* is a necessary component in the overall process by which nature becomes possible. The pure intuitions of time and space will not by themselves yield a judgment or knowledge of objects, for these are merely the forms of sensibility. To know that anything is an "X" requires a rule by which to identify what is universal in the particular, what makes "X" the sort or type of entity it is. This is the very point of the famous maxim at B75 according to which "without sensibility no object would be given to us; and without understanding no object would be thought. Thoughts without content are empty; intuitions without concepts are blind."

According to Kant, the empiricists cannot account for such unified conceptual knowledge. They attempt to explain it on the basis of mere associations and habits, but the process actually works the other way. In order for objects to be connected in experience, there must first be experiences; there must first be a "something" that is thinkable. To think an object it is necessary that mere sensations be given a conceptual structure provided by cognition itself. For some sort of associationist thesis to be plausible, these other conditions must be in place a priori. It is only by applying concepts that the understanding can abstract from the particulars of sensation what is universal.

There is still more that must be considered, for any so-called "association of ideas" requires some means by which one distinguishes the object from one's mental representations. There must be some means by which to distinguish inner mental life from outer reality. This requires *spatial* intuition, as well as the cognition of objects as standing in causal relations and as persisting in time. In a word, it is the rule-governed application of the pure categories that renders what is otherwise mere appearances as the actual experience of a something.

It is by way of the *synthetic unity of apperception* that Kant attempts to establish the basis on which thoughts are *someone's*. On this significant point, he and Descartes are not too far apart. In keeping with his transcendental mode of analysis, Kant begins with a fact and then proceeds to show that, were some condition or process not satisfied, the fact could not come about; more generally, *if there is to be X, then Y is necessary. There is X, therefore Y.*

Conceivably, the various features of entities in the external world *could* be represented in different consciousnesses. Of the red rose, Jack could be mindful of the red, Jill of the fragrance, Mary of the shape, and Tim of the texture. In such a case, none of them would be conscious of the red rose as such. Indeed, even taking counsel with each other, none could arrive at the actual experience of the red rose. For such an experience to be possible, the various features of the manifold must be unified in a given consciousness. And, because such experiences are commonplace, it is clear that there is, indeed, just this *synthetic unity of apperception.*

Recall Hume's account with its skeptical tendencies: What makes any perception someone's perceptions is that it happens to be bundled together in a persisting associational framework. Consider the metaphor of the parade. The parade takes on a form—a formation—as a result of the synchronized movements of the marchers. The overall formation is preserved even as one marcher drops out and another steps in. So, too, with the unity of consciousness. It is not a property of the subject but of an ensemble of sensations.

Kant's position is entirely different. It is an essential feature of the human mind that its experiences are unified in consciousness. A mere and contingent congeries of associational bonds could never ground the universal and necessary concepts on which understanding depends. Indeed, at this point, Kant actually seems ready to endorse the *Cogito* for, as he says,

> otherwise, something would be represented in me which could not be thought at all, and that is equivalent to saying that the representation would be impossible, or at least would be nothing to me. (B132)

However, Descartes' *Cogito* is an epistemic device deployed against skepticism, whereas Kant's aim is to unearth what is metaphysically foundational for experience and thought. Kant is not attempting to construct the empiricist's percipient or the Cartesian theater of the Ego. Where Descartes's argument pertains to "being conscious" Kant's is more properly understood as pertaining to "being conscious *that.*"[8] He repeats the point that "intuition" refers to any representation that is given prior to all thought (B132). But to think is to think of something, and this requires a mode of apprehension that goes beyond mere representations. Through the intuitions, representations become possible. These then rise to the level of knowledge when there is, in Kant's words,

> the determinate relation of given representations to an object. (B137)

How are "objects" to be understood in this context? An object is the structured outcome of the unification of what is given by the manifold. Thus, the manifold of color, shape, texture, and so on,— through the spatiotemporal mode of representation—becomes united to constitute an object, in this case, say, an apple. The relations among the representations are determinate owing to the pure concepts of the understanding.

With this there is that determinate relation of a given representation to an object, and so it now can be said that there is objective knowledge.

Not only are the various elements of the objects of thought synthesized, but a given object is encountered under radically different conditions at different times. It retains its identity as a "this" or "that" not as a result of supplying the senses with invariant properties, but by being cognitively comprehended as a "this," even as *the same* "this."

Kant is clear on the need for a process by which otherwise various and varying representations are held together. He describes the process of synthesis as

> the act of putting different representations together, and grasping what is manifold in them in one cognition. (A77/B103)

The process of synthesis is one that gave Kant and some of his contemporary readers more than the usual degree of difficulty. In a letter to Marcus Herz (May 26, 1789) he repeats a question that has been raised by Salomon Maimon who had many criticisms of the *Critique*. Just how does Kant account for the agreement between the a priori intuitions and the a priori concepts? How is it that sensuous representations are properly taken up in the right way by the pure concepts of the understanding? Maimon is prepared to accept that this takes place but raises a question about what, in Kant's analysis, renders this agreement *necessary*.

> To this I answer: All of this takes place in relation to an experiential knowledge that is only possible for us under these conditions, a subjective consideration, to be sure, but one that is objectively valid as well, because the objects here are not things in themselves but mere appearances; consequently, the form in which they are given depends on us. . . . On the other hand, they are

dependent on the uniting of the manifold in consciousness, that is, on what is required for the thinking and cognizing of objects by our understanding. Only under these conditions, therefore, can we have experiences.[9]

If the process of synthesis is not to be arbitrary and merely subjective—if the resulting synthesis generates the same object for all comparably situated observers—there must be a framework and rules by which the elements of the manifold are pulled and held together. The framework is given by the table of categories in which are located the *pure concepts of the understanding.* One can now begin to see how Kant's famous "Transcendental Deduction of the Categories" unfolds. We begin with an indubitable feature of the understanding, namely, the stability of representations and the (virtually) universal manner in which comparably positioned observers judge the objects of experience. The question addressed to the empiricist is whether such stable and universal cognitions are plausibly explained on the basis of no more than repeated encounters with things. Clearly, empiricists have no explanation for how we move from "mere forms of thought" to such objective concepts or how the contents of our perceptions come together with objects; how they

> establish connection, obtain necessary relation to one another, and, as it were, meet one another. (A92)

The required connection—the "necessary relation"—is that between the object and the cognizing of it. Kant argues that there are only two possible ways for such a connection to come about:

> Either the object alone must make the representation possible, or the representation alone must make the object possible. (A92)

The first of these is illustrative of the Locke–Hume empiricist position. There is no more than an empirical connection such that the relation is neither necessary nor a priori. The second possibility has the representations (*Vorstellungen)* not creating the object (as some sort of illusion) but rendering the object knowable *as an object* (B125). This sense of "knowable" is to be distinguished from "apprehended" or "beheld" as in the instance of *Anschauungen*. Thus, the conditions necessary for the knowledge of an object require a priori categories, and the "deduction" here is just the quasi-juridical argument that would defend these a priori categories as the enabling conditions of all human understanding.

Kant summarizes:

> There are two conditions under which alone knowledge of an object is possible; first, intuition, through which it is given, though only as appearance; secondly, *concept*, through which an object is thought corresponding to this intuition. . . . The question now arises whether *a priori* concepts do not also serve as antecedent conditions under which alone anything can be, if not intuited, yet thought as object, in general. (A93–4/B125–6)

As he says at A112, in the absence of the categories, the perceptions (*Vorstellungen*)

> would be without an object, merely a blind play of representations, less even than a dream.

There is lingering controversy on the question of the relationship between appearances and objects of experience. The controversy goes back to Kant's own day but was raised to new heights by Peter Srawson's *The Bounds of Sense*.[10] Kant states the problem clearly enough at B142 where it raises the question of the distinction between appearances and experience proper, where the latter possesses an objectivity that the former lacks. The text would seem to leave no doubt but that the distinction is between a subjective mode or representation and a cognitively *constructed* but nonetheless *objective* representation. On this point, Kant is unequivocal:

> All Sensible Intuitions are subject to the Categories as Conditions under which alone their Manifold can come together under one Consciousness. (B142)

But as Strawson would have it, this unnecessarily complicates a process that is better understood by acknowledging that

> the unified items are just the experiences reported in our ordinary reports of what we see, feel, hear, etc.[11]

Needless to say, this is surely an option Kant might have considered had he not already left no doubt but that appearances as such offer no means by which to establish that there is actually an external world of objects seen, felt, heard, and so on. Rather, it is the concepts that yield the objective ground of experience, or, put another way, the ground on which the possibility of objective experience depends.

Concepts arise from nonempirical ("pure") foundations. The constant in the act or achievement of understanding is a *judgment*, to be considered in more detail in the next chapter. Here it is enough to say that Kant accepts the traditional (Aristotelian) classification of logical judgments, but then uses these to derive a corresponding table of pure concepts. The table of judgments is given at A70/B95:

Quantity
Universal
Particular
Singular

Quality	*Relation*	*Modality*
Affirmative	Categorical	Problematic
Negative	Hypothetical	Assertoric
Infinite	Disjunctive	Apodeictic

The twelve "pure concepts" flowing from these exhaust the conceptual resources of the understanding, resources setting limits on just how anything can be conceptualized:

Categories of Quantity	*Categories of Quality*	*Categories of Relation*
Unity	Reality	Inherence & Subsistence
Plurality	Negation	Causality & Dependence
Totality	Limitation	Community (Agent/Patient)

Categories of Modality
Possibility-Impossibility
Existence-Nonexistence
Necessity-Contingency

Here, then, is the framework within which empirical content is organized, the conceptual framework within which human knowledge claims can be asserted. However, the framework itself raises yet another vexing question. Out of the welter of appearances, how is one somehow able to forge an actual *judgment* regarding things in the external world? To do this, appearances must not simply be organized and integrated but organized and integrated *in just the right way*. The physical world is not cognitively prepackaged, it just *is*. But at the level of one's knowledge of that world, if it is to be objective, there is not only packaging but such a similitude of packaging among human creatures to generate nothing less than a universal modes of understanding.

A crude analogy might be useful here. Consider a matrix of mailboxes, twelve in all, with the incessant arrival of items bearing no names as such, no specific addresses. All that is known in advance is that, just in case items are properly assigned, the contents from the separate items will form coherent messages conveying meanings that are universally comprehensible to native users of the language.

If the analogy is serviceable, it helps to clarify what Kant refers to in relation to the *Schematism of the Pure Concepts*.[12] This *schematism*, previously considered in Chapter 3, is designed to show how ". . . an object is contained under a concept."[13] The concept must be "homogeneous" with the representation of the object; there must be something represented in the concept itself, which is similar to the representation of the object subsumed under it. The German text reads,

> In allen Subsumtionen eines Gegenstandes unter einen Begriff muß die Vorstellung des ersteren mit der letzteren gleichartig sein.

Which might be clearer if rendered as,

> In all subsumptions of an object under a concept, there must be in the former something that is kindred (*gleichartig*) with the latter.

Recall from Chapter 3 that Kant uses the example of a dinner plate. The *empirical* concept of such an object is *gleichartig* with the *pure* geometrical concept of a circle. At work here is a thesis advanced in modern times by *Gestalt* psychologists to indicate the manner in which objects are represented in the processing performed by the nervous system. The *Gestalt* principle is that of *isomorphism*.[14] The theory requires not that the neural representation of the objects of perception be in any sense of the same shape—it is not a "picture" theory—but that there is a functional relationship between the two representations. Of course, "functional" tends to be one of those elastic terms, sometimes deployed to conceal an excusable ignorance. As intended here, a *functional* relationship can be illustrated by the relationship between, on the one hand, an abstract mathematical formulation and, on the other, a physical system that instantiates the formulation. Consider two radically different physical systems designed to reflect electromagnetic waves from metal surfaces. Suppose the power of the transmitted signal is known, as is the power of the signal thereupon reflected from the surface. Suppose further that there is a general equation that predicts these outcomes for a very wide range of such transmissions and is of this form:

$$P_r = \frac{P_t G^2 \lambda^2 \sigma}{(4\pi)^3 R^4} = \frac{P_t A^2 \sigma}{4\pi \lambda^2 R^4}$$

This is the *radar equation*. Any and every device, capable of transmitting energy within a given band of frequencies, and possessing a means by which to measure the power (P_i) of the return signal, qualifies as a radar, just in case this equation describes the relationship between the transmission and the reception of signals. Two otherwise entirely different systems in the circumstance are nonetheless *functionally* the same.

Kant's example of a dinner plate as an empirical entity and the geometrical form of circles stand in this sort of "isomorphic" relationship. The empirical dinner plate is one in which all points on the edge of the plate are the same distance from the center. This is a property that is represented formally by way of mathematics and experientially by way of perception. So the question of moment is just how the empirical finds its way to the right (*pure*) conceptual bin.

Now consider two billiard balls striking each other. Here is that Humean setting that is critically assessed by way of the Second

Analogy. Kant readily acknowledges that such pairs of events are not *sensibly* presented as causally related. More generally,

> No one will say that a category, such as that of causality, can be intuited through sense. (B177/A138)

Thus, there must be a nonempirical source or power or process by which such paired events come to be cognized as causally related. What is given is the brute empirical fact of an event. Also available but not "given" is what can be drawn from the pure categories. For there to be the right sort of linkage,

> there must be some third thing, which is homogeneous on the one hand with the category, and on the other hand with the appearance, and which thus makes the application of the former to the latter possible. . . . Such a representation is the *transcendental schema*. (B177/A138)

It links the a priori and the a posteriori, the empirical and the pure, the concrete and the formal.

The *schemata* are absolutely essential if appearances are ever to lead to knowledge of any objective fact in the world. Kant states the matter unequivocally:

> Indeed, it is schemata, not images of objects, which underlie our pure sensible concepts. No image could ever be adequate to the concept of a triangle in general. It would never attain that universality of the concept which renders it valid of all triangles. (A141)

When one views a triangle, its projection on the retina changes as the head moves, as the distance changes between the object and the observer, as the conditions of lighting are altered, as the eye's own level of adaptation varies, as the angle of regard is shifted, and so on. The myriad images thus formed and the incessant changes each of them undergoes could not possibly ground a concept of triangle as such, universally applicable to figures of the right sort.

The *schema* of time proves to be that "third thing" having kinship with both the empirical and the pure. This becomes clear when considering the category *Quantity*. The pure schema of all magnitude as a concept is *number*. The representation of alterations in quantity involves what Kant refers to as "the successive addition of homogeneous units" (B182/A143). Any empirical "X" varies in magnitude by adding or subtracting more of those similar or kindred units of which it is comprised. Addition, as a successive process, is a process *in time*. The schema of *necessity* makes possible the cognizing an object as existing at all times, just as the schema of *actuality* is the existence of an object at a determinate time. This analysis leads Kant to the general conclusion that the *schemata* constitute the necessary conditions whereby any concept comes to be related to objects. In this way, the concepts are meaningful and significant, resulting in that universal intersubjective agreement that is the mark of objective knowledge. Absent empirical content to work with, the categories have no function at all. This part of the argument is integral to the larger project of establishing the limits of human knowledge. The powerful rational resources of the human mind are capable of deepening understanding and enlarging the domain of knowledge, but only insofar as these resources are stocked with the empirically accessible facts of the world.

To this point, Kant has addressed the question of just what must be assumed in accounting for the fact that appearances can be subsumed under concepts, thereby giving the concepts themselves a real-world significance. A strong case (i.e., a compelling legal brief) has been filed against all attempts to attain knowledge of the world by reason alone. There still remains ample room for mismanaging the appearance–concept pairings. Demonstrating how synthetic judgments come about by way of empirical and conceptual interactions does not provide a means for determining which resulting judgments are valid and which are false or groundless. What is required beyond this *schematism* of the pure understanding is a *system* of all principles of the understanding, a system that identifies the rules by which the pure categories are to be applied. The process by which judgments are formed and the standard for assessing their validity requires additional work, a standard of *judgment*, the subject of the next chapter.

CHAPTER 7

JUDGMENT

In the previous chapter and elsewhere, the concept of judgment has been used somewhat loosely. Judgment within the *Critique* is basic, however, and calls for a more precise understanding. This, in turn, calls for a return to the distinction between *analytic* and *synthetic* propositions and that key question, "How are synthetic judgments a priori possible?" One returns to this question because Kant's larger argument supporting the claim that our knowledge of objects is, alas, *objective* is a claim regarding a class of propositions that are themselves *judgments*. Where these propositions are *synthetic*, they purport to be about reality.

Kant thus makes the distinction between judgments that *clarify* and those that *amplify* (A7/B11). Analytical judgments (e.g., that unmarried man is a bachelor) clarify the predicate term by joining it to a subject term that already expresses its meaning. Judgments of amplification are information bearing. When true, they add to the store of knowledge beyond what is available in the subject term. "Air has weight" is illustrative, for nothing in the judgment, "There is air in the chamber," carries with it the fact that, therefore, "There is weight in the chamber."

A further distinction is that analytic judgments are universally and necessarily true and, thus, could not be the product of experience. Their truth is established independently—a priori—not empirically. Whatever is available by way of experience can rise no higher than the level of a contingent fact that, after all, could have been otherwise and may in the future be otherwise. As Hume was at pains to establish, synthetic judgments are inherently contingent and probabilistic. This sets the larger goal for Kant that Paul Guyer summarizes this way:

> So how can Kant show that the first principles of mathematics, science and philosophy itself are synthetic propositions known *a priori*, not merely *a posteriori*; that is, how can he refute Humean skepticism: that what may seem to us to be universal and necessary principles are in fact nothing but contingent and incomplete generalizations. . . ?[1]

Any argument able to address the challenge head on has as it first requirement making clear that knowledge is different from perception and that those representations at the level of perception must finally stand in proper relation to the objects represented. There must be, as Kant says,

> the determinate relation of given representations to an object. (B137)

Knowledge, after all, is the agreement that obtains between objects and their ultimate representation in thought. One must be clear as to what counts as an "object" in all of this. For Hume, any and all "objects" of inquiry—entities about which one might pretend to know anything—are of one of two kinds: Matters of fact or relations among ideas, that is, that which figures either in synthetic or in analytic propositions. The latter offer nothing new, and the former provide no *logical* (rational) claim to truth. How, then, to avoid complete skepticism? Hume's answer expresses stoic resignation:

> The great subverter of Pyrrhonism or the excessive principles of skepticism is action, and employment, and the occupations of common life. These principles may flourish and triumph in the schools; where it is, indeed, difficult, if not impossible, to refute them. But as soon as they leave the shade, and by the presence of the real objects, which actuate our passions and sentiments, are put in opposition to the more powerful principles of our nature, they vanish like smoke, and leave the most determined skeptic in the same condition as other mortals.[2]

In other words, the ultimate standard is neither reason nor sense but *practice*. The ultimate standard of truth, or at least the best warrant for accepting a synthetic proposition as true, is that it leads to or is consistent with the deeper needs and sentiments of creatures such as ourselves. What moves one to action are not the products of reason but the passions. Action arises from sentiments and desires, the action typically expended in order to satisfy desire.

Hume rejected the traditional view of reason and passion being competing forces in directing behavior, for reason cannot move a muscle. In graphic and memorable terms, he set this principle down in a work that was not available to Kant, his *Treatise* of 1739. But it is clear that Kant was well aware of Hume's position as defended in the *Treatise* where Hume made the case this way, italics added here to highlight that famous Humean aphorism that still inspires partisanship:

> Nothing can oppose or retard the impulse of passion, but a contrary impulse; and if this contrary impulse ever arises from reason, that latter faculty must have an original influence on the will, and must be able to cause, as well as hinder any act of volition. But if reason has no original influence, 'tis impossible it can withstand any principle, which has such an efficacy, or ever keep the mind in suspense a moment. Thus it appears, that the principle, which opposes our passion, cannot be the same with reason, and is only call'd so in an improper sense. We speak not strictly and philosophically when we talk of the combat of passion and of reason. *Reason is, and ought only to be the slave of the passions, and can never pretend to any other office than to serve and obey them.*[3]

To accept this without qualification is to absorb all science, all philosophy into the domain of the practical that is itself finally governed by sentiment and desire. Here the ultimate warrants of belief are pragmatic. The seeming universality of the core judgments of human beings would thus express nothing beyond a shared biology—a shared nature—with which philosophical truths conflict at their peril. To use the already serviceable example of the honey bee, the creature finds nectar in something rendered "real" when radiated in the ultraviolet part of the spectrum; human beings find it when it is illuminated by wavelengths elsewhere on the spectrum. The needs of the bee and of the gardener launch the search for nectar. Both may be said to have "knowledge" as such just in case they succeed in practice.

For Kant, an account of this sort would seem to begin at mid-sentence. It fails to establish what amidst the sensory clutter qualifies as an *object* at all. From a purely physical perspective, the physics of the thing changes from moment to moment as does the percipient. There must be some a priori basis on which various elements of the overall physical array are joined. With this understanding, Kant is then able to define an *object* as *that in the concept of which the manifold of a given intuition is united.* Thus, the manifold of color, shape, texture, and so on—through the spatiotemporal mode of representation—is united to constitute an object.

This same manifold must also be unified within a single consciousness if there is to be an objective relationship between the manifold of representations and the given object. Only then does that *determinate relation of given representations to an object* become present in consciousness as an item of objective knowledge. However, the unification of the manifold as given in intuition cannot be supplied by sensibility itself. That is, sensibility, as the potentiality for experience, does not include any means by which a manifold is forged into a unified whole. As unification is both necessary and a priori, Kant refers to the power or process by which it takes place as *pure apperception* and says,

> The unity of this apperception I likewise entitle the *transcendental* unity of self-consciousness, in order to indicate the possibility of *a priori* knowledge arising from it. For the manifold of representations, which are given in an intuition, would not be one and all *my* representations, if they did not all belong to one self-consciousness. (B132)

What is shown to be necessary, then, is the synthetic unity of consciousness as the precondition of all knowledge. Kant illustrates this by way of a line. Space as a pure intuition is not an object of knowledge but only the necessary enabling condition of sensibility itself. If there is to be knowledge of something *in space*—a line, for example—it must be drawn or constructed. Now the unity of the act that results in the drawn line must match up with a unification of the manifold in consciousness, the result now being knowledge of an object. Kant concludes,

> The synthetic unity of consciousness is, therefore, an objective condition of all knowledge. It is not merely a condition that I myself require in knowing an object, but is a condition under which every intuition must stand in order *to become an object for me*. (B138)

This all moves a great distance from what Hume took to be the bare essentials, and it has nothing whatever to do with passion, sentiment, or pragmatic standards of success. The unity is *transcendental*, not a contingent feature of the subjectivity of experience. Although it is by way of the synthetic unity of apperception that the manifold of experience is "mine," the unity is nonetheless *objective*.

For all this to be achieved, there must be a unified concept forged out of the material supplied by experience but universalized and necessitated by the proper subsumption under the pure concepts of the understanding. Here the needed work of *synthesis* is done by what Kant refers to as the imagination (*Einbildungskraft*). It is essential to the synthesis of a manifold of sensations into a *this* or a *that*. As Kant says,

> Synthesis in general . . . is the mere result of the power of imagination, a blind but indispensable function of the soul, without which we should have no knowledge whatsoever, but of which we are scarcely ever conscious. (A78)[4]

Kant assigns to the imagination the power of drawing together certain elements in an otherwise disconnected assortment of possible sensations, drawing together just those elements that constitute a knowable *something*. Imagination does not yield knowledge but makes it possible. It is only when the synthesis of the manifold is then brought into (under) the pure categories of the understanding that *knowledge* as such arises.

The categories, however, must be applied to *something*, for it is only a *something* that stands (in categorical terms) as, for example, a unity, a reality, something subsisting, having actual existence, and so on. These, as noted in the previous chapter, are drawn from the table of the categories. They are drawn from the framework that exhausts the a priori concepts and at once sets boundaries and universalizes whatever is objective in human knowledge.

Kant is not indifferent to the wider range over which the function of imagination operates. It is not merely a mode of picturing, it is also part of the process of invention. As he says,

> If the imagination is not simply to be *visionary*, but is to be *inventive* under the strict surveillance of reason, there must always previously be something that is completely certain, and not invented . . . namely, the *possibility* of the object itself. (A770/B798)[5]

Where strict discipline is not imposed on reason, any number of utterly empty hypotheses might pass for understanding, for some putatively "deeper" insight. The cautionary note sounded by Kant is that the very inventive power of the imagination—the power of synthesizing inventively—is an asset when tied to the possibility of an object of experience, but dangerous when totally liberated from such constraints. The dangerous form of liberation leads to what Kant refers to as errors of *subreption* (German *Erschleichung*), a term borrowed from Roman and Canon Law. "Subreption" appears at A643/B671 in the *Critique* and draws attention to specific defects of *judgment:*

> All errors of subreption are to be ascribed to a defect of judgment, never to understanding or to reason.[6]

The term when found in legal contexts refers to the *vitium reptionis*, generally translated as "the crime of fraud" or an offense arising from a gross misrepresentation of the facts. As Kant would have the term understood, it is a form of delusion based on the misuse or illicit use of judgment. The proper deployment of the various perceptual and cognitive powers results in the correct subsumption of perceptual content within the framework of the pure categories of the understanding. Reason, properly disciplined, draws permissible inferences from the resulting concepts of the understanding. The outcome is *knowledge*. When rightly employed, the perceptual and cognitive powers match up *the right way* with the real world and ground the knowledge claims of the developed sciences.

However, there is a strong tendency to stretch these processes beyond the normal boundaries and seek what Kant refers to as "transcendent ideas" that go beyond the realm of actual or possible experience. The result is to regard the thus conceived *transcendent* as if it were real; it is to defraud oneself, to perpetrate a subreption.[7] Therein lies the danger. But therein also lies possibilities of great value, for, correctly managed, these transcendental ideas

> have an excellent and, indeed, indispensably necessary regulative employment; namely that of directing the understanding toward a certain goal . . . (giving) the concepts of the understanding . . . the greatest unity combined with the greatest extension.[8]

Reason is controlled by the canons of logic, by the law of contradiction. The understanding, however, makes use of concepts whose source is empirical. This, then, is the means by which knowledge is acquired and also limited. Think of a mirror, which is the example Kant offers. Looking into it, there is the vivid appearance of what lies behind the observer, and at a great distance. One is now aware not merely of what is before one but of an entire volume of things and events. All of this is conveyed by no more than reflections from a glassy surface, but the overall process leads to an apprehension of a greater unity, a greater connectedness among things. Kant uses this imagery to illustrate what he takes to be a basic presupposition of reason, namely, that what is unified within its own limited field is expressive of a wider and total unity, connected by universal laws. It is this presupposition that one *brings to* an examination of nature, not one *derived from* that examination.[9]

A wider field of the total unity of things connected by universal laws is clearly not something directly perceived, nor is it the result of any number of discrete perceptions, no matter how numerous. Rather, it is a judgment that goes beyond the given and seeks to locate what is behind the given. It is in his third critique, the *Critique of Judgment*, that Kant distinguishes between and among what he calls *determinate, reflective,* and *teleological* forms of judgment. He recognizes the need for some foundational or a priori belief or disposition on which the very project of investigating nature would seem to depend. The pure and disciplined rational faculty, combined with concepts firmly tied to possible experience, is too constricted. Empiricists offer a mental life that is stimulus bound and rationalists a mental life of abstractions. It is by way of the imagination that actual mental life moves freely and beyond the simplicities that systematic philosophies tend to impose.

One makes not merely *determinate* judgments but also *reflective* judgments that transcend the level of experience. With determinate judgment, there is the connection of the individual object of experience with the general or universal category of which it is a member. "All men are mortal" illustrates such a connection: Each particular human being is an instance of "mortal." Mortality, here, is a determinative predicate.

Reflective judgments are different. Now one moves from the particular but in search of an intelligible principle with which to understand the particular more fully. Were the search to end in a universal concept, the judgment would again be determinative. Rather, a concept such as "the finality of nature" or "a principle of harmony" supplies a presupposition with which to comprehend the particular instance. Finally, there is the mode of judgment that Kant calls *teleological*, judgments that presuppose *purpose* behind the orderly and lawful productions of nature. The mental life in which these powers are exercised is one in which (as Kant puts it) there is a *free play* of concepts, "lawlessly lawful," and conducive to real pleasure. Here is where art begins and the strictures of metaphysics are left if not in limbo then in reserve. A further consideration of these forms of judgment will be useful.

First, it should be noted that Kant's foray into nondeterminate forms of judgment did not await his entry into the field of aesthetics, nor was it confined to aesthetics and morality. As early as 1755, in his *Nova Dilucidatio,* he is found advancing a straightforward teleological account of the very possibility of causal influences. Against Leibniz's thesis that any change in a substance must arise within itself, Kant argues that there is nothing within a given substance that would somehow render it a causal partner of some other substance. Rather, such harmony or fitness between and among distinguishable substances must be attributed to and seen as expressive of an initial and "divine" understanding.[10] Even apart from such specific passages, it is surely obvious that Kant understood the aptness of teleological explanations of a broad range of biological facts.

It is in the aesthetic domain, however, that Kant fully recognized the need to enlarge the scope of his theory of judgment and the role of the imagination. The need to address aesthetic judgments had several sources. Within the contemporary intellectual context the subject had been given prominence (and even a name) by Alexander Baumgarten (1714–62) whose philosophical system defended the view that reason, as such, does not reach the aesthetic character of one's perceptual contact with the world. Baumgarten argued for a new science able to address this fact, a science he dubbed *Aestheticae*.[11] Comparably influential was a famous set of essays published by Joseph Addison in *The Spectator* in 1712. These focused on the pleasures of the imagination, comparing them favorably with those of the understanding. As Addison would have aesthetic experience understood,

> There is nothing that makes its way more directly to the soul than *beauty*, which immediately diffuses a secret satisfaction and complacency through the imagination, and gives a finishing to anything that is great or uncommon. The very first discovery of it strikes the mind with an inward joy, and spreads a cheerfulness and delight through all its faculties. There is not perhaps any real beauty or deformity more in one piece of matter than another, because we might have been so made, that whatsoever now appears loathsome to us, might have shown itself agreeable. . . . This is nowhere more remarkable than in birds of the same shape and proportion, where we often see the male determined in his courtship by the single grain or tincture of a feather, and never discovering any charms but in the colour of its species.[12]

Consider this passage now in the context of the *Critique of Judgment* where Kant writes,

> If we wish to discern whether something is beautiful or not, we do not relate the representation of it to its object by means of rational understanding. Instead, we relate the representation though imagination (acting perhaps in conjunction with reason) to the subject and its feeling of pleasure or displeasure. The judgment of taste, therefore, is not a cognitive judgment, is not logical, but is *aesthetic*—which means that it is one whose determining ground cannot be other than subjective. Every reference of representations is capable of being objective, even that of

sensations (in which case it signifies the real in an empirical representation). The one exception to this is the feeling of pleasure or displeasure. This denotes nothing in the object, but is a feeling which the subject has within itself and in the manner in which it is affected by the representation.[13]

It is clear to Kant that the *determinate* judgments connecting representations to objects cannot account for the quite different connection between representations and aesthetic feelings of pleasure or displeasure. The former judgment reaches a connection between cognition and the "outer" world; the aesthetic judgment, between the inner world of both representations and feeling.

Contrasted with determinate judgments (central to the *Critique of Pure Reason*) are the four forms of *reflective* judgment that seek to find an unknown universal able to include particulars. Determinate judgments account for what is given in experience according to causality. Reflective judgments take the same data but now understood as arising from a cause that executes a more fundamental *design*, the operation of an *intelligence*. Thus, something is judged as (ethically) good, as (aesthetically) beautiful, as (aesthetically) sublime. *Teleological* judgments go beyond even this. To the property of design is now added *purpose* and the autonomy expressed in authentically purposive undertakings. There may be a Newton for the heavens, but not for a single blade of grass! On this point, Kant could not be more explicit:

> It is indeed quite certain that we cannot adequately cognise, much less explain, organised beings and their internal possibility, according to mere mechanical principles of nature; and we can say boldly it is alike certain that it is absurd for men to make any such attempt or to hope that another *Newton* will arise in the future, who shall make comprehensible by us the production of a blade of grass according to natural laws which no design has ordered. We must absolutely deny this insight to men.[14]

This, however, all goes well beyond the proper role of judgment and imagination in the domains of metaphysics and science. Yet, even in these more restricted domains, Kant recognizes that something is missing if the account is limited to the subsuming of representations under concepts. He asks by what authority the pure categories of the understanding can be taken as something other than merely subjective frameworks. The question goes beyond what is established by way of the *Transcendental Analytic* for, as Kant says, the categories by themselves do not convey any knowledge of actual things but do so only when applied to what is empirically represented. The categories properly understood constitute the *possibility* of empirical knowledge. Thus:

> Space and time, as conditions under which alone objects can possibly be given to us, are valid no further than for objects of the senses, and therefore only for experience. . . . The pure concepts of understanding are free from this limitation. . . . But the extension of concepts beyond our sensible intuition is of no advantage to us. For as concepts of objects they are then empty, and do not even enable us to judge of the objects whether or not they are possible. They are mere forms of thought, without objective reality. (B147–9)

How, then, is it possible to move from such "mere forms of thought" to objective concepts? By what means do the contents of perception come together with objects? How, that is, can they "establish connection, obtain necessary relation to one another, and, as it were, meet one another" (A92)? The needed connection is between what is presented in experience (the *Vorstellungen*) and the actual "articles" or, as it were, the actual "subject matter" (*Gegenstände*) of what is presented. The required connection—the "necessary relation"—is that between the object and the cognizing of it .

Kant has already argued that there are only two possible ways for such a connection to come about: "Either the object alone must make the representation possible, or the representation alone must make the object possible" (A92). The first of these is illustrative of the Locke–Hume empiricist position according to which there is no more than an empirical connection such that the relation is neither necessary nor a priori. The second possibility would have the representations (*Vorstellungen)* not creating the object (as some sort of illusion) but rendering it knowable *as an object* (B125). This sense of "knowable" is to be distinguished from "apprehended" or "beheld" as in the instance of *Anschauungen*. The pure intuitions (via the *Transcendental Aesthetic*) are necessary for sensations to be received as appearances. What the pure intuitions make possible and necessary for *appearance* is what the pure categories make possible and necessary for *understanding*.

Kant is now able to summarize the overall problem this way:

> There are two conditions under which alone knowledge of an object is possible; first, intuition, through which it is given, though only as appearance; secondly, *concept*, through which an object is thought corresponding to this intuition. . . . The question now arises whether *a priori* concepts do not also serve as antecedent conditions under which alone anything can be, if not intuited, yet thought as object, in general. (A93–4/B125–6)

The move here is to establish the grounds on which objects can be *thought* as objects and, given the conceptual grounding of thought, then to understand that the mode of thought is itself a priori and necessary. As he says at A112, in the absence of the categories, the perceptions (*Vorstellungen*) would not contain any object at all, only the "blind play of representations, less even than a dream."

This leads directly to the "Transcendental Deduction" of the pure categories. The pure intuitions establish the conditions of sensibility, absent which there can be no representation at all. By way of what Kant calls *imagination* (an expression of the power of *spontaneity* as previously discussed), there is the synthesis of these representations, but there is still more required for knowledge proper. What is required is the unification of the manifold, under the pure categories such that there can be a *judgment*. Knowledge entails judgment (A69/B93). In other words, more is required than merely pulling various fragments together; they must be synthesized in such a way as to ground judgments. Achieving the proper unity yields what Kant calls *the pure concept of the understanding*. The concept is "pure" in that it is not an empirical given but something necessarily brought to bear on what has been given by way of sensuous intuition. To judge of anything as a determinate something is made possible by what Kant refers to as the "logical functions" of judgment, these being forms of judgment made possible by the pure categories of the understanding. Thus, there are precisely the same number of pure concepts of the understanding as there are logical functions in all possible judgments.

This brings one back to the question of just how is it that there is just the right unification and assignment of presentations to categories, according to the "logical functions" of all possible judgments? Alas, as noted in Chapter 4, Kant credits this to the gift of "mother wit," supplying the rules by which experiences are properly subsumed under general concepts. In this way it is the table of judgments that sets the a priori boundary conditions for concepts.

It is surprising at first, in a work of such analytical rigor, to discover that, in the final analysis, the faculty or power of judgment is to be understood in terms of "mother wit" (*Mutterwitz*). Whether this is a debt to or an echo of Scottish Commonsense philosophy—Reid's "mint of nature"—it is clearly a concession to the nature and functions of judgment itself. The term "mother wit" is discussed under the heading of "Transcendental Judgment in General" (A133–5/B172–4), which is the first part of book 2 of the *Transcendental Analytic*. Kant begins by noting the difference between understanding and judgment. The former involves the application of rules. The latter is the faculty or power of subsuming cognitions under rules. The task of judgment is to determine whether something does or does not stand under a given rule. This is a task that cannot be completed by way of formal logic. Logic, after all, operates not on empirical content, but on propositions and abstractly. Accordingly, at every turn it is necessary to form a judgment as to what goes with what.

> And thus it appears that, though understanding is capable of being instructed, and of being equipped with rules, judgment is a peculiar talent, which can be practiced only, and cannot be taught. It is the specific quality of so-called mother wit, and its lack, no school can make good. (A133/B172)

Judgment, in a word, is improved by practice, but strongly depends on native powers. Kant speaks of doctors, lawyers, and political leaders fully equipped with facts and principles and with formidable powers of understanding. They may even be gifted teachers of their subjects. Still, they may be deficient in what Kant refers to as the *natural* power of judgment. They may understand the universal in the abstract, but be unable to distinguish whether a given concrete case comes under it (A134/B173). Where one is deficient in these respects, examples may serve to sharpen the judgment somewhat. For such persons examples serve, Kant says, as a "go-cart" permitting them to make some trial-and-error progress toward soundness. Those with the natural power require no such contrivances.

We have seen that the table of categories provides all the logical functions entering to any judgment. As Kant says, the pure categories "specify the understanding completely, and yield an exhaustive inventory of its powers" (A80). Now, whereas formal logic cannot provide rules for judgment, *transcendental* logic is able to correct judgments by subjecting them to specific rules in the use of the pure understanding. Unlike formal logic, transcendental logic engages concepts that must match up a priori with actual objects. The objective validity of such objects is not established empirically, for it is only by way of the pure categories that they stand as "objects" of experience at all. It is by way of transcendental logic that the ". . . conditions under which objects can be given in harmony with these concepts" are formulated (A136). Absent the establishment of such harmony or fitness, the concepts would be utterly lacking in content. They would stand as logical forms of understanding but not as pure concepts.

It is important to rehearse the argument from the subjectivity of mere perceptions to what is objective experience, from what is personal to what is intersubjectively valid. The process itself is a function of the *imagination*. It is through the imagination that concepts and intuitions are synthesized according to a universal rule—which Kant refers to as a *schema*. This is the way the understanding rises to the level of empirical knowledge.

To make this clearer, consider the *Prolegomena* (297 to 302). Here Kant draws a fundamental distinction between *judgments of perception* and *judgments of experience*. Judgments of perception are merely subjectively valid. When one judges honey to be sweet there is the connecting of two entities, the physical object that is honey and a subjective sensation of sweetness. There is no guarantee that others will have the same experience or that anyone will on repeated encounters or that one's sensation is not the result of something other than the honey. There is no guarantee that judgments of perception will enjoy any degree of intersubjective agreement. Quite simply, they are not the stuff of which a science of nature is made.

Judgments of experience are different. With these what is given by way of sensuous intuition is then subsumed under concepts based on the pure categories of the understanding universally operative within the realm of human cognition—significant pathologies

aside. Think of each hand preadapted to very different tempera-
tures, then placed together in lukewarm water; one hand feels hot
and the other cold. It is by way of judgments of experience—these
made possible by the universal categories of the understanding—
that the judgments of perception are overruled.

Only when perceptions are thus subsumed under concepts may
the resulting judgment be a judgment of *experience*. A creature may
have rich perceptual resources and thus "register" various appearances, but these become experiences only when absorbed into a
conceptual scheme that is finally the framework for all knowledge.
Unlike the judgments of perception, the judgments of experience
hold good not only for a given person but for every one. There is
now objective validity, which, says Kant, is the same as *necessary
universality*. It is in this sense, then, that the possibility of nature is
tied to the possibility of experience.

Moving full circle, all this should be weighed in relation to the
distinctions between and among *determinate, reflective*, and *teleological* judgment. The latter two are not so rigidly "formulated" and
thus can reach beyond considerations of harmony and fitness. That
reach is liberating, to be sure, but a price is paid: What escapes its
grasp is *knowledge*.

CHAPTER 8

WHOSE EXPERIENCE?
THE SELF AND OUTER SENSE

In his informing entry on Kant, James Van Cleve summarizes Kant's concept of the "transcendental ego," contrasting it with the "empirical" self readily reached by way of introspection:

> In the philosophy of Kant, the transcendental ego is the thinker of our thoughts, the subject of our experiences, the willer of our actions, and the agent of the various activities of synthesis that help to constitute the world we experience. It is probably to be identified with our real or noumenal self (see Kant, *Critique of Pure Reason*, A492/B520, where "the transcendental subject" is equated with "the self proper, as it exists in itself"). . . . Kant called it transcendental because he believed that although we must posit such a self, we can never observe it.[1]

At the conclusion of Chapter 4 several questions related to this were raised but not addressed. One has to do with Kant's requirement that all empirical representations are spatiotemporal. Why not just temporal? Even more vexing is the question of how the various sensations are integrated and unified in consciousness. Perhaps most vexatious is the question of just how all this inheres in *his*, *her*, and *your* consciousness. Do plausible answers require recourse to Descartes's *Cogito* and the room it creates for the Cartesian form of skepticism? It is clear enough (Chapter 7) that, if there are to be concepts, there must be a means by which to fashion them out of representations. Thus, some sort of categorical framework is necessary if entities are to be cognized as *objects*. Kant's table of categories, a refinement of what Aristotle had proposed, might support learned quibbles, but it would seem to match up reasonably well with the properties that enter into an intersubjectively stable identification of entities. So far, then, there is a reasonable if rather thickly argued account of the ascent from the level of appearances to that of understanding. Additional resources are required, however, if there is to be *knowledge,* for understanding is grounded in rules. A different rule book directs the application of rules to specific cases, thus being the business of *determinative judgment.* As noted, this is an innate faculty that derives benefit from practice but is at base the gift of "mother wit."

Just when all this seems to be the last word on progress from sensation to objective knowledge, something new and seemingly "psychological" enters into the equation if there are to be concepts at all, namely, *apperception* and its shadowy relatives, the "empirical" ego, the "transcendental" ego, the *self,* and so on. This chapter begins with Van Cleve's economical summary of what may be the thorniest pages in the *Critique.* A bit of retracing is the way to begin.

By way of the pure intuitions of time and space, sensations are transformed into appearances. Only when these are subsumed under the pure categories of the understanding is there an *experience* of what is present in the external world. The necessary conditions by which there is the very possibility of experience are the pure concepts of the understanding (B161). A creature without the a priori categories could have the same sensations and appearances as we do, but not the same experiences. And the final step? The necessary concepts, through the transcendental unity of apperception, come to stand as *my* and *your* concepts.

For Hume what makes perceptions someone's perceptions is that they happen to be bundled together in the right associational framework. The unity of consciousness is not a property of the subject but of an ensemble of sensations. Kant's position is that an essential feature of the human mind is the unification of experiences in consciousness. If such unification is to obtain across subjects, it is obvious that something beyond the vagaries of contingent associations be at work.

All attempts to derive these pure concepts of understanding from experience, and so to ascribe to them a merely empirical origin, are entirely vain and useless. . . . How is this association itself possible? . . . I therefore ask, how are we to make comprehensible to ourselves the thoroughgoing affinity of appearances, whereby they stand and *must* stand under unchanging laws?" (A112–13)

This question leads Kant to that especially complex aspect of the *Critique*, the *synthetic unity of apperception*. It is here that we must establish how thoughts are *someone's* thoughts without adopting Cartesianism. Absent such unchanging laws (operating within the ever-changeable *empirical* self), there could be no unification of the manifold of representations within a given and undivided consciousness. Were it otherwise, "hot" might be in consciousness A, "sweet" in B, "aromatic" in C, but with *coffee* nowhere to be found in experience.

The importance Kant attaches to the synthetic unity of apperception cannot be exaggerated. He leaves no doubt about it when he states that it is

that highest point, to which we must ascribe all employment of the understanding, even the whole of logic, and conformably therewith, transcendental philosophy. Indeed, this faculty of apperception is the understanding itself. (B134)

Why it is given this status becomes clear from the argument that leads up to it. To begin with, whatever else might be said of representations, they must of necessity relate to what Kant refers to as a *possible* empirical consciousness. That which we are in principle incapable of relating to consciously is, for that very reason, nonexistent at least to us. Empirical consciousness—the consciousness of actual representations—stands in a necessary relationship to transcendental consciousness. That is,

it is absolutely necessary that in my knowledge all consciousness should belong to a single consciousness, that of myself. (A118, note a)

The "bare representation 'I'" is what makes possible the "collective unity" of all other representations. That is, if there is to be a unification of multiple representations, the unity must be in a single consciousness, a (transcendentally) given "I." This is not a factual claim about introspection. Rather, it pertains to the logical form of all knowledge as necessarily relating to the faculty or power by which unification becomes possible. This faculty is *apperception*.

It is not always clear just how Kant wants apperception to be understood over the many passages in which it figures. It is not always clear just what kind of mental act it refers to. Gregory Klass would have the term understood this way:[2] Asking what is the nature of any act that Kant dubs "apperception," the answer is that it is an act of the sort, "*I think P*," where P refers to a *representation*. Contact with the external world is by way of representations. For these to rise to the level of experience it is necessary that they be subsumed under concepts. In this way, one can now say of the representation "P," *I know P*, this being an act of *apperception*.

That apperception is an *act* is an important consideration in getting clear on Kant's understanding of the process. Unlike inner sense, it is responsible for all combinations of intuitions in general. It is a faculty or power that is prior to sensible intuitions.

> Inner sense, on the other hand, contains the mere form of intuition, but without combination of the manifold in it, and therefore, so far, contains no *determinate* intuition. (B154)

It is only when there is consciousness of the result of the synthesis of the manifold that inner sense attains a comprehended state or condition with content. What is required is what Kant refers to as an *act* of the imagination (B154), which is known not as a representation but directly by way of the act itself. "It is conscious to itself, even without sensibility" (B153). It is worth repeating that, at any given moment, a veritable flood of stimulation reaches the percipient, and thus, there must be a priori grounds by which all this is unified. The *transcendental unity of apperception* refers, then, to what are finally the necessary conditions for the unification of the elements of the empirical apperception. That this must operate a priori is established by the fact that nothing at the level of appearances contains within it the means by which to establish such a unification.

Surely sensibility, as the potentiality for experience, does not include any means by which the contents of the manifold are thus unified. As unification is both necessary and a priori, the power or process by which it takes place is *pure*. Moreover, the unification is not, as it were, disembodied or depersonalized. Apperception as an

act takes place through the resources of a given entity, a given kind
of entity. Thus,

> The manifold of representations, which are given in an intuition,
> would not be one and all *my* representations, if they did not all
> belong to one self-consciousness. (B132)

Still more is required, for at this point there is the nagging question
of just how such unities actually do stand as *yours* or *mine*. Then,
too, there is the question of constraints, if any, on the apperceptive
functions of unification, and it is here that Kant clarifies the role
of imagination. Intuitions, as he says, count for nothing unless they
are "taken up" in consciousness (A116). This is a necessary precur-
sor to knowledge itself. But there is the additional requirement that
we be,

> conscious *a priori* of the complete identity of the self in respect
> of all representations which can ever belong to our knowledge.
> (A116)

This is obvious, for unless every representation were joined in a single consciousness there could be no synthetic unity at all. It would
be as if each word in a message were delivered to a different person.
Of course, more is required, for all the words could result in a mere
jumble even though delivered to one person. What is additionally
required, then, is that the relevant faculty or power be of such a
nature as to be prepared to assemble (synthesize, unify, join, con-
nect) in all possible ways. Otherwise, there would be objective features that could not be derived from the manifold. The power or
faculty able to accommodate all such combinations is what Kant
calls the *imagination*:

> The transcendental unity of apperception thus relates to the pure
> synthesis of imagination, as an *a priori* condition of the possibil-
> ity of all combinations of the manifold in one knowledge. (A118)

It now becomes clearer as to what Kant intends in the statement, "It
must be possible for the 'I think' to accompany all my representations" (B132). Indeed, it seems fair to say that at this point, he actually accepts the *Cogito* for, as he says,

otherwise, something would be represented in me which could not be thought at all, and that is equivalent to saying that the representation would be impossible, or at least would be nothing to me. (B132)[3]

For Descartes, however, the *Cogito* functions as an epistemic device deployed against skepticism, whereas Kant's aim is to unearth what is metaphysically foundational for experience and thought. Kant is not adopting the empiricist's percipient or a Cartesian theater of the Ego. Where Descartes's argument pertains to "being conscious" Kant's is more properly understood as pertaining to "being conscious *that*."[4] In this respect, referring to apperception with the statement, *I know P*, might just as well be replaced with, *I am conscious that P*.

At B132 Kant again presents "intuition" as referring to any representation given prior to all thought, for it is what thought is *about*. To think is to think of something, and this requires a form of apprehension, which is what the term "intuition" is getting at. Through the intuitions, representations become possible. As we have seen, these rise to the level of knowledge when there is, in Kant's words, ". . . the determinate relation of given representations to an object" (B137). Kant repeatedly attempts to make clear just how "object" is to be understood. He is perhaps most clear at A204 where he notes again that appearances, as such, have no existence outside our power of representation. An appearance is entirely observer dependent. Appearances are, he says, *sensible representations*. By subsuming such representations under the pure categories, an object of thought—a bit of knowledge—arises. The character imposed by the categories renders the object a "something in general":

> Now we find that our thought of the relation of all knowledge to its object carries with it an element of necessity; the object is viewed as that which prevents our modes of knowledge from being haphazard or arbitrary, and which determines them *a priori* in some definite fashion. (A104)

An "object" is that in the concept of which the manifold of a given intuition is united. Thus, the manifold of color, shape, texture, and so on, through the spatiotemporal mode of representation, becomes united to constitute an object; in this case, say, an apple; a determinate kind of thing rather than a haphazard or arbitrary congeries of dis-connected appearances. This same now integrated, synthesized manifold must be unified within a single consciousness if there is to be an objective relationship between the manifold of representations and the given object. In this way there is the determinate relation of a given representation to an object; there is objective knowledge.

Here, then, are the a priori and necessary conditions in virtue of which unified experiences are *someone's*. Furthermore, again drawing attention to the difference between apperception and inner sense, we learn that

> The transcendental unity of apperception is that unity through which all the manifold given in an intuition is united in a con-cept of the object. It is therefore entitled *objective*, and must be distinguished from the subjective unity of consciousness, which is a determination of the inner sense. (B139)

It is the representation of the spatiotemporally given—that which originates first as appearances—that must be unified within a uni-tary consciousness. It is in this (empirical) sense that the result is a *synthetic* unity of consciousness. This is a precondition of all knowl-edge; otherwise, there would be concepts without content. Indeed, absent unification in consciousness, the manifold of representations would never be melded into a coherent whole. It would lack "that unity which only consciousness can impart" (A103). Kant concludes,

> The synthetic unity of consciousness is, therefore, an objective condition of all knowledge. It is not merely a condition that I myself require in knowing an object, but is a condition under which every intuition must stand in order *to become an object for me*. (B138)

The unity is *transcendental*, not a contingent feature of the subjec-tivity of experience. In all such passages in which the qualifier is *"transcendental"* it is useful to keep in mind what was set down at the outset:

> I call all knowledge *transcendental* if it is occupied, not with objects, but with the way that we can possibly know objects even before we experience them. (A12)

In so identifying the process to reach all that we can possibly know of objects, Kant contends that, although it is by way of the synthetic unity of apperception that the manifold of experience is *some-one's*, the unity itself is nonetheless objective. It is a requirement of every and any intuition (thus, *everyone's and anyone's*) intuition. In this connection, recall from Chapter 6 Kant's two "Supreme Principles"—one controlling all that comes under sensibility and one that controls all that comes under understanding:

> The former requires that the manifold of intuition "should be subject to the formal conditions of space and time"; the latter that "all the manifold of intuition should be subject to conditions of the original synthetic unity of apperception." (B136)

At a commonsense level, it would seem obvious that there must be a stable and enduring personal identity or "self" or "ego" in whom these processes take place, for every idea is, after all, *someone's*. This commonsense notion came under philosophical scrutiny in ancient times and then with special concern owing to Locke and Hume. The issue may be said to begin with the legendary Theseus who liberated Athens by landing in Crete and killing the Minotaur. As Greek cities celebrated the feat year after year, questions arose as to whether the constantly repaired ship of Theseus was still the same ship! At what point was there so much new wood as to consti-tute a new vessel?

Well, what, then, of persons? Daily life introduces changes, some of them radical and even psychological. The contents of conscious-ness are in constant flux. Still, one seems to remain one's *self* through it all. John Locke attempted to account for personal identity entirely on the basis of the contents of consciousness, thereby avoiding what he took to be the unsupportable concept of "real essences." The sense in which Mary is Mary is not that she is recognized as having the "real essence" of Mary but that she has the connected experi-ences (memories) unique to a given life, which, in this case, is named "Mary." On Locke's account, the mind is furnished solely by expe-rience. It must follow, therefore, that one's personal identity, too, must be fashioned from the stock of such experiences.[5] He illustrates the point with the thought experiment involving the Prince and the Cobbler. In the course of sleep each has the contents of mind relo-cated into to the mind of the other. It is clear to Locke that on arising the next day each would be the same man but not the same person. Although their corporeal identities would remain unchanged, their *personal identity* would now have been entirely transformed.

David Hume went further with the empiricistic account, insisting that in every search for his "self" he could find nothing but a *bundle of sensations.*[6] How, then, is this "self" continuous, even as the sensations vary? Hume's associationistic theory features a law of *cause and effect* that is finally reducible to the *constant conjunctions* of events in experience. Once formed, however, the chains or bundles retain their character even as one item or link is removed and replaced by another. The metaphor of the parade formation is illustrative. Just as the parade formation remains intact when one marcher is removed and replaced by another, so the continuity of "self"—as but a bundle of perceptions—is preserved even when one or another element is jettisoned and another is put in its place. No essential "self" need be posited, for the "self"—far from being some mysterious substance that ideas inhere in—is no more than the bundles of ideas held together by associative bonds.

Where Hume's theory is patently psychological, Kant's analysis is far removed from a merely descriptive psychology. His is a metaphysical analysis designed to establish the necessary and sufficient conditions, as well as the limiting conditions, on knowledge claims. Satisfied that Hume's account of causation itself required far more by way of metaphysical underpinnings, Kant brings the same transcendental mode of analysis to bear on the issue of the "self." It is surely not enough to acknowledge that any mental event has to be someone's, for it could be someone's without that one actually knowing it! (Imagine tickling someone in a trance, but able to "feel" tickled). Quite apart from the empirical features of one's "self," is there a metaphysically adequate argument that renders the right sort of self-consciousness necessary? To answer this, we return to the *Transcendental Aesthetic,* which sets out the form of all representations, that form being spatiotemporal.

But why must there be both spatial and temporal intuitions? In *The Bounds of Sense* Peter Strawson raises this fundamental question and offers a thought experiment featuring a world experienced only by way of audition. He puts the case this way:

> The Kantian doctrine that space and time are not only forms of intuition, but *a priori* forms of intuition. We are confronted not

merely with the thought of an intimate link between the idea of particular items, capable of being encountered in experience, and the idea of there being temporally and spatially ordered items. We are confronted with the thought of this link being so vital that it cannot be broken without nullifying the whole conception of experience. . . . But . . . the hearing of the sequence of notes, for example, may seem to be a case of the type of experience which can be coherently considered in isolation from everything else. Is it not conceivable that experience in general should consist exclusively of such sequences of auditory experience? And where then would be any necessary (or even possible place) for the notion of spatial ordering of particular items encountered in experience?[7]

This is just such a challenge that invites a further inquiry into the subtlety of Kant's analysis. It is a challenge that leads perhaps to a clearer account of the transcendental case for the necessity of self-consciousness. Consider the argument in the *Transcendental Deduction* addressing the fundamental question, in Kant's words, of "How I can be an object to myself at all" (B155). To get to the heart of the question, he begins with what he knows will seem paradoxical, namely, the contention that "inner sense" represents to consciousness the "self" as appearance and not "as we are in ourselves" (B153). The consequence of such a stipulation is that we are, as it were, merely passive observers of sensations taking place under the skin. Commenting critically, but without citing sources, Kant says that psychology avoids this by mistakenly conflating inner sense and apperception, two processes, as we have seen, that Kant has carefully distinguished. Beginning with the changes taking place in one's own inner states, he says,

> For all inner perceptions, we must derive the determination of lengths of time or of points of time from the changes which are exhibited to us in outer things. (B156)

The argument for this is developed further within the context of the *Refutation of Idealism* at B276–9. Summarizing it, we find

First: I am conscious of existing in time, this being an empirically determined item of consciousness;

Second: Consciousness of something enduring in time, requires a standard of permanence;

Third: That standard cannot be provided by the same empirical sources, for these afford only *representations* now calling for something distinct from them. That is, were the standard internal to me, it would be as a representations and could not ground knowledge of my own existence *in time*, for that would require an independent standard;

Finally: For me to be have consciousness of myself as enduring, there must therefore be actually existing and enduring external things.

It is this argument that has Kant claiming to turn idealism against itself. If the core thesis of idealism is that we can have knowledge only of the contents of our own consciousness—our own inner experiences—then whatever we might claim regarding the outer world is by way of inference. It is the thesis that takes the claimed existence of objects in space to be either doubtful or false (B274). For Descartes, the only empirical certainty is the "*sum*" of the *cogito ergo sum*, established by inner sense. What Kant claims to have shown, however, is that it is outer experience that is immediate "... and that only by means of it is inner experience ... possible" (B277). The "I am" of consciousness is granted, but it provides absolutely no knowledge of the subject whatever. If the "I" of the *Cogito* is to be knowable as an object of experience, it must be by way of representations dependent on the pure intuitions. Thus, it requires the representation of determination in time, and it is this that requires outer objects.

Kant is especially awkward in his phrasing here, but in a separate note (B278) he gives a mundane example that makes the point more clearly. The only way we are able to perceive time-based effects is by way of changes that take place in the outer relations of objects, for example, the motion of one entity against a background that is immobile or the daily motion of the sun against the background of stable objects on earth. So, too, with the "I" of consciousness. Knowledge of the "I" as an subject of experience, as with all knowledge, depends on the pure intuitions. Knowledge of an *enduring* self requires something permanent, and this, in turn, requires the permanent in outer sense. This becomes clearer when considering the concept of *substance*:

To demonstrate the objective reality of this concept, we require an intuition in space. For space alone is determined as permanent, while time and therefore everything that is in inner sense, is in constant flux. (B291)

So, too, with the concept of causation, which pertains to an alteration of something. At bottom, the alteration is a species of motion, itself requiring the sensuous intuition of space. Again,

All alteration, if it is to be perceived as alteration, presupposes something permanent in intuition, and . . . in inner sense no permanent intuition is to be met with. (B292)

In a Strawsonian world of sound only, the auditory experiences could only be *mine* if space is granted as a necessary a priori intuition through which the permanent in outer space stands as the necessary condition for recognizing myself as an enduring subject of experience. Absent this, there is "experience" but not known by me to be *my* experience, for there is no known enduring "I" in which the appearance inheres.

In the end, one of the abiding ambiguities in the *Critique* arises from Kant's passages on self-consciousness, the "empirical" self, and, alas, the (possibly) "noumenal" self. All normal waking persons are in some sense aware (or, with focused attention, can make themselves aware) of various states of feeling, desire, imagination, and so on. The objects of such awareness are actual states, sometimes directly traced to events in various parts of the body and the brain. All this comes under the heading of "empirical self-consciousness."

It is clear that the issue of the "I" was especially weighty for Kant. There is evidence of his taking various positions on the matter long before composing the *Critique.* Worth considering in this connection is the collection of fragmentary notes passed down as the *Duisburg Nachlaß*, which reveals a deeply reflecting Kant, more or less taking counsel with himself. Alison Laywine has written most informingly on some of these fragments as they pertain to the *self.* She summarizes Kant's position on inner sense, by which there is the immediate apprehension of the truth of "I am." More, there is the distinction between the "I" as an intelligence and what are otherwise merely the sensations tied to events in the physical body.

But then Kant goes further, now to the concept of *substance* and to what seems to be an acceptance of actual *noumenal* knowledge of the self:

> Substance is the first subject of all inhering accidents. But this I is an absolute subject to which all accidents and predicates can be attributed and that can be the predicate of no other thing. Thus the I expresses the substantial. For the substratum that underlies all accidents is the substantial. This is the one case in which we can immediately intuit substance. We can intuit the substantial and the subject of no [sc. other] thing, but in me I intuit substance directly. Thus the I expresses not only substance, but also the substantial itself. Indeed, what is more, the concept that we have of any substance at all we borrow from this I. This is the original concept of substances.[8]

Years later, in the relevant sections of the *Critique,* Kant makes clear that he has no doubt, metaphysical or otherwise, regarding his own existence. He knows that he is something more than an appearance, and he certainly knows that he is something other than an illusion. The abiding issue, then, has nothing to do with the ontological question of Kant's existence, but with the epistemological question of how or if Kant knows *himself.* In conformity with the conditions on which knowledge depends, he has no empirical access to the *noumenal* self, but only to himself as *appearance.* So there is a fundamental difference between being "conscious" of oneself and having knowledge of oneself (B158). He provides a clarifying note (a) at B158 where he acknowledges that his existence is "given" by the very act of determining it. At issue is what he calls the *mode* by which this is determined, namely, the manifold that belongs to it which is not so given. Required is a *self-intuition* by way of the a priori intuition of time. Although he cannot derive from this the actual proof of himself as a self-active being, he is able to represent to himself the "spontaneity" of his thought. Recall that spontaneity is "the power of knowing an object through . . . representations" (A50/B74). It is an expression of the *productive imagination* (B152). It is, he says, "owing to this spontaneity that I entitle myself an *intelligence*" (B158a).

What is clear is that knowledge of oneself is not different from knowledge of objects, for in both instances knowledge requires representations of what is present in the form of appearances. Acknowledging that we know objects external to ourselves only insofar as we are affected by them in a manner generative of appearances, it follows that a knowledge of ourselves requires that ". . . we are inwardly affected *by ourselves*. . . . We know our own subject only as appearance, not as it is in itself" (B156). There is, then, the "I" that thinks and is necessarily presupposed; the *transcendental* "I" is required if there is to be the possibility of the transcendental unity of apperception, and there is the *empirical* "I," known by way of the representations:

> Just as for knowledge of an object distinct from me I require . . . an intuition by which I determine that general concept, so for knowledge of myself I require, besides the consciousness . . . an intuition of the manifold in me. . . . I exist as an intelligence. . . . Such an intelligence, therefore, can know itself only as it appears to itself in respect of an intuition which is not intellectual and cannot be given by the understanding itself. (B158–9)

Nonetheless, there is in addition to the natural realm of causes and effects that intelligible realm of reasons and purposes. Thus, as a prelude to the possibility of morality itself, this passage moves the "self" well beyond the narrow boundaries of sensibility:

> Every efficient cause must have a *character*, that is a law of its causality, without which it would not be a cause. . . . We should also have to allow the subject an *intelligible character*, by which it is indeed the cause of those same actions in their quality as appearances. . . . We can entitle the former that character of the thing in the field of appearances, and the latter its character as thing in itself. (A539/B567)

The *transcendental ego*, as the necessary entity in which there can take place the transcendental unity of apperception, is not an object of knowledge. The *empirical ego* that is knowable is not known as in itself it really is but only by way of inner sense. It is a subject of psychological, not metaphysical consequence. To go beyond this and seek to establish as a knowable fact either the numerical identity of the *self* over time or the independence of the mind (soul) from external determinations is to push knowledge beyond its legitimate range and to locate the senses in realms in which they are blind. It is to exemplify those *paralogisms*—beginning with that very concept of a *substance*—that arise from reason's failure to discipline itself.

CHAPTER 9

THE DISCIPLINE OF REASON: PARALOGISMS, ANTINOMIES, AND FREEDOM

Graham Bird has written that

> The Paralogisms are at the center of Kant's account of the self, and that topic is plainly central to the whole argument of the *Critique*.[1]

Kant defines a paralogism as, ". . . a syllogism which is fallacious in form, be its content what it may" (A341/B399). His specific target is the *transcendental* paralogism. This is one in which there is a transcendental ground, but one that leads to a formally invalid conclusion. The pernicious process begins, says Kant, with

> syllogisms which contain no empirical premises, and by means of which we conclude from something which we know to something else of which we have no concept, and to which, owing to an inevitable illusion, we yet ascribe objective reality. (A339/B397)

The offense takes a characteristic form. The syllogisms in question are lacking in empirical premises. If this were not bad enough, reason now moves from something known to something about which we have no concept at all! Then, in a paroxysm of triumphant delusion, the theorist assures the world that something objective about reality is now *known*. As such syllogisms are transcendentally grounded, acceptance of them is

> in the nature of human reason, and gives rise to an illusion which cannot be avoided . . . but may be rendered harmless.

To see how calls for a virtually "clinical" appraisal of reason's defects. Although Kant's analysis throughout the *Critique* pertains to creatures such as ourselves, it is not an analysis that would reduce the transcendental unity of apperception to a contingent feature of subjective experience. Rather, it is by way of the synthetic unity of apperception that the manifold of experience is someone's, but the unity itself is nonetheless objective:

> It is not merely a condition that I myself require in knowing an object, but is a condition under which every intuition must stand in order to become an object for me. (B138)

It is through the imagination that *concepts* and *intuitions* are *synthesized*, according to a universal rule, which Kant refers to as a *schema*. This is the way the understanding attains *empirical knowledge* inter-subjectively validated. In failing to realize the dependence that all knowledge claims have on the proper assimilation of appearances to pure concepts, both the empiricists and the rationalists wandered in darkness and confusion. In something of a pathologist's report, Kant then sets down what he terms the *paralogisms of pure reason*. It is by way of these that Kant reveals more fully that *critique* by which to uncover not only the limits of reason, but its tendency to overstep its legitimate grounds. "Legitimate" here should be taken in the literal sense: that which under the color of law the impartial judge would regard as warranted.

Although the paralogisms and the antinomies are developed late in the *Critique* the groundwork is done early, just after the *Transcendental Aesthetic*. Following his Introduction Kant begins the treatise with the section titled, *Transcendental Doctrine of the Elements*, part 1 devoted to the *Transcendental Aesthetic*. In part 2 he introduces the transcendental logic and this is a good place to begin sorting out where the antinomies fit within the larger work.

As noted in earlier pages, Kant divides logic into general logic and transcendental logic, the former further divided into "Analytic" and "Dialectic." Analytic logic was bequeathed by Aristotle and stands as *the canon of judgment*. It is the mode of analysis with which to preserve whatever truths are contained in propositions as well as the means by which to avoid fallacies and impermissible inferences. "Dialectic" is another matter entirely. The formal logic that is a *canon* of judgment is now used not as a *canon* but, says Kant, as an *organon*—a method of discovery, which, in the end, becomes "the sophistical art of giving to ignorance . . . the appearance of truth" (A61/B86). In book 2 of *The Transcendental Dialectic* (A339/B397), Kant lists the three "Pseudo-rational Dialectical Syllogisms" productive of illusory knowledge. They are products of the misuse of logic, the corruption of a canon of judgment into what is finally the counterfeit of a method of discovery. Each of the pseudorational dialectical syllogisms is a lesson and a cautionary note.

The first such syllogism is illustrative of all *paralogisms.* It finds one drawing inferences from transcendental concepts to particulars; inferences, that is, from concepts that are utterly lacking in empirical content to objective particulars. The *Cogito* is illustrative. The transcendental concept of a substance is now used to establish Descartes as a particular thinking thing, independent of physical properties. Thus, by way of a (doomed) rational psychology one would "prove" the immateriality and immortality of a particular "soul" through the transcendental concept of *substance.* It should be clear, however, that "substance" as a concept depends on permanence. Permanence requires the pure intuition of time, now applied the sensuous intuitions. Thus, the paralogism rests on a concept without empirical content.

The second type of pseudorational syllogism now finds one drawing inferences from a series of appearances to the transcendental concept of the absolute totality of conditions for a given appearance. This is illustrative of what Kant dubs the *Antinomies of Pure Reason.* Finally and momentously, there is a third form of pseudorational inference that moves from the synthetic unity of all that one does know by way of the understanding to what one could not possibly know by way of the same concepts—an inference to the *ens entium,* to *God* by another name—and here we have the *Ideal of Pure Reason.*

The first paralogism, *contra* Descartes's *Cogito,* critically assesses what Kant refers to as the rational doctrine of the soul. Here one sees why Graham Bird regards the account of the *self* as central to the whole argument of the *Critique.* Metaphysics in the rationalist tradition, notably as represented by Descartes, takes the "self" to be either self-evident or somehow known a priori by way of reason alone, requiring no empirical content. On this account, the self is not known as an appearance or as an empirical representation, but through some undisclosed rational process. Thus, such arguments, if syllogistic, begin without any empirical premise whatever. More than this, the traditional rationalists sought to establish that the soul can be known as a *substance*, simple and indestructible. Of course, were such knowledge actually available through reason alone, Kant's entire project would collapse. It would amount to the claim that *noumena* are directly given in experience.

Kant's appraisal of such claims is embedded in that core question, *How are synthetic a priori propositions possible?* Through the *Transcendental Aesthetic*, he first establishes the ideality of time and space and thus the possibility of synthetic propositions a priori in mathematics. The pure intuitions similarly necessitate the Euclidean character of all spatial appearances. The *Transcendental Analytic* is then advanced to establish the a priori grounding of objective knowledge. The question then revives the issue raised in the Prize Competition, namely, whether there are similar synthetic a priori propositions possible in metaphysics and whether metaphysics might aspire to the scientific and systematic *knowledge* of mathematics and the physics. The *Transcendental Dialectic* leaves no doubt: The answer is an unequivocal *no*. Synthetic a priori propositions in metaphysics are not possible at all, for "Concepts without intuitions are empty" (A52/B76).

Concepts can be applied solely to appearances as these are grounded in the pure intuitions. Moreover, there can be no "general knowledge" derived from the pure categories, for these are devoid of the very objects that are accessible solely by way of experience. Finally, knowledge depends on the full cooperation of both sensibility and understanding, not on either alone. Accordingly, what lies beyond sensibility is beyond knowledge. The concepts and principles of the understanding are mere forms of thought and cannot yield knowledge of objects. He makes this clear at B147:

> For if no intuition could be given corresponding to the concept, the concept would still be a thought, so far as its form is concerned, but would be without any object, and no knowledge of anything would be possible by means of it. So far as I could know, there would be nothing, and could be nothing, to which my thought could be applied.

Thus, such "transcendental" use of the understanding independent of sensibility is simply a mistake, generative of the illusions

of reason. Seeking knowledge of things independently of experience—seeking "noumena"—is doomed to fail (A246/B303) and this
includes the search for the "noumenal self" of Descartes, Leibniz
and others in the rationalist school of metaphysics. Alas,

> the proud name of ontology, which presumes to offer synthetic
> *a priori* cognitions of things in general . . . must give way to the
> more modest title of a transcendental analytic. (A247/B304)

What is to replace the Cartesian and Leibnizian ontology of the self
is not reached by undisclosed powers of reason. The modest "transcendental analytic" has been met within earlier chapters. It has
as its main components that *Analytic of Concepts* (which includes
the Transcendental Deduction of the Categories) and the *Analytic
of Principles*, which includes the Analogies of Experience and the
Anticipations of Perception. Rather than unearthing a noumenal
self, Descartes and Leibniz were simply displaying "discoveries"
made inevitable by just these forms of cognition. They confused
the logical self of propositions, with the ontological discovery of a
noumenal self.
   Consider again the first paralogism:

> The soul or "self" is a *substance,* simple and enduring. Of course,
> *substance,* as one of the Categories, is of itself without content.
> Substances, "have in themselves no objective meaning, save in so
> far as they rest upon an intuition, and are applied to the manifold
> of this intuition, as functions of synthetic unity. In the absence of
> this manifold, they are merely functions of the judgment, with-
> out content. (A439)

So, even granting that thoughts inhere in the "I," this "I" as substance entails nothing as regards the origin or persistence of itself.
"I" as a logical subject of thought reveals nothing about the real
subject. Accordingly, rational psychology ". . . owes its origin simply to misunderstanding. The unity of consciousness . . . is only
unity in thought, by which alone no object is given, and to which
therefore, the category of substance, which always presupposes a
given intuition, cannot be applied" (B421–2).
   The second paralogism pertains to the putative simplicity of
the soul, described by Kant as, the "Achilles" of all dialectical

inferences (A351). The main argument for this simplicity has a distinctly "scholastic" ring, contrasting "Composites" and "Simples" in action. Although the body's motion is the result of the movement of all its parts, "thought" is not thus divisible; that is, were the total thought the combination of thoughts held by more than one subject, there would be no unity of thought and so on. The conclusion drawn from this is that

> It is therefore possible only in a single substance, which, not being an aggregate of many, is absolutely simple. (A352)

But the required conclusion does not follow. First, the proposition that requires the unity of a thinking subject if multiple representations are to yield a single representation is not "analytic." In other words, the concept of the unity of a thinking subject is not synonymous with or included in the concept of multiple representations condensed into a single representation. (Photographs taken from different angles can be merged into a composite without reference to the unity of a thinking substance.) Therefore, the proposition is not established by way of the principle of identity (A353). In other words, it is not a claim capable of vindication by the law of contradiction, which is to say by reason alone. Nor can it, as a synthetic proposition, be known a priori, for a single representation could be derived by the concerted action of a collective. Nor is it empirically confirmed, for nothing in experience is generative of logical necessity.

Clearly, then, the alleged simple substance is not the content of an experience but merely a subjective condition of knowledge. The thesis that would take the unity and simplicity of the soul to be a piece of objective knowledge rationally established is defeated. What is left is an empty "I," a mere something.

> It is obvious that in attaching "I" to our thoughts, we designate the subject of inherence only transcendentally, without noting in it any quality whatsoever—in fact, without knowing anything of it either by direct acquaintance or otherwise. . . . Simplicity of the representation of the subject is not knowledge *eo ipso* of the simplicity of the subject itself. . . . Thus the whole of rational psychology is involved in the collapse of its main support. (A353–60)

This should blunt all hope of extending knowledge

> through mere concepts—still less by means of the merely subjective form of all of our concepts—consciousness—in the absence of any relation to possible experience.

The third paralogism offers nothing less than an enduring self or soul and it fares no better. Kant takes the following as the paradigmatic argument:

> That which is conscious of the numerical identity of itself at different times is in so far a person. Now, the soul is conscious, etc. Therefore it is a person. (A361)

But is there, indeed, an enduring, persisting "self" (soul) that is thus knowable a priori and by reason alone? Clearly, the numerical identity of something can be known *a posteriori* by any percipient who perceives what is permanent among appearances that are otherwise in flux (A362). However, although it is true that, amidst the flux of appearances, there is an "I" that connects them all, this "I" is a mere thought, which, for all one could know, is in the same state of flux as the other thoughts, which by means of the "I" are linked up with one another (A364). Hume's associationist model should be able to establish such connections. Accordingly, there may be a strong argument for the "self" or person, even a *transcendental* self, as necessary in accounting for the unity of apperception, but not as an object of *knowledge*—for not as an object at all. Self-knowledge does not entail the continuity of personal identity.

> We can never parade it as an extension of our self-knowledge through pure reason, and as exhibiting to us from the mere concept of the identical self an unbroken continuance of the subject. (A366)

As for the soul's immortality (the limitless continuity of that substantial, simple "self"), this would not follow even granting its unity and simplicity:

> The supposed substance . . . may be changed into nothing, not indeed by dissolution, but by gradual loss of its powers. . . . For

consciousness itself has always a degree, which always allows of diminution, and the same must also hold of the faculty of being conscious of the self. . . . Thus the permanence of the soul, regarded merely as object of inner sense, remains undemonstrated, and indeed indemonstrable. (B414)

The fourth paralogism, "Of Ideality," was considered at length in Chapter 5, for it is at the center of that skepticism answered by Kant's *Refutation of Idealism.* In the form of a paralogism, the skeptic's position reduces to the insistent claim

that, the existence of which can only be inferred as a cause of given perceptions, has a merely doubtful existence. (A367)

Kant's refutation of idealism exposes this instance of paralogism as predicated on assumptions defeated by the very cognitive resources needed to render the challenge intelligible.

What all four paralogisms make clear is that reason, liberated from necessary discipline, seeks to go beyond its own transcendental grounding to what is finally "transcendent" and therein lies illusion. The early project that Kant set for himself and briefly referred to in correspondence with Hertz was to test and set the limits of sense and reason. In the paralogisms the mature expression of this aim is now evident in relation to the possibility of rational psychology. This is then extended to include his critical perspective on the possibility of rational cosmology, and rational theology as set forth in his treatment of the *Antinomies of Pure Reason.*

The antinomies are taken up under "Dialectic." Kant surely had the ancient Sophists in mind when choosing the word, which is from the Greek, *dialegesthai*—conversing. He has in mind that argumentative mode of conversation found, for example, in the paradoxes of Zeno or in the part given to Protagoras in the dialogue named after him. The use of formal logic not as canon but as organon renders dialectic a *logic of illusion* (A62) calling for a *critique of dialectical illusion*, which is precisely what the paralogisms and the antinomies are intended to provide.

Transcendental Logic sets the rules or laws for how concepts relate to objects, as well as the validity and scope of such knowledge as might arise from such relations. This provides the right starting point for entry into the *Antinomies.* They are presented in book 2 of the *Transcendental Dialectic*, just after the Paralogisms. The fatal element in the paralogisms is conjecture without content, metaphysical conjectures regarding the soul—its simplicity and permanence—devoid of representations. With the antinomies, there are conjectures seemingly robust in empirical content but now infected with yet another set of fallacies tending toward what Kant calls "the euthanasia of pure reason."

Where book 1 of the *Transcendental Dialectic* is addressed to the *concepts* of pure reason, book 2 is an examination of the *inferences* of pure reason, and the pitfalls thus encountered. The paralogisms generate illusions regarding the *subject* of thought—the self or soul. Now a different class of illusions arises "when reason is applied to the *objective* synthesis of appearances" (A407/B433).

The paralogisms pertain to the unwarranted reach of reason toward a noumenal self or soul; the antinomies offer unwarranted rational inferences toward the objects of knowledge, toward what Kant calls *the world*—this being, "the absolute totality of all existing things" (A420). "The world" is to be understood, then, as the ultimate source of all appearances, all objects, and all events. Stated in these terms, the question of questions is whether the world can be known through pure reason.

Kant is certainly not heading toward skepticism here; quite the contrary. Aware of such a charge, he makes the distinction between what he calls the skeptical *method* and *skepticism* itself. He again invokes the legal metaphor, making clear that what he is advancing is less a logical argument then a juridical one.

> This method of watching, or rather provoking, a conflict of assertions, not for the purpose of deciding in favor of one or the other side, but of investigating whether the object of controversy is not perhaps a deceptive appearance which each vainly strives to grasp . . ., and in regard to which, even if there were no opposition to be overcome, neither can arrive at any result—this procedure, I say, may be entitled the *skeptical method*. Is altogether different from *skepticism*—a principle of technical and scientific ignorance, which undermines the foundations of all knowledge. (A423–4/B451–2)

Kant charts reason's illusory progress when it misapplies the pure categories of the understanding. The illusions of theoretical reason now surface in futile attempts to discover or identify objects entirely inaccessible to the forms of sensuous intuition. He classifies these objects as drawn either from the school of Plato or that of Epicurus (A471–B499), two philosophies in which each "says more than it knows." Plato allows reason to indulge in ideal explanations of natural appearances, which can never rise to the level of scientific knowledge. It must remain at the level of speculation. The world of Epicurus is equally speculative, what with its invisible elements and ambiguous swerve. Each of these grand theories, and all such productions of dogmatic metaphysics, are able to generate a coherent and compelling set of conclusions about the way things really are, only to face equally coherent and compelling conclusions that are diametrically opposed. Hence, the antinomies. Hence, "the *euthanasia* of pure reason" (B434).

The autopsy report begins with the paralogisms, reason's fatal attempts to attain complete knowledge by applying concepts removed from the very possibility of experience. The process of euthanasia begins with reason now appropriating from the understanding of concepts whose valid function pertains to intuitions. The understanding is the faculty that "enables us to *think* the object of sensible intuition . . ." (A51/B75). The pure intuitions constitute the necessary conditions of all sensibility, but confer only form and not content on appearances. It is the required further work of the mind to move from the level of appearances to the production of representations, and this is the power that Kant refers to as *spontaneity*. Were it not for this, we would be unable to *think* the very objects of sensible intuition. In this way, understanding depends on spontaneity. In this way the intuitions are represented in thought through the application of general concepts. Thinking just is this representing of a thing through the use of general concepts. The proper deployment of the pure concepts of the understanding is to subsume intuitions under them thereby making the objective world thinkable, to make possible nothing less than experience itself.

However, the categories are not included within the forms of sensibility, and, therefore, they cannot provide the conditions under which objects are "given." Objects may appear without the participation of the understanding. Thus, all that is sensible is not for that reason thinkable, nor is all that is thinkable for that reason sensible. The pure concepts issue from the understanding, not from reason as such, and this creates the possibility of metaphysical mischief.

Reason is able to liberate concepts of the understanding from the limitations imposed by any possible experience, that is, from the limitations imposed by the pure intuitions. By way of this liberation, reason can extend the concepts beyond the empirically accessible, and therein is the prospect of illusory knowledge, of *illusion*.

The autopsy report includes what Kant refers to as a given or prevailing condition—the *gegeben Bedingt*—here the empirical "given." The understanding subjects the manifold of appearances to synthetic unity. This is fine as far as it goes. But now reason goes beyond this, reaching for absolute totality. It is not enough to subsume representations under general concepts and thereby possess a genuine experience, an experience, which, owing to the universality and necessity of the categories, is intersubjectively shared. Rather, reason now extends itself to reach nothing less than the totality—the world. In so doing, it converts the concept—otherwise empirically grounded—into a transcendental idea (A409/B436) liberated from what is given in intuition. It seeks to go beyond the conditions of knowledge to achieve an understanding that is, as it were, unconditional. It seeks what Kant calls the unconditioned. In a word, reason now would comprehend the *transcendent*! But as this "unconditional" is nowhere met with in experience, what has been achieved is not knowledge at all, let alone knowledge of the unconditional. Rather, it is but a categorical mode or model of thought. Having established how the process works, Kant is then in a position to examine his four *Antinomies of Pure Reason* to illustrate the illusions arising from each. The four are divided into two classes: two that are *mathematical* antinomies, and two that he calls *dynamical*. The first two are mathematical in that they pertains to that world of objects in space and time. Thus: Is the world finite? Is it limitless? Is everything divisible? Are there indivisible entities whole unto themselves? The dynamical antinomies arise from very different questions. Is the world to be understood as the outcome of strict and mechanical causation? Must there be behind everything some one causal power, itself free of causal constraints? If there is such freedom, then does that uncaused source necessarily stand outside the order of spatiotemporal causation? Is there, then, an absolutely necessary being standing as the uncaused originator?

The four antinomies are not conflicts between reason and sensibility but "pathologies" of reason itself. What conflicts with the limits of sensibility is the assumption that there can be a valid search for knowledge of things in themselves. What is turned up by such a search is empirically empty and thus not subject even to dispute at the level of knowledge. The four antinomies present pairs of arguments, each coherent and compelling, but with each member of the pair contradicting its mate in the form of a thesis and antithesis.

The first antinomy is the *cosmological*:
Thesis: The world has a beginning in time and a limit in space;
Antithesis: The world is infinite in temporal duration and spatial extent (A426–7/B454–5).

The second antinomy is *ontological*:
Thesis: Substances in the world are ultimately composed of simple parts.
Antithesis: Nothing simple is ever to be found in the world, thus everything is infinitely divisible (A434–5/B462–3).

The third antinomy is that of *causality*:
Thesis: Causality in accordance with laws of nature is not the only kind of causality, but there must also be a "causality of freedom."
Antithesis: Everything in nature takes place in accord with deterministic laws alone (A444–5/B462–3).

The fourth antinomy is that of *theology*:
Thesis: There must be a necessary being as the cause of the whole sequence of contingent beings, either as its first member or underlying it.
Antithesis: No such being exists inside or outside the world (A452–3/B480–1).

In the paralogisms of pure reason Kant put rational psychology on notice and offered a refutation of any proposition by which the self could be known noumenally. Now, by way of the antinomies, he sets the same limits on cosmology, ontology, causality, and theology. Reason must learn to discipline itself lest it generate sheer illusion as a counterfeit of knowledge.

The analysis of each of the antinomies is detailed, but the overall approach is fairly straightforward. In the first antinomy the dispute is between the thesis that the world has a beginning in time and a limit in space. The antithesis is that it is infinite in temporal duration and spatial extent. In contemporary terms, this is not unlike the competing theories of "Big Bang" and the cosmos as eternal. It should not be difficult to anticipate how Kant would treat this antinomy. Both thesis and antithesis take for granted the reality of a mind-independent realm of time and space. Thus, the core assumption behind both defies what has been established as the necessary preconditions for sensibility itself. As both thesis and antithesis regard space and time as infinite, meaning, among other things, that they are real features of an external world, the transcendental aesthetic is all that is needed to establish that both positions are nonstarters if they presume to be knowledge claims.

The thesis of the first antinomy is that the world (which is *everything*) has a beginning. This requires that the collection of all events leading up to it—which is to say the entire past—must be completed at the very point at which the "world" comes about. But if this same world (i.e., *everything* in the spatiotemporal universe) fills infinite space, it would require infinite time to achieve the required synthesis of all "parts." Thus, the temporal series could never be completed. One begins to sense that those who traffic in such grand generalizations are directed not by the rules of judgment but by the anarchic deployment of reason itself.

In the second antinomy, the dispute is between the thesis that substances in the world are ultimately composed of simple parts; the antithesis, that nothing simple is ever to be found in the world, such that everything is infinitely divisible. In these "mathematical antinomies" *neither* side can claim truth, because reason is attempting to apply to time and space something unconditioned, thus failing to realize that the entire framework is a product not of possible experience but of the cognitive resources of the percipient (A504–5/B532–3). It is again the success of the *transcendental aesthetic* that dooms the partisans on both sides.

What of freedom versus determinism? The thesis here is that *causality in accordance with laws of nature* is not the only kind of causality. There must also be a "causality of freedom" underlying the whole series of natural causes and effects. Against this, the antithesis requires that everything in nature takes place in accordance with strict deterministic laws alone (A444–5/B462–3). Both thesis and antithesis are defensible by seemingly compelling arguments, but neither can be established in the sense of "known to be true." Indeed, both can be seen as compatible on Kant's "double-aspect" account (A553–8/B581–6). On this understanding, reason is the abiding condition of all volitional actions, which is to say that volitional action proceeds from *reasons for acting*. It is this that renders actions *intelligible*. Unlike the empirical character of the actions as appearances, their intelligible character is not grounded in the a priori intuitions. Reason thus operates "freely" in that it is not dynamically determined by natural causes as these are given through the intuitions. Although this is not "proof" of freedom, it is an account of that aspect of actions that can be conceived as "free" while being compatible with accounts based on the principle of natural causation.

One is inclined in light of Kant's treatment of causality here to locate him squarely in the court of *compatibilism* on the question of free will and determinism. The "fit" with usual forms of compatibilism is not a good one, but there have been suggestive interpretations that would improve it.[2] The most direct route to such a reading is by way of a *dual aspect* mode of explaining actions. Kant encourages this by distinguishing between the phenomenal world of appearances, where causality operates without exception, and a noumenal realm in which actions are intelligible only on the assumption of freedom. Something about this view is very tempting, but, again, the actual arguments of the *Critique* make such a position rather forced. It is not at all clear that the terms "compatibilism" and "incompatibilism" should even be applied to his position.[3] There are those who find in Kant's third antinomy something akin to the *anomalous monism* defended by Donald Davidson.[4] Read in this light, there is again a double aspect at the level of explanation but not a dualistic ontology. There is but one ultimate reality to which we have only indirect and cognitively predetermined access. However, on this very reading, the larger question seems hopelessly unsettled, for on Kant's account, that "ultimate" reality surely need not be the reality of physics. It is precisely the burden of the sections devoted to the paralogisms and the antinomies to make clear that a firm position on a matter of this sort cannot be reached by the human understanding. To the extent that it is permitted by reason, it is now reason set adrift from the moorings of knowledge and the knowable world.

If one is required to take a stand on just what Kant's position was, prudence dictates caution. Perhaps the way toward greater clarity as to Kant's final position on a matter of this centrality is away from the determinative judgments tied to sensual modes of apprehension and toward the teleological judgments required in the moral and aesthetic realms. After all, there is nothing in the

Critique suggesting that Kant's conception of aesthetics is but one "aspect" of a comprehension that is also attached to what is otherwise a physical object. The latter carries nothing of sentimental or affective value, nothing conducive to feelings of sublimity in the presence of the beautiful, nothing finally conducive to the recognition of an object or state of affairs or action as in itself *good.*

Paul Guyer seems to be on surer interpretive footing when attributing to Kant an argument according to which,

> if we are to view nature as a whole, as a system, then we must find a point—a "final end" (*Endzweck*)—for that system, but the only thing that could possibly play that role is the one thing of unconditional value, namely human freedom, and its full effect, the highest good.[5]

What of the alternatives of God or a Mindless Universe? The thesis is that there must be a necessary being as the cause of the whole sequence of contingent beings, either as its first member or underlying it. Against this is the antithesis is that no such being exists inside or outside the world (A452–3/B480–1). Claims of such a nature are clearly not grounded in spatiotemporal conditions of sensibility. They refer to a noumenal realm and, as such, either thesis may be true (A558/B586), but, of course, beyond the reach of reason's powers of proof (A531/B559, A603/B631).

One must be cautious here. Kant's philosophy of religion—a term suggesting rather greater systematicity than the published record would warrant—is, needless to say, worthy of and has received careful scholarly attention.[6] It is a subject that he addressed often and over a course of many years, even lecturing on the topic during his early years at the University of Königsberg. His *Religion within the Boundaries of Mere Reason* (1793)[7] marked a point of high controversy resulting in a formal rebuke by Frederick William II, with instructions to Kant to write no further on religious subject. Kant complied until the death of Frederick William in 1797.[8] Sampling his writing on this subject over a period that runs to nearly forty years, one is inclined to be reserved in attempting to establish his own religious faith. His parents were Pietists and the well-known position of Pietism on formalism and ritual orthodoxies is expressed in a number of Kant's publications and letters. But Pietism's grounding of moral strictures in religion is there as well, Kant leaving no doubt but that he regarded faith in God as foundational for moral conscientiousness.

Kant was careful to make clear that "existence" as such is not a predicate, thus challenging various ontological arguments for the existence of God. To have the concept of "X" does not include existence as a necessary or contingent property. One may believe that one's watch is gold-plated (thus possessing the concept of a gold-plated watch) whereas it is actually brass. The concept of the watch is the same in both instances, though there is no actually existing gold-plated watch. In brief, to have a fully developed concept of God does not entail God's existence. Kant moves in this direction over a course of years, the one clear trend being increasing doubt about the power of philosophy to settle such questions—and an increasing conviction that all previous attempts descend into paralogisms and antinomies. On a question of such *transcendent* proportions, he is best understood as resigned to the view that neither sensory sources of knowledge nor neat logical arguments can hope to be decisive.

Remaining faithful to the constraints he has imposed on "theoretical reason," Kant turns to the different powers and functions of *practical reason* that grounds his moral philosophy. Where the former must operate by way of those appearances and representations within the domain of causal necessitation, practical reason arises in the realm of the *intelligible* in which explanations are grounded in reasons, not causes. It is the acknowledged duality of human persons that locates them at once in the natural realm of *causes* and the intelligible realm of *reasons*. A person dropped from a height will fall with an acceleration determined by the laws of physics. What occurs in this context is the reaction of a natural body to physical forces. A person at a choice point, reflecting on the available options and seeking to choose that which will satisfy the requirement of morality, now acts on the basis of a *reason* for acting, which is different from the causes at work on merely physical objects. Indeed, the only way the course of action is rendered intelligible is by identifying the reasons that gave rise to it.

Occupants of the intelligible realm of reasons and purposes are presumed to be autonomous. Even if the arguments surrounding the antinomies render proof of moral freedom impossible, that freedom is nonetheless *thinkable*, and that is sufficient for moral purposes. Liberated from the spatiotemporal domain of strict determination, free actions now occupy a different domain and rest on principles that are assessed according to conceptions of the moral ideal. Consider a being who, at every possible choice point, acts according to a morally perfect standard. Call such an entity "God," now rendered possible by way of the possibility of moral perfection itself.

The idea of a morally perfect standard leads to a consideration of that *categorical imperative* that so occupied the Kant of the second *Critique*. This is the imperative that transcends the physicality and associated desires and impulses of a purely natural creature and enters into the moral deliberations of a being free to set its own laws, its own *laws of freedom*. This, too, is a subject inviting treatment extending far beyond present purposes. In Kant's later years, in the unfinished *Opus Postumum*, there is a conceptual movement in the direction of a philosophy of religion—a proof of God, even—based on the categorical imperative and such ontological possibilities arguably derivable from it.[9]

The relationship between the will and the actions arising from it can be framed in two distinct ways and regarded from two entirely different aspects: From one standpoint, the account is given in terms of natural causation leading to the satisfaction of desires; from the other, the account is in terms of adherence to moral precepts, an adherence that presupposes moral freedom. A total skepticism regarding moral freedom, however, can only arise from the fallacious deployment of theoretical reason, but the moral account falls well beyond the theoretical use of reason. Causal accounts are predicated on the assumption that for anything to exist it must be the result of some preexisting condition. This, as a species of *transcendental proof*, would presume to be independent of empirical principles (A615/B643). However, neither "freedom" nor "determinism" thus understood can be represented as "absolutely necessary," given the possible modes of representation. Accordingly, neither has *objective* standing. Neither rises higher than a *subjective principle of reason*. (A616/B644).

If reason's overreaching is to be avoided, what is necessary is what Kant refers to as *The Discipline of Pure Reason* and the *Rejection of Dogmatic Empiricism*. Hume had awakened Kant from his dogmatic slumber. Thus awakened, Kant will have Hume at the center of his thoughts when he observes that

the fate that awaits upon all skepticism likewise befalls Hume, namely, that his own skeptical teaching comes to be doubted, as being based only on facts which are contingent, not on principles which can constrain to a necessary renunciation of all right to dogmatic assertions. (A768/B796)

In light of these arguments, Kant's diffidence regarding God and immortality is in conformity with the aims and conclusions of his critical philosophy. To leave the domain of the sensible and sensuous intuition, one moves not on the sure path of knowledge but along the less if more exciting map of the imagination.

Through an analysis of practical reason one finds cogent arguments for actions falling in the *intelligible* realm of moral purposes and the freedom they presuppose. Situated morally, outside the framework of spatiotemporal causality, one is permitted to speculate without contradiction as to an enduring existence after death. To the extent that this conjecture is coherent and thinkable, there is a necessary link to what Kant calls that *Supreme Cause of Nature—God*—as the source of all impulses toward moral perfection. Neither experience nor pure reason, as now properly assessed by a sound metaphysical method, can establish any of this, which, after all, is to note yet again the limits of sense and reason—the very point of the first *Critique*.

NOTES

PREFACE

1. Peter Strawson (1966), *The Bounds of Sense*. London: Methuen & Co. Ltd., 11.
2. On this point, see Manfred Kuehn (1987), *Scottish Common Sense in Germany, 1768–1800: A Contribution to the History of Critical Philosophy*. Montreal: McGill-Queen's University Press.
3. This account is given in *The Autobiography of Heinrich Steffens (1773–1845)*, a Danish traveler and writer who attended Fichte's lectures and who was later to hold a professorship in Berlin. His ten-volume autobiography is not available in English. The Fichte material appears in the third volume of his *Was Ich Erlebte* and was published in 1841 by Joseph Max Co., Breslau. It is available on microfilm and on the internet at http://www.archive.org/stream/3198850_3#page/256/mode/1up
4. Leslie Stevenson (1983), "Empirical Realism and Transcendental Anti-Realism." *Proceedings of the Aristotelian Society,* 57, 131.
5. For ease of use, in most instances the location of quoted passages from the *Critique* are given in the body of the text rather than as footnotes. Except where indicated otherwise, all references to the *Critique of Pure Reason* are from Immanuel Kant, *Critique of Pure Reason,* trans. Norman Kemp Smith (2003). New York: Palgrave Macmillan. The standard convention is adopted, the letters A and B referring respectively to the first and second editions of the *Critique.*

CHAPTER 1

1. Jonathan Bennett (1968), "Strawson on Kant." *The Philosophical Review,* 77, 40–9.
2. Kenneth Westphal (2003), "Epistemic Reflection and Transcendental Proof," in *Strawson and Kant*, ed. H.-J. Glock. Oxford: Oxford University Press, 127.
3. I. Kant, *Prolegomena to Any Future Metaphysics.* The Paul Carus translation of 1902 is available at http://philosophy.eserver.org/kant-prolegomena.txt
4. Letter of June 7, 1771, to Marcus Herz, in *Immanuel Kant Correspondence*, ed. and trans. Arnulf Zweig (1999). Cambridge: Cambridge University Press, 126–8.

5. Graham Bird (1995), "Kant and Naturalism." *British Journal for the History of Philosophy*, 3, 399–408.
6. Ibid., 407.
7. This standard mode of citation is used throughout, where A and B refer, respectively, to the first and second editions of the *Critique*.
8. Karl Ameriks (2000), *Kant and the Fate of Autonomy*. Cambridge: Cambridge University Press, especially 41–52.
9. Frederick Beiser is of the view that the dispute is "sterile and irresolvable," the text of the *Critique* admitting of both interpretations. Frederick Beiser (2002), *German Idealism: The Struggle Against Subjectivism*. Cambridge: Harvard University Press, 22.
10. Peter Mittelstaedt (2009), "Cognition versus Constitution of Objects: From Kant to Modern Physics." *Found Phys,* 39, 847–59.

CHAPTER 2

1. Kant, *The Conflict of the Faculties* (1798), trans. Mary Gregor (1992). Lincoln: University of Nebraska Press, 69–70.
2. For the teaching of Johann Arndt, see his *True Christianity*, trans. Peter Erb (1979). New York: Paulist Press. An English translation of Spener's *Pia Desideria* by T. G. Tappert was published in 1964 by Fortress Press. For portions of that work and important related works see Peter C. Erb (1983), *The Pietists: Selected Writings*. New York: Paulist Press.
3. F. Ernest Stoeffler (1973), *German Pietism During the Eighteenth Century*. New York: Brill, 39.
4. This intention is given in the subtitle of his *Einleitung der Vernunftlehre* (*Introduction to the Doctrine of Reason*) published in German in 1691.
5. The secondary literature on Thomasius in English is thin. This has been valuably repaired by Ian Hunter (2008), *The Secularisation of the Confessional State*. Cambridge: Cambridge University Press. The quoted passage is from page 23.
6. Kant, *Critique*, Bxxxvi.
7. See Ronald Calinger (1969), "The Newtonian-Wolffian Controversy." *Journal of the History of Ideas*, XXX, 319–30.
8. Perhaps the most accessible English translation of Wolff's (1728) works is his *Preliminary Discourse on Philosophy in General*, trans. Richard J. Blackwell (1963). Indianapolis: The Bobbs-Merrill Company, Inc.
9. Christian Wolff, The passage is translated by Lewis White Beck as "German Metaphysics." Available at http://plato.stanford.edu/entries/wolff-christian/
10. Ibid., section 46.
11. Kant, *Critique*, 33.
12. For Knutzen's influence, see Manfred Kuehn (2001), *Kant: A Biography*. Cambridge: Cambridge University Press. See also L. W. Beck (1960), *Early German Philosophy: Kant and His Predecessors*. Cambridge, MA: Harvard University Press.

13. See Isaiah Berlin (2000), *Three Critics of the Enlightenment: Vico, Hamann, Herder*. Princeton: Princeton University Press. Perhaps an echo of this is heard when Kant says that he must suspend knowledge in order to make a place for faith, "Ich mußte also das Wissen aufheben, um zum Glauben Platz zu bekommen."
14. Kant, *Prolegomena*.
15. Source for Prize Competition.
16. Kant, *Prolegomena*.
17. A fully informed account is Brigitte Sassen (2000), *Kant's Early Critics: The Empiricist Critique of the Theoretical Philosophy*. New York: Cambridge University Press. See also Manfred Kuehn (1987), *Scottish Common Sense in Germany, 1768–1800: A Contribution to the History of Critical Philosophy*. Kingston and Montreal: McGill-Queen's University Press.
18. Descartes, Geometry.
19. Leibniz, New Essays.
20. *The Leibniz-Arnauld Correspondence*, ed. and trans. H.T. Mason (1967). Manchester: Manchester University Press, letter 62.
21. Leibniz, *Monadology*.
22. Leibniz, *New Essays*.
23. Cited by Manfred Kuehn (2001), *Kant: A Biography*. Cambridge: Cambridge University Press, 86.
24. Leibniz, Letter to Arnauld in *The Leibniz-Arnauld Correspondence*.
25. *Leibniz-Clarke Correspondence*.
26. Leonard Euler (1997), *Letters of Euler to a German Princess: On Different Subjects in Physics and Philosophy*, trans. Henry Hunter. Thoemmes Continuum; Facsimile of 1795 edition.
27. In David Shavin (1999), *Fidelio*, 8, 2.
28. Moses Mendelssohn, *Philosophical Writings*.
29. Moses Mendelssohn (1997), section 2, "On the Self-Evidence of Metaphysical Principles"; in *The Cambridge Edition of the Works of Immanuel Kant in Translation*, ed. David Walford and Ralf Meerbote. Cambridge: Cambridge University Press, 277.
30. Kant, Prize Competition essay.
31. Michael Friedman.
32. Michael Friedman (2007), *Studies In History and Philosophy of Science*, part B: *Studies In History and Philosophy of Modern Physics*, 38(1), 216–25. For Newton's employment of conceptual analysis see Robert DiSalle (2002), "Newton's Philosophical Analysis of Space and Time," in I. B. Cohen and G. E. Smith (ed.), *The Cambridge Companion to Newton*. Cambridge: Cambridge University Press, 33–56.
33. I am in substantial agreement with those who, like Michael Friedman, consider the First *Critique* having the exact sciences at the center of its concerns. See his (1992) *Kant and the Exact Science*. Cambridge, MA: Harvard University Press.
34. Kant, *Correspondence, 94*.
35. Kant, Inaugural dissertation.

36. Section 3, paragraph 14, trans. William J. Eckoff (1894). New York.
37. Kant, CPR.
38. Leibniz, "Of Universal Synthesis and Analysis," in G. *Leibniz: Philosophical Writings*, ed. H. R. Parkinson (1973). London: Everyman, 16.
39. Trans. T. H. Green and H. H. Hudson (1934). Chicago: Open Court.
40. Johann Gottfried Herder, *Letters on the Advancement of Humanity*, letter 79, in Cassirer, 84.

CHAPTER 3

1. Kant, CPR, Introduction.
2. Immanuel Kant, "Public Declaration Concerning Fichte's *Wissenschaftslehre*," in *Correspondence—Immanual Kant*, ed. and trans. A. Zweig (1999). Cambridge: Cambridge University Press, 12, 370–1.
3. As he would put it at 260 in the *Prolegomena,* "I openly confess, the suggestion of David Hume was the very thing, which many years ago first interrupted my dogmatic slumber, and gave my investigations in the field of speculative philosophy quite a new direction."
4. *Prolegomena*, Introduction.
5. Ibid.
6. Immanuel Kant, "Metaphysical Foundations of Natural Science," in *Kant's Prolegomena and Metaphysical Foundations of Natural Science*, trans. Ernest Belfort (1883). London: George Bell, 139.
7. Immanuel Kant, *Correspondence*, ed. and trans. Arnulf Zweig (1999). Cambridge: Cambridge University Press, 301.
8. Saul Kripke (1980), *Naming and Necessity.* Cambridge: Harvard University Press, 32–7.
9. Willard Quine, "Two Dogmas of Empiricism," chapter 2 in *From a Logical Point of View.* Cambridge, MA: Harvard University Press. On page 29 he refers to the "air of hocus pocus" that stalks the distinction.
10. C. D. Broad, "Are there Synthetic a priori Truths?" pages 102–117 in a *Symposium of the Aristotelian Society* (Supplementary Volume 15, 1936), 102–53. C. D. Broad, A. J. D. Porteous, and R. Jackson Broad's contributors. I have inserted "not" ("*could not possibly*") to express what is clearly Broad's intention here.

CHAPTER 4

1. Erich Adickes (1894). "Bibliography of Writings by and on Kant Which Have Appeared in Germany Up to the End of 1887 (VIII.)." *Philosophical Review,* 3(4), 434–58. Well known, of course, is the influence Kant had on Coleridge.
2. Sabastian Gardner.
3. Kant, *Prolegomena,* Introduction.

4. Barry Stroud, "Transcendental Arguments," in *Kant on Pure Reason,* ed. Ralph C. S. Walker (1982). Oxford: Oxford University Press, 117–31. However, I do not share Stroud's estimation of the defects in the transcendental method of argument as I hope to make clear below and in Chapter 5.
5. Carnap's "thing language" is a conventionalist account of meaning is based on the concept of linguistic frameworks. See Rudolph Carnap (1956), "Empiricism, Semantics and Ontology," in *Meaning and Necessity: A Study in Semantics and Modal Logic* (enlarged edition). Chicago: University of Chicago Press.
6. Kant, *Correspondence*, 398.
7. Ibid.
8. Kant, CPR.
9. This has been suggested by Karl Ameriks (2005) in "A Common Sense Kant?"*Proceedings and Addresses of the American Philosophical Association*, 79(2), 19–45.
10. James Van Cleve (2003), *Problems from Kant.* New York: Oxford University Press, 106.
11. An excellent essay on this aspect of Kant's theory is Derek Pereboom (1988), *Kant on Intentionality Synthèse*, 77, 321–52.
12. Paul Guyer (1987), *Kant and the Claims of Knowledge.* Cambridge: Cambridge University Press, 11.
13. Martin Gardner (1952), "Is Nature Ambidextrous?" *Philosophy and Phenomenological Research,* 13, 200–11.
14. Rene Descartes, *Meditations on the First Philosophy.* Fifth Meditation. In *The Philosophical Writings of Descartes* (volume 2, pages 44–5), trans. John Cottingham, Robert Stoothoff, and Dugald Murdoch (1984). Cambridge: Cambridge University Press.
15. Aristotle, *Physics*, trans. R. P. Hardie and R. K. Gaye. Cambridge: Harvard University Press, book 4, part 12. He is subtle on this point: "For time is not motion, but 'number of motion': and what is at rest, also, can be in the number of motion. Not everything that is not in motion can be said to be 'at rest'—but only that which can be moved, though it actually is not moved."
16. Sebastian Gardner (1999), *Kant and the Critique of Pure Reason.* London: Routledge, 76.
17. Gödel 1990 (volume 2, page 236), cited by Mauro Dorato, "Kant, Gödel and Relativity," ed. P. Gardenfors, K. Kijania-Placek, and J. Wolenski (2002), *Proceedings of the invited papers for the 11th International Congress of the Logic Methodology and Philosophy of Science*, Synthese Library, Kluwer Dordrecht, 329–46.
18. Gary Hatfield, "Kant on Perception of Space (and Time)"; In *Cambridge Companion to Kant and Modern Philosophy*, ed. Paul Guyer.
19. See Teri Merrick (2006), "What Frege Meant When He Said: Kant Is Right about Geometry." *Philosophia Mathematica*, 14(1), 44–75.
20. Paul Guyer summarizes his position in *Kant* (2006) London: Routledge, 63–8. Henry Allison's (2004) "dual-aspect" thesis is discussed in his

Kant's Transcendental Idealism. New Haven: Yale University Press, 35–8.

21. Leslie Stevenson and Ralph Walker (1983), "Empirical Realism and Transcendental Anti-Realism." *Proceedings of the Aristotelian Society,* 57, 131–57. The passage is from page 139.

22. The three positions that scholars take on this are represented in the cited works by Guyer, Allison, and Beiser. The first defends a dual ontology, and the second a dual aspect; the third regards the *Critique* as insufficiently clear to decide the matter.

23. I. Kant, *Critique of the Power of Judgment,* trans. Paul Guyer and Eric Matthews (2001). Cambridge: Cambridge University Press, section 1, division 1, "Analytic of Beauty."

24. Kant, *Correspondence,* 203.

25. Barry Stroud (1968), "Transcendental Arguments," *Journal of Philosophy,* 65.

26. See, for example, Barry Stroud (1999), "The Goal of Transcendental Arguments," ed. Robert Stern, *Transcendental Arguments: Problems and Prospects.* Oxford: Oxford University Press.

27. Kant's juridical sense of a transcendental argument is discussed by D. Henrich, "Kant's Notion of a Deduction," in *Kant's Transcendental Deductions,* ed. Förster (1989). Stanford: Stanford University Press, 29–46.

CHAPTER 5

1. See Simon Blackburn (1990), "Hume and Thick Connexions." *Philosophy and Phenomenological Research,* 50(Supplement), 237–50. Blackburn would have Hume a "quasi-realist" on this point.

2. *Enquiry.* Section 12, part 1, 119.

3. Karl Ameriks, *Interpreting Kant's Critiques.*

4. Ibid., 98.

5. An instructive study of the argument is provided by G. Dicker (2008), "Kant's Refutation of Idealism." *Noûs,* 42, 80–108.

6. Allison, 7.

7. A sample of informing analyses are H. E. Allison (1983), *Kant's Transcendental Idealism. An Interpretation and Defense.* New Haven: Yale University Press. P. Guyer (1983), "Kant's Intentions in the Refutation of Idealism," *The Philosophical Review,* XCII/3, 329–83. K. Ameriks (2003), "Kant's Transcendental Deduction as a Regressive Argument," in *Interpreting Kant's Critiques.* Oxford: Clarendon Press, 51–66.

8. Jonathan Vogel (1993), "The Problem of Self-Knowledge in Kant's 'Refutation of Idealism': Two Recent Views." *Philosophy and Phenomenological Research,* 4, 875.

9. The generic idealism under consideration is what he refers to as *material* idealism. He identifies two forms. One version renders doubtful and indemonstrable the actual existence of material objects in space. He calls this problematic idealism of the sort advanced by Descartes.

The second version declares external material objects to be impossible. This is the dogmatic idealism of Berkeley.
10. Henry Allison (page 294) addresses this interpretation and argues against it, but on grounds different from those advanced here.
11. The paralogisms and antinomies are the subject of Chapter 8. ·
12. A brief and informing discussion of this point is provided by Paul Guyer (2008) in his Introduction to *Knowledge, Reason and Taste: Kant's Reply to Hume*. Princeton: Princeton University Press.
13. CPR at Bxl where the scandal extends to reason itself.
14. This conclusion is reached by way of a transcendental argument. Space as such is not given in the stimulus and thus must be an intuition—an a priori mode of apprehension—found in the subject.
15. Mark Sacks has discussed the importance of the first analogy at this point in the proof. See Mark Sachs (2006), "Kant's First Analogy and the Refutation of Idealism." *Proceedings of the Aristotelian Society,* 106(1), 113–30.
16. Thomas Reid, *An Inquiry into the Human Mind. On the Principles of Common Sense*, ed. Derek Brookes (2000). Edinburgh: Edinburgh University press.
17. No such limit is imposed on what might be conjured in consciousness. Some have argued that Kant misunderstood Descartes's position and that consciousness of a unitary self is no more problematic than consciousness of other entities. See, for example, Terence Wilkerson (1980), "Kant on Self-Consciousness." *The Philosophical Quarterly,* 30(118), 47–60. But the question at issue is whether such objects of consciousness count as objective knowledge.
18. For a detailed critical discussion see Q. Cassam (2007), *The Possibility of Knowledge.* Oxford: Clarendon Press.

CHAPTER 6

1. John Locke (1689), *An Essay Concerning the Human Understanding.* Oxford: Oxford University Press, book 2, xxxiii, 5.
2. David Hume (1739), *A Treatise of Human Nature.* Oxford: Oxford University Press, 662.
3. David Hume, *Enquiry,* section 22.
4. Kant, to Marcus Herz, February 21, 1772, in *Correspondence,* ed. Arnulf Zweig (1999). Cambridge: Cambridge University Press, 132–3.
5. Ibid.
6. Again, see Karl Ameriks (2005), "A Common Sense Kant?" *Proceedings and Addresses of the American Philosophical Association*, 79(2), 19–45; Manfred Kuehn (1987), *Scottish Common Sense in Germany, 1768–1800: A Contribution to the History of Critical Philosophy.* Montreal: McGill-Queen's University Press.
7. See especially Norman Daniels (1989), *Thomas Reid's "Inquiry": The Geometry of Visibles and the Case for Realism.* Stanford: Stanford University Press.

8. See Graham Bird (2006), *The Revolutionary Kant*. Chicago: Open Court, 367.
9. Kant, *Correspondence*, 313.
10. Peter Strawson.
11. Ibid., 32.
12. Kant's development of this is in chapter 1 of "The Analytic of Concepts," in book 2 of the "Transcendental Analytic" (A137/B176–A147/B187).
13. Ibid., A137/B176.
14. See chapter 5 of Wolfgang Kohler (1992), *Gestalt Psychology*. Chicago: Liveright Publishing Corporation.

CHAPTER 7

1. Paul Guyer, *Kant*, 49.
2. David Hume, *An Enquiry Concerning Human Understanding* (1751), ed. L. A. Selby-Bigge (1974). Oxford: Oxford University Press, 425.
3. David Hume (1739), *A Treatise of Human Nature*, ed. L. A. Selby-Bigge (1896). Oxford: Clarendon Press, book 2, part 3, section 3.
4. Immanuel Kant, *Critique of Pure Reason* (1781–7), trans. Norman Kemp Smith (2003). New York: Palgrave-Macmillan.
5. Ibid.
6. Kant, *Critique of Pure Reason*.
7. Ibid.
8. Ibid., A644–5/B672–3.
9. The argument for this is developed in his *Critique of Judgment*, section 5: "The Principle of the Formal Purposiveness of Nature Is a Transcendental Principle of Judgement." The edition used here is I. Kant (2001), *Critique of the Power of Judgment*, trans. Paul Guyer and Eric Matthews (2001). Cambridge: Cambridge University Press.
10. The essay is titled, *Principiorum primorum cognitionis metaphysicae nova dilucidatio.* Königsberg: Johann Heinrich Hartung, 1755, ii, 38 (Ak. 1:387–416) and is translated as, "New Elucidation of the First Principles of Metaphysical Cognition." J. A. Reuscher (trans.) in Lewis White Beck (1992), *Kant's Latin Writings* (2nd ed.). New York: Peter Lang, 42–83. The contra-Leibniz passages are at 412–13.
11. Alexander Baumgarten was the first to use the term "aesthetics" as a discipline and mode of systematic inquiry. It appears in his (1735) *Meditationes philosophicae de nonnullis ad poema pertinentibus*, given by K. Aschenbrenner and W. B. Holther (trans.) as *Reflections on Poetry* (1954). Berkeley: University of California Press.
12. Joseph Addison, *The Spectator* (1712), 411–21. The passage is from paper 3 and is available at http://www.mnstate.edu/gracyk/courses/web%20publishing/addison413.htm
13. Kant, *Critique of Judgment*. The passage is from section 1, division 1, "Analytic of Aesthetic Judgment—Analytic of the Beautiful."
14. Immanuel Kant, *Critique of Judgment,* trans. Werner Pluhar (1790/1987). Indianapolis, Indiana: Hackett, section 75, 282–3.

CHAPTER 8

1. James Van Cleve, *Blackwell's Companion to Metaphysics*, ed. Jaegwon Kim and Ernest Sosa (1995). Oxford: Blackwell.
2. Gregory Klass (2003), "A Framework for Reading Kant on Apperception: Seven Interpretive Questions." *Kant-Studien*, 94, 80–94.
3. Note that Stephen Engstrom (1994) among others sees that Kant is not attempting to refute Descartes's skepticism here. *Journal of the History of Philosophy*, 32, 359–80.
4. See Graham Bird, 367.
5. John Locke (1689), chapter 27, "On Identity and Diversity," in *An Essay Concerning Human Understanding*. Oxford: Oxford University Press.
6. David Hume (1739), book 1, section 6, *A Treatise of Human Nature*, ed. Selby-Bigge (1896). Oxford: Oxford University Press.
7. Peter Strawson, 50.
8. Alison Laywine (2006), "Kant's Laboratory of Ideas in the 1770s," in the *Blackwell Companion to Kant*. Oxford: Blackwell. The passage is from page 72. The original is taken from volume 17 of the Academy Edition of Kant's *Works* (R4674–84).

CHAPTER 9

1. Graham Bird, 625.
2. Particularly interesting in this connection is Harold Langsam (2002), "Kant's Compatibilism and His Two Conceptions of Truth." *Pacific Philosophical Quarterly*, 81(2), 164–88.
3. See, for example, Simon Shengjian Xie (2009), "What Is Kant? A Compatibilist or Incompatibilist?" *Kant-Studien*, 100(1), 53–76.
4. For this interpretation, see Hud Hudson (1994), *Kant's Compatibilism*. Ithaca: Cornell University Press. For Donald Davidson's anomalous monism, see his "The Material Mind," in *Actions and Events* (1980). Oxford: Clarendon Press.
5. Paul Guyer, *Kant*, 349.
6. See, for example, Pamela Anderson and Jordan Bell (2010), *Kant and Theology*. London: Continuum Publishing; Frederick C. Beiser (1997), *The Fate of Reason: German Philosophy from Kant to Fichte*. Cambridge, MA: Harvard University Press, chapters 2–4, pages 44–126; Gordon Michalson (1999), *Kant and the Problem of God*. Oxford: Blackwell.
7. Immanuel Kant, *Religion within the Boundaries of Mere Reason: And Other Writings*, trans. *Allen Wood* and *George Di Giovanni* (1999). Cambridge: Cambridge University Press.
8. For an informing discussion, see Manfred Kuehn, *Kant—A Life*, 378.
9. In this connection, see Eckhart Forster (2000), *Kant's Final Synthesis: An Essay on the Opus Postumum*. Cambridge, MA: Harvard University Press, especially chapter 5, "The Subject as Person and the Idea of God," 117–47.

BIBLIOGRAPHY

Addison, Joseph (1712). *The Spectator*, 411–21. Available at http://www. mnstate.edu/gracyk/courses/web%20publishing/addison413.htm

Adickes, Erich (1894). Bibliography of Writings by and on Kant Which Have Appeared in Germany Up to the End of 1887 (VIII.). *Philosophical Review*, 3(4), 434–58.

Allison, Henry (1983). *Kant's Transcendental Idealism. An Interpretation and Defense*, New Haven: Yale University Press.

Allison, Henry (2004). *Kant's Transcendental Idealism*. New Haven: Yale University Press.

Ameriks, Karl (2005). "A Common Sense Kant?" *Proceedings and Addresses of the American Philosophical Association*, 79(2), 19–45.

Ameriks, Karl (2003). *Interpreting Kant's Critiques*. Oxford: Oxford University Press.

Ameriks, Karl (2000). *Kant and the Fate of Autonomy*. Cambridge: Cambridge University Press.

Arndt, Johann (1979). *True Christianity*, trans. Peter Erb. New York: Paulist Press.

Baumgarten, Alexander (1735). *Meditationes philosophicae de nonnullis ad poema pertinentibus*, trans. K. Aschenbrenner and W.B. Holther (1954) as *Reflections on Poetry*. Berkeley: University of California Press.

Beck, L.W. (1960). *Early German Philosophy: Kant and His Predecessors*. Cambridge, MA: Harvard University Press.

Beiser, Frederick (2002). *German Idealism: The Struggle against Subjectivism*. Cambridge, MA: Harvard University Press.

Bennett, Jonathan (1968). "Strawson on Kant." *The Philosophical Review*, 77, 40–9.

Bird, Graham (1995). "Kant and Naturalism." *British Journal for the History of Philosophy*, 3, 399–408.

Blackburn, Simon (1990). "Hume and Thick Connexions." *Philosophy and Phenomenological Research*, 50(Supplement), 237–50.

Calinger, Ronald (1969). "The Newtonian-Wolffian Controversy." *Journal of the History of Ideas*, XXX, 319–30.

Cassam, Q. (2007). *The Possibility of Knowledge*. Oxford: Clarendon Press.

Dahlstrom, Daniel O. (ed.) (1997). Cambridge: Cambridge University Press.

Davidson, Donald (1980). *Actions and Events*. Oxford: Clarendon Press.

Dicker, G. (2008). "Kant's Refutation of Idealism." *Noûs*, 42, 80–108.

DiSalle, Robert (2002). "Newton's Philosophical Analysis of Space and Time," in I. B. Cohen and G. E. Smith (eds), *The Cambridge Companion to Newton*. Cambridge: Cambridge University Press.

Engstrom, Stephen (1994). "The Transcendental Deduction and Skepticism." *Journal of History of Philosophy*, 32, 359–80.

Erb, Peter (1983). *The Pietists: Selected Writings*. New York: Paulist Press.

Euler, Leonard (1997). *Letters of Euler to a German Princess: On Different Subjects in Physics and Philosophy*, trans. Henry Hunter. Thoemmes Continuum; Facsimile of 1795 edition.

Forster, Eckhart (2000). *Kant's Final Synthesis: An Essay on the Opus Postumum*. Cambridge, MA: Harvard University Press.

Friedman, Michael (2007). "Studies in History and Philosophy of Science." *Part B: Studies in History and Philosophy of Modern Physics*, 38(1), 216–25.

Friedman, Michael (1992). *Kant and the Exact Science*. Cambridge, MA: Harvard University Press

Gardner, Sabastian (1999). *Routledge Philosophy Guidebook to Kant*. London: Routledge.

Guyer, Paul (1983). "Kant's Intentions in the Refutation of Idealism." *The Philosophical Review*; XCII/3, 329–83.

Guyer, Paul (2006). *Kant*. London: Routledge.

Guyer, Paul (2008). *Knowledge, Reason and Taste: Kant's Reply to Hume*. Princeton: Princeton University Press.

Hatfield, Gary. "Kant on Perception of Space (and Time)," in *Cambridge Companion to Kant and Modern Philosophy*, ed. Paul Guyer. Cambridge: Cambridge University Press.

Henrich, D. (1989). "Kant's Notion of a Deduction," in *Kant's Transcendental Deductions*, ed. Förster. Stanford: Stanford University Press.

Herder, J. G. (2004). "Letters on the Advancement of Humanity" (Letter 79), in *Another Philosophy of History and Selected Political Writings*, trans. Ioannis D. Evrigenis, and Daniel Pellerin. Indianapolis: Hackett.

Hudson, Hud (1994). *Kant's Compatibilism*. Ithaca: Cornell University Press.

Hume, David (1739). *A Treatise of Human Nature*, ed. Selby-Bigge (1896). Oxford: Oxford University Press.

Hume, David (1751). *An Enquiry Concerning Human Understanding*, ed. L. A. Selby-Bigge (1974). Oxford: Oxford University Press

Hunter, Ian (2008). *The Secularisation of the Confessional State*. Cambridge: Cambridge University Press.

Kant, I. (1790). *Critique of Judgment*, trans. Werner Pluhar (1987). Indianapolis: Hackett.

Kant, I. (2003). *Critique of Pure Reason*, trans. Norman Kemp Smith. New York: Palgrave Macmillan.

Kant, I. (2001). *Critique of the Power of Judgment,* trans. Paul Guyer and Eric Matthews. Cambridge: Cambridge University Press.

Kant, I. (1755). *Principiorum primorum cognitionis metaphysicae nova dilucidatio* (Königsberg: Johann Heinrich Hartung), translated as

"New Elucidation of the First Principles of Metaphysical Cognition," J. A. Reuscher (trans.) in Lewis White Beck, (1992) *Kant's Latin Writings* (2nd ed.). New York: Peter Lang.

Kant, I. *Prolegomena to Any Future Metaphysics*, trans. Paul Carus, trans, Available at http://philosophy.eserver.org/kant-prolegomena.tx

Kant, I. (1999). "Public Declaration concerning Fichte's *Wissenschaftslehre* . . . ," in *Correspondence—Immanual Kant*, ed. and trans. A. Zweig. Cambridge: Cambridge University Press, 12, 370–1.

Kant, I. (1999). *Immanuel Kant Correspondence*, ed. and trans. Arnulf Zweig. Cambridge: Cambridge University Press.

Kant, I. (1883). "Metaphysical Foundations of Natural Science," in *Prolegomena and Metaphysical Foundations of Natural Science*, trans. Ernest Belfort. London: George Bell,

Kant, I. (1798). *The Conflict of the Faculties*, trans. Mary Gregor (1992). Lincoln: University of Nebraska Press.

Klass, Gregory (2003). "A Framework for Reading Kant on Apperception: Seven Interpretive Questions." *Kant-Studien*, 94, 80–94.

Kohler, Wolfgang (1992). *Gestalt Psychology.* Chicago: Liveright Publishing Corporation.

Kripke, Saul (1980). *Naming and Necessity.* Cambridge, MA: Harvard University Press.

Kuehn, Manfred (1987). *Scottish Common Sense in Germany, 1768–1800: A Contribution to the History of Critical Philosophy.* Montreal: McGill-Queen's University Press.

Langsam, Harold (2002). "Kant's Compatibilism and His Two Conceptions of Truth." *Pacific Philosophical Quarterly, 81*(2), 164–88.

Laywine, Alison (2006). "Kant's Laboratory of Ideas in the 1770s," in *Companion to Kant.* Oxford: Blackwell.

Leibniz, G. W (1973). "Of Universal Synthesis and Analysis," in G. H. R. Parkinson (ed.), *Leibniz: Philosophical Writings.* London: Everyman.

Leibniz, G. W. (1998). *The Leibniz-Clarke Correspondence: Together with Extracts from Newton's Principia and Opticks*, ed. H. G. Alexander. Manchester: University of Manchester Press.

Leibniz, G. W. *New Essays on Human Understanding.* Available at http://www.earlymoderntexts.com/pdf/leibne.pdf

Locke, John (1689). *An Essay Concerning Human Understanding.* Oxford: Oxford University Press.

Mendelssohn, Moses "On the self-evidence of metaphysical principles," in *The Cambridge Edition of the Works of Immanuel Kant in Translation*, ed. David Walford and Ralf Meerbote. Cambridge: Cambridge University Press.

Mendelssohn, Moses (1997). *Moses Mendelssohn: Philosophical Writings*, ed. Daniel Dahlstrom. Cambridge: Cambridge University Press.

Merrick, Teri (2006). "What Frege Meant When He Said: Kant Is Right about Geometry." *Philosophia Mathematica*, 14(1), 44–75.

Mittelstaedt, Peter (2009). "Cognition versus Constitution of Objects: From Kant to Modern Physics." *Found Phys*, 39, 847–59.

Pereboom, Derek (1988). "Kant on Intentionality." *Synthèse*, 77, 321–52.

Reid, Thomas (2000). *An Inquiry into the Human Mind on the Principles of Common Sense*, ed. Derek Brookes. Edinburgh: Edinburgh University press.

Sacks, Mark (2006). "Kant's First Analogy and the Refutation of Idealism." *Proceedings of the Aristotelian Society*, 106(1), 113–30.

Shavin, David (1999). *Fidelio*, 8(2).

Spener, Philip Jacob (1964). *Pia Desideria*, trans. T. G. Tappert. Minneapolis: Fortress Press.

Steffens, H. (1841). *The Autobiography of Heinrich Steffens (1773–1845)*. Breslau: Joseph Max, Co. Available at http://www.archive.org/stream/3198850_3#page/256/mode/1up

Stevenson, Leslie (1983). "Empirical Realism and Transcendental Anti-Realism." *Proceedings of the Aristotelian Society*, 57, 131–57.

Stoeffler, F. E. (1973). *German Pietism during the Eighteenth Century*. New York: Brill.

Strawson, Peter (1966). *The Bounds of Sense*. London: Methuen & Co. Ltd.

Stroud, Barry (1999). "The Goal of Transcendental Arguments," in Robert Stern (ed.), *Transcendental Arguments: Problems and Prospects*. Oxford: Oxford University Press.

Stroud, Barry (1982). "Transcendental Arguments," in Ralph C. S. Walker (ed.), *Kant on Pure Reason*. Oxford: Oxford University Press.

Stroud, Barry, (1968). "Transcendental Arguments." *Journal of Philosophy*, 65.

Van Cleve, James (1995). *James Blackwell's Companion to Metaphysics*, ed. Jaegwon Kim and Ernest Sosa. Oxford: Blackwell.

Van Cleve, James (2003). *Problems from Kant*. New York: Oxford University Press.

Vogel, Jonathan (1993). "The Problem of Self-Knowledge in Kant's 'Refutation of Idealism': Two Recent Views." *Philosophy and Phenomenological Research*, L(4).

Walker, Ralph (1983). "Empirical Realism and Transcendental Anti-Realism." *Proceedings of the Aristotelian Society*, 57, 131–57.

Walker, Ralph (ed.) (1982). *Kant on Pure Reason*. Oxford: Oxford University Press.

Westphal, Kenneth (2003). "Epistemic Reflection and Transcendental Proof," in H.-J. Glock (ed.), *Strawson and Kant*. Oxford: Oxford University Press.

Wilkerson, Terence (1980). "Kant on Self-Consciousness." *The Philosophical Quarterly,* 30(118), 47–60.

Wolff, Christian (1728). *Preliminary Discourse on Philosophy in General*, trans. Richard J. Blackwell. Indianapolis: The Bobbs-Merrill Company, Inc.

Wolff, Christian *German Metaphysics*, trans. L. W. Beck. Available at http://plato.stanford.edu/entries/wolff-christian/

Xie, Simon (2009). "What Is Kant? A Compatibilist or Incompatibilist?" *Kant-Studien*, 100(1).

INDEX

absolute (space, time, motion) 15,
  23, 24, 72, 74, 81, 93
aesthetics 142, 178
Ameriks, Karl P. ix, x, 5, 6, 97
analogies of experience 51, 67–75,
  169
analytic judgments 135
analytic logic 166
analytic of concepts 108, 117, 169
analytic of principles 169
analytic propositions 21, 41, 42,
  45–50, 52, 54, 73, 135, 136
analytic-synthetic distinction 41,
  42, 45, 50
anschauung 30, 31, 61 *see also*
  intuition
anticipations of perception 67, 169
antinomies 22, 97, 166, 167, 172–8,
  180
appearances 25, 44, 45, 46, 48, 59,
  60, 62, 63, 64, 67, 68, 69, 72, 74,
  75, 78, 79, 82–9, 96, 97, 102–9, 113,
  121, 122, 124, 127, 129, 130, 131,
  133, 145, 149, 151, 152, 155, 156,
  163, 166, 167, 171, 173, 175, 180
apperception 68, 89, 123, 124–6,
  138, 139, 151, 152–7, 159, 163, 166,
  171
A priori synthetic propositions xii,
  35, 38, 39, 45, 46, 49, 52, 54, 57,
  66, 72, 75, 89
architectonics 57
aristotle 10, 12, 69, 81, 117, 150, 166

Arnauld, Antoine 20, 23

Baumgarten, Alexander 16, 143
beauty 88, 143
Berkeley, George 5, 27, 92, 93, 94,
  96, 102, 105, 108, 111, 119, 121

categories (pure categories of the
  understanding) 46, 57, 59, 60,
  66, 97, 106, 116, 121, 124, 125,
  133, 134, 139, 140, 144, 146, 148,
  151, 155, 168
causation 21, 22, 40, 43, 44, 47, 65,
  68, 69, 71, 95, 102, 103, 109, 113,
  115, 137, 143, 144, 158, 163, 172,
  173, 176, 177, 178, 179, 180
Clarke, Samuel 24
cognition 7, 8, 14, 16, 20, 30, 32,
  33, 34, 42, 46, 52, 56, 61, 65, 96,
  107, 115, 121, 125, 127, 128, 144,
  147, 148, 169
compatibilism 178
concepts 9, 13, 18, 26, 35, 36, 40,
  52, 60, 61, 65, 73, 74, 76, 77, 79,
  80, 83, 84, 86, 89, 90, 91, 96,
  102, 108, 112, 115–34, 139–42,
  145–7, 149–53, 167, 168, 171,
  172–5
Copernicus 32, 33, 34

Deduktionschriften 124
Descartes, Rene xii, 5, 17, 19, 20,
  22, 23, 37, 51, 58, 80, 89, 92, 93,